Success Tweets

Explained

140 Bits of Common Sense

Career Success Advice

All in 140 Characters or Less

Explained in Detail

Bud Bilanich

The Common Sense Guy

Front Row Press

191 University Blvd., #414 • Denver, CO 80206 • 303.393.0446

Dedication

As always, this book is for Cathy

xoxoxoxoxoxoxoxoxoxoxoxoxoxoxoxoxoxoxoxoxo

xoxoxoxoxoxoxoxoxoxoxoxoxoxoxoxoxoxoxoxoxoxo

xoxoxoxoxoxoxoxoxoxoxoxoxoxoxoxoxoxoxoxoxoxo

xoxoxoxoxoxoxoxoxoxoxoxoxoxoxoxoxoxoxoxoxoxo

xoxoxoxoxoxoxoxoxoxoxoxoxoxoxoxoxoxoxoxoxoxo

xoxoxoxoxoxoxoxoxoxoxoxoxoxoxoxoxoxoxoxoxoxo

xoxoxoxoxoxoxoxoxoxoxoxoxoxoxoxoxoxoxoxoxoxo

That's 140 hugs and kisses…

Table Of Contents

Introduction

In 2010, I published *Success Tweets: 140 Bits of Common Sense Career Success Advice, All in 140 Characters or Less,* and offered it as a free download. Over 5,000 people have taken me up on my offer since.

I've received many thank you notes and nice compliments on the book. I've also received a few questions. People emailed to ask for clarification on a few of the tweets.

So I decided to write a series of blog posts explaining my thoughts on each of the 141 tweets in *Success Tweets.* I began the series in April 2010 and completed it in November. That took 28 weeks and over 120,000 words. I spent this time and effort because I want to give you all of my best thinking on what it takes to become a life and career success.

You can see the Success Tweets Blog at www.SuccessTweets.com. I had such great feedback on the Success Tweets Blog that I've decided to compile the blog posts into an eBook.

I view this eBook as a companion piece to *Success Tweets.* Keep it next to your copy of *Success Tweets.* You can refer to it when you want to further explore the ideas in a specific tweet.

Like *Success Tweets*, this eBook is my gift to you. I hope it helps you create the life and career success you want and deserve.

Bud Bilanich
Denver Colorado USA
November 2010

Success Tweet 1

Define exactly what life and career success mean to you. It's easier to hit a clear, unambiguous target.

Career success begins with clarity of purpose and direction. As the tweet says, it's easier to hit a clear, unambiguous target. Successful people know what they want in life. However, career success means different things to different people.

When I graduated from Penn State in 1972, I chose to do a year of service. I became a VISTA (Volunteers In Service To America) Volunteer. I worked for a grass roots community group in North Philadelphia. I had a successful year. I wrote a proposal that was funded by the US Department of Health, Education and Welfare. We received a grant to do Sickle Cell Anemia awareness and screening in the community. The grant provided some much-needed jobs in the community. More important, we were able to identify local people who carried the Sickle Cell gene and make them aware of its consequences.

I enjoyed the experience tremendously; so much so that I took a job as a VISTA trainer, training new volunteers. I was a full time, but we used several independent training consultants and coaches to help us with our work. These folks worked out of their homes, traveling to the assignments. I liked their lifestyle. They were able to do work they loved helping people learn new skills – and they had the freedom and flexibility that came with being self-employed. Of course, they had to generate enough income to fund their lifestyle, but that appealed to the entrepreneur in me.

By the time I was 25, I knew that I wanted to become an independent coach and consultant. I knew that I needed some additional education and experience to be able to do this successfully. So I went back to school and received an MA and PhD. I worked in the Training and Development Departments of three Fortune 500 companies, moving up the ladder, taking increasingly more responsible positions. All this was in preparation for that day in March 1988 when I resigned my job and struck out on my own.

22 years later, I'm doing what I decided I wanted to do when I was 24- or 25-years-old. I'm doing some things that I didn't imagine way back then – blogging and writing books.

However, my life today is much as I imagined it in 1975. My clarity of purpose was very instrumental in helping me become the career success – and career success coach – I am today.

I have a friend who is a serial entrepreneur. He started a software business when he was 27. He built it up and sold it to a major computer manufacturer by the time he was 35. He has since started and sold four other companies. His clarity of purpose lies in the challenge of creating something new, building it into a viable, sustainable business and then moving on.

I have another friend who recently retired as the Executive VP of Human Resources for a Fortune 50 company. We were chatting a few days ago. She told me that when she was in college, she decided that she was going to join a good company and work her way up the ladder. She took an entry-level HR job with a company she liked. It took her over 25 years, but she eventually became the most senior HR person in that company. Her clarity of purpose and definition of success was different from mine and the serial entrepreneur's, but she reached her goal.

My second friend told me that her son has yet a different definition of success. He is not interested in climbing the corporate ladder, or in being an entrepreneur. He wants an interesting job where he can contribute, but he doesn't want to spend inordinate amounts of time at work. He wants to spend as much time with his family as he can. His definition of success is different from his mother's.

I've just told you four stories about four different people. All four of us are professional successes – according to our clarity of purpose.

As a career success coach, I often tell my clients that there is no one correct definition of career success. There are as many definitions as there are people in this world. Your definition of career success is what's right for you – not anyone else. I would not have been happy building and selling a number of businesses in succession, climbing a corporate ladder or working for a large company in an individual contributor position. However, as you can tell from the stories of the three people above, they were. They knew what they wanted and they went after it.

That's why defining your clarity of purpose is so important. Your clarity of purpose provides both a foundation and launching pad for your career success. The old saying,

"If you don't know where you're going, you won't know when you get there," is a cliché, but true. Getting clear on your personal definition of career success is the first step to becoming a career success.

The common sense, career success coach point of this tweet is simple. Career success begins with a clear idea of how you define success for you personally. Tweet 1 in *Success Tweets* says, "Define exactly what life and career success mean to you. It's easier to hit a clear, unambiguous target." If you haven't already done so, I suggest you take some time and think about your clarity of purpose. How do you define life and career success for yourself? Keep that purpose and definition of career success in mind as you move forward in your life and career.

Success Tweet 2

The more clear you are about what success means to you personally, the easier it will be to create the life and career you want.

In the first post in this series, I told how I decided that I wanted to be an independent career success coach early in my career. I was fortunate in that I had several good role models – people with whom I was working who had the career to which I aspired. It was reasonably easy for me to be very clear on what I wanted out of my life and career.

I always advise my career success coach clients to develop a clear mental image of themselves as a success. I tell them that this image should be as vivid as they can make it.

When I was 25, I conjured up an image of myself as a career success coach, motivational speaker, and management consultant. I worked in my home office – where I wrote and developed the programs I delivered at client locations. This office had a floor-to-ceiling wall of books that I could use for easy reference. It also had a state-of-the-art IBM Selectric typewriter and a big, clunky telephone. PCs and the Internet were science fiction in 1975.

I also saw myself having one-to-one coaching discussions with senior leaders in a variety of organizations, conducting training and team-building sessions in conference rooms at their locations. Amazingly, many of the people in the sessions were smoking. I had very vivid images of standing in front of large audiences at sales meetings doing talks. I saw myself at a book store signing a book I had written. I also saw myself on airplanes, traveling to my coaching, speaking and consulting gigs.

All of these vivid images came true. My office is much as I had imagined it – except it has two PCs and cell phone, not a Selectric typewriter and clunky phone. The wall of books is there – overflowing. I've written 11 of the books on the shelf. People don't smoke in my coaching, training and team-building sessions anymore; and I use PowerPoint instead of handwritten flip charts, but the big stuff is the same as I've imagined it. I've coached people and spoken to audiences all over North America, in Latin America, Europe and Asia. I am a million-mile flyer with Continental Air Lines.

I'm living my dream – in large part because I dared to dream it all those years ago.

You can begin creating your vivid mental image of yourself as a career success with affirmations. Affirmations are positive self talk. The idea behind affirmations is that when you think of the things to which you aspire, like becoming a career success, and then tell yourself that you are a career success, you will believe that you can become a career success. More importantly, you will be more likely to do the work it takes to make that aspiration come true.

A couple of years ago, I wrote a book called *Star Power, Common Sense Ideas for Career and Life Success.* I used a star to depict the ideas in the book. I urged readers to think of themselves as a star and to aspire to becoming a career and life star. I like the star metaphor. Daily, I repeat the following affirmation to myself: "Bud Bilanich is a star."

I've done a lot of work in making this affirmation a reality – redoing my website, developing better promotional materials, speaking, writing books, blogging and podcasting.

I've also done something a little unusual. A few years ago, right after *Star Power* was published, I went to the "Name a Star" website and named a star after myself. Now I can say, "Bud Bilanich is a star" and really believe it, because Bud Bilanich really is a star. It's easy for me to visualize myself as a star, because I am a star.

Bud Bilanich, the star, is Catalog Number TYC 868-1011-1 in the constellation Leo. Bud Bilanich has a Visual Magnitude indicator of 11.2. Right Ascension is 11h 58m 21s. Declination is 11degrees, 43,'18." I don't have a clue what all of these things mean, except the constellation Leo, which I chose because my birthday is August 14. But I do know one thing. Bud Bilanich is a star!

How's that for an affirmation?

Affirmations work. I have become a minor star in the career success coach world. You don't need to go to the lengths I did to make them work either. Just decide what you want, visualize yourself as having it, and tell yourself you have it. Then do whatever it takes to make your affirmation come true.

Affirmations alone, however, are not enough to guarantee your career success. You have to do the work. Spend the time necessary to accomplish your goals. Volunteer for projects that will get you noticed. Become an expert on your company, its competitors, and your industry. In other words, bust your butt, and you will succeed.

To develop a clear picture of you as a career success, you need to carefully think through your priorities – and then align your behavior to ensure that you are living according to them. To do so, ask yourself two very important questions:

1. What do I want to do in this life?
2. What is the result I want to achieve?

The answers to these two questions will not only guide the big decisions you make, they will serve as a guide for living your life on a day-to-day basis.

Here's another way to look at it. Imagine that you're nearing the end of your life. You feel happy, content and satisfied. You don't fear death because you've had a happy and prosperous life. You've lived and loved and feel that you've been blessed.

Once you get yourself into this frame of mind, look back at your life and what you've accomplished. Of all these accomplishments, what matters the most to you? What challenges did you overcome along the way to these accomplishments? How did you do it? What messages did you send to others by the way you lived your life?

This visualization exercise will help you in clarifying your purpose and direction in this life. It's important because it helps you create a vivid mental image of what success looks like for you personally. This is not day-dreaming. It is real work. You are designing your future in your mind.

When I was younger, I realized that my purpose in life is simple – to help others grow and succeed. I am a teacher and a helper. I enjoy helping others succeed. I'm good at it. It's very fulfilling. When I'm at the end of my life, I expect that I'll look back with great joy at the number of people I helped succeed.

I keep this mental picture in mind as I go about my day-to-day business. I ask myself a simple question almost every day. "Bud, did the things you did today support your life's purpose of helping others learn, grow and succeed?"

If I answer, "yes," I consider it a successful day. If I answer "no," I think about what I can do the next day to get back to living my purpose.

Successful people have a clear and vivid mental image of what success means to them. They live their life's purpose every day. If you haven't clarified your purpose in life, this is a good time to start. Once you get clear on your purpose, live it every day in all your actions.

What's your dream? Have you created a vivid mental image of it?

I suggest that you take some time for yourself. Ask and answer these three questions:

- Where do I want to be 10, 20 and 30 years from now?

- What will it look like and feel like when I'm there?

- What will my life be like?

Ask and answer these and any other questions that will help you develop a clear, vivid mental image of your success. This is not day-dreaming. It is real work. You are designing your future in your mind.

The common sense point of this tweet is simple. Successful people define what success means to them. Then they develop a compelling and clear mental image of their success. They use this mental image to help keep their dreams alive and to keep moving forward to what they want in their lives and careers. Remember Tweet 2 in *Success Tweets*, "The more clear you are about what success means to you personally, the easier it will be to create the life and career you want." Get clear on what your career success looks like, and then create it. Keep this mental picture with you as you go about your day-to-day business. Every once in a while, ask yourself if what you did that day brought you any closer to your mental image of you as a career success. In this way, you'll be keeping your dream alive – and moving toward your career success goals.

Success Tweet 3

Think of your purpose as your personal mission; why you are on this earth. Your direction is your vision for the next 3 to 5 years.

As a career success coach, I'm here to help other people succeed in realizing their purpose. I think this is a pretty mighty purpose. I may help someone who someday may become President, or a Supreme Court Justice, or find a cure for cancer, or just be a loving and caring parent. This purpose anchors me. It keeps me going when I get frustrated, or when I feel like quitting, or when I start to feel that it's OK to be "good enough," not great.

The other day, I was having a conversation with one of my career success coach clients. We were discussing clarity of purpose and direction. She said that she read a blog post on clarity of purpose and direction that I wrote and got confused by all of the different words that came up when she thought about clarity – words like purpose, direction, mission and vision.

This got me thinking. If she gets confused about the semantics of clarity of purpose and direction, I bet others do too. Below, I have defined these terms for you in a manner that will help you create your personal clarity of purpose and direction.

As I begin, please note that these are the working definitions that I use with my career success clients. You may have seen other definitions for these terms. I am presenting these definitions here to help you better understand how I use them in my model – not as the "correct" definition of these terms.

For our purposes here, I define the word "mission" as follows…

- Your **reason** for existing.
- Your **passion**.
- **Why** you are on this earth.

This isn't always easy to discover.

If you're young and still trying to figure out your mission, don't worry. It takes time. That's why I always tell people to be open to new ideas and thoughts, as you never know what you might pick up.

If you'd told me when I was in high school that my mission would be to help others succeed, I would have laughed. It took several courses in college and a year of service as a VISTA Volunteer for me to figure it out. That's when I began my career in the human development field.

Your mission needs to come from deep inside you. It is unlikely to change over the long run. I've had lots of different jobs in lots of companies and have been self-employed for over 20 years. Through all the changes, one thing has remained constant – my desire and passion for helping others succeed. In my heart of hearts, I know that I am on this earth to help others navigate the ambiguities of life in order to reach their goals.

Here is my mission...

> To help others achieve the career and life success that they want and deserve by applying their common sense.

It hasn't changed since I was 23 years old. This mission reflects who I am and why I get up every morning. It's what's right for me.

What's right for you? What is your passion? What is your reason for living? Why are you on this earth?

Think of your vision as...

- Where you are going.
- What you will achieve in the next 1, 5, 10, 20 years.

Unlike your mission, your vision will change over the course of your life and career. Early in my career I was working for the government training other people to be VISTA Volunteers; my three-year vision was to get a Master's Degree at night and to parlay that into a training and development job in business. Notice that this vision fit into my mission of helping others succeed in their lives and careers, but it had a specific short-term time frame.

When I was in my 30's my vision shifted. It became "to create a successful career success coaching, consulting and speaking business." Your vision needs to be consistent with your mission. However, unlike your mission, your vision should change as you grow and develop in your career.

Finally, your vision should always be a BHAG – a big hairy audacious goal. I first saw this term in Jim Collins and Jerry Porras' great book, *Built to Last*. You need to create a vision that will challenge you and motivate you – it should be big and hairy and audacious. What's a big hairy audacious goal for your next year? Five years? Ten years?

My current vision comes in a one-year and a five-year time frame.

> Create a profitable Internet business that will allow me to share my optimistic message on career and life success and help as many people as I can.

> Make 100% of my income from the Internet five years from now.

Notice how my one-year vision is consistent with my mission of helping others succeed in their lives and careers. It's also a BHAG – for me at least. While I have amassed knowledge about career and life success over a lifetime of work and study, turning that knowledge into information products that I can sell over the Internet is something completely new for me. I'm learning about Internet marketing as I go. With a little luck and a lot of persistence, I am confident that this will be a breakout year for me as an Internet marketer.

I'm also confident that in five years; I'll be doing almost all of my business on the Internet. I'll be traveling for business only when I choose to do so. This will be a radical departure from the 45 to 50 weeks of business travel that I've done for so many years.

So where does all this leave us when it comes to thinking about clarity of purpose and direction? Here's how I suggest you think about it.

Your purpose is your mission – your reason for living, your passion, what you are on this earth to do; something that is unlikely to change over the long run.

Your direction is your vision – short- and medium-term goals that define the direction you will take your life and career.

There is a common sense career success point to this tweet. Successful people define a clarity of purpose and direction for their lives and careers. Your clarity of purpose and direction should include both a personal mission (your purpose) and a personal vision (your direction). Your mission is your reason for living, why you are on this earth. It is unlikely to change over the long run. Your vision is a short- or medium-term goal that defines the direction you will take over the next three to five years. It will change as you grow and develop in your life and career. Your vision must be consistent with your mission.

Success Tweet 4

The mightier your purpose, the more likely you are to succeed. It will give you a strong foundation when the winds of change shift.

Your clarity of purpose and direction provide your foundation. From them, you can build the successful life and career that you want and deserve. The more clear and the more mighty your purpose and direction, the stronger your foundation.

I'm a sixties guy. After all these years, my favorite recording artist is still Bob Dylan. My favorite Dylan song – and maybe my favorite song ever -- is "Forever Young." He rerecorded and re-released it recently. Pepsi has picked it up and is using it in its ads that run on NFL games. I used one of the lines from it to introduce my bestselling book, *Straight Talk for Success* – "May you build a ladder to the stars and climb on every rung."

Check out some of the other lyrics...

"May your hands always be busy.

May your feet always be swift.

May you have a strong foundation

When the winds of change shift."

By now you may be saying, "Get to the point, Bud." So I will. You should begin your success journey by clarifying your purpose in life. Why are you on this earth? What are you meant to do? I believe that the more mighty this purpose, the more you are likely to succeed. A mighty purpose gives you that strong foundation "when the winds of change shift."

Brad Swift of the Life On Purpose Institute (www.lifeonpurpose.com) makes a great point about clarity of purpose...

> "Taking a bold stand for living on purpose starts by knowing your purpose with crystal clarity -- knowing it so well that if someone woke you up at 3:00 in the morning and asked you what your life purpose is, you'd be able to tell them.

21

And if someone who knew you well heard what you said, they'd realize that your life was a true, authentic reflection of that purpose."

There are two common sense points on which I want to focus here. First, your clarity of purpose should be so big, so mighty, so important to you, that it is deeply ingrained in your psyche. It has to be part of who you are. Second, you have to live your clarity of purpose 24/7/365. This takes commitment; commitment to determining your life's purpose, and commitment to living it.

If you were to wake me at 3:00 in the morning, shine a light in my face and ask me for my life's purpose, I'm sure I would say, "Helping people create successful lives and careers." It's that much a part of me. My elevator speech begins, "Hi, I'm Bud Bilanich, the Common Sense Guy; I help people create successful lives and careers by applying their common sense."

For me, this is a mighty purpose. I'm helping other people find career success -- and fulfillment in their lives. That's important work in my book. I take immense satisfaction out of seeing others learn, grow and succeed. In another life I might have been a teacher or athletic coach. In this life, I help people create the life and career success that they want and deserve.

There is an old saying that goes something like, "The problem is not in setting your goal too high and not reaching it. The problem is setting your goal too low and achieving it." I can't remember the exact quote or the attribution. I'll send a copy of *Success Tweets* to the first person who leaves a comment telling us the exact quote and the attribution. Please respond by leaving a comment, not by sending me an email. I want the answer to be visible to everyone who reads this blog.

What is your purpose? Is it mighty? I hope so.

The common sense career success coach point of this tweet is simple. Successful people think big. They ground themselves in a mighty purpose. Tweet 4 in *Success Tweets* says, "The mightier your purpose, the more likely you are to succeed. It will give you a strong foundation when the winds of change shift." Take this advice to heart. Ground yourself with a mighty purpose. It's better to aim too high and fall a little short than it is to aim too low and reach your goal. Or, as Mario Andretti once said, "If you're in complete control, you're probably not going fast enough." Think about it.

Success Tweet 5

Your vision should be a BHAG; a Big Hairy Audacious Goal. Make it something that is really worth accomplishing.

Let's back up for a second and talk about the difference between your personal mission and personal vision. Your mission is your reason for existing, your passion, why you are on this earth. As I've said, my mission is to help others achieve the life and career success they want and deserve. Your mission is your purpose in life. Once you settle on a personal mission, you should think very long and hard before you change it.
Your personal vision is the direction in which you are going in the short to medium term – usually the next three to five years. Unlike your mission, your vision should change with the times. It should be consistent with your mission, but should reflect the new goals you set for yourself as you move forward in your life and achieve some measure of career success.
As the tweet says, your vision should always be a BHAG – a big hairy audacious goal. You need to create a vision that will challenge you and motivate you – it should be big and hairy and audacious. What's your big hairy audacious goal for the next year? Three years? Five years? Ten years?
I like the word "audacious" in the BHAG idea. According to Dictionary.com, audacious is defined as: "extremely bold and daring, brave, fearless, original, without restriction to prior ideas, highly inventive, unrestrained, uninhibited, bold in defiance of convention." Do these words inspire you or frighten you? I hope they inspire you to be bold and daring, fearless and original when it comes to creating your personal vision. Don't be constrained by convention, or restricted by prior ideas. Be highly inventive.

I've shared my current vision in a previous post. It comes in a one-year and a five-year time frame.

> Create a profitable internet business that will allow me to share my optimistic message on career and life success and help as many people as I can.
> Make 100% of my income from the Internet five years from now.

This Vision is a BHAG for me; it's audacious. I'm on a steep learning curve when it comes to Internet marketing. Accomplishing my personal vision is going to take more than a little luck -- and a lot of persistence. But that's OK – I realize my vision is a BHAG, and I'm willing to take the risk of stating it in public and committing to doing the work to make it a reality. I'm choosing to be bold and daring as I enter the next phase of my life.

So what does this mean for you? It means that you too should be bold and daring as you create your personal vision. Don't be constrained by convention; see yourself as an audacious success three to five years in the future. That's how you become a career success.

Your mindset makes all the difference. You need to be willing to commit to doing things differently. As the saying goes, you need to be willing to give up what you are for what you can become. The first step in creating a personal vision that is a BHAG is to determine your goal for the time frame you choose. As you see, I've created a one-year and five-year goal. Your goal should be very focused. It should be difficult to achieve – or it's not a BHAG. Your personal vision should stretch you past your comfort zone. It should be life-changing. It should build on the momentum you have going. It should excite and stimulate you. It should be something that is really worth accomplishing.

The common sense career success coach point here is simple. Successful people clarify their purpose and direction in life. Your purpose is your personal mission. Your direction is your personal vision – what you will accomplish in the next three to five years. As Tweet 5 in *Success Tweets* says, "Your vision should be a BHAG; a Big Hairy Audacious Goal. Make it something that is really worth accomplishing." Your personal vision should be bold and daring, original, not restricted by your past way of thinking, highly inventive, unrestrained and uninhibited. In short – think big, think outside the box, think about what you can become, not what you are today.

Success Tweet 6

Make sure that your personal mission and vision are what you want – not what someone else wants for you.

This is really important. You need to live your own life and create your own career success. Over the years, I have had way too many career success coach clients who felt as if they were trapped in careers that they didn't really choose. That's not a good way to build career success. You have to love what you do. You have to be passionate about what you do. This love and passion has to come from deep inside you.

This means that you need to choose the career you love – not what others want you to love. Parents, friends and peers mean well when they try to steer you into a career they think is right for you. But, parents, friends and peers are not you. You know what's best for you.

Many people apply to medical or law school because their parents want them to become a doctor or a lawyer. However, after a year or two of school, or worse yet, a year or two of practice as a doctor or a lawyer, some of these people figure out that they aren't living their life purpose, they're living the life their parents want for them. And, they have a mountain of student loan debt. These folks become angry and bitter. They spend a lifetime going through the motions, never really developing that sense of happiness and career success that comes from doing what they love and what they choose to do.

We all have to find our passion in life and pursue it. I had a double major at Penn State, broadcast journalism and human development. My senior year I had an internship at a television station in Scranton PA. I did well in the internship. As luck would have it, one of the reporters announced his plans to leave the station right about the time I was to graduate. The News Director liked me and offered me a reporter job. I was flattered and really tempted to take it. This was a rare opportunity. In those days, most people coming out of college had to spend a few years in radio news prior to moving to TV. Yet, I was lucky enough to receive an offer at a TV station right out of school.

However, there was one small problem. I had already committed to doing a year of service as a VISTA Volunteer. I could have backed out of that commitment, but my personal ethics wouldn't let me do so. I turned down the TV news job. The News Director and my Journalism advisor at Penn State did their best to convince me that this was a special opportunity and that there would be no guarantee that I would be able to secure a similar offer one year later. They had my best interests in mind. They wanted me to get off to a running start in the world of TV news.

I chose to stick to my commitment of a year of service. And I'm glad I did. That year of service opened my eyes to career possibilities I didn't know existed. After my year of service, I took a job that helped me identify my purpose in life – helping others grow and succeed. To paraphrase Tweet 5, I made sure that my personal mission and vision were what I wanted – not what my professor, boss, and parents for that matter – wanted for me.

These people were all well-meaning. My professor saw some promise in me. He liked my writing style. He thought I would be a great TV news writer. Besides that, he saw his students' work in the broadcast journalism field as part of his legacy. The News Director saw an opportunity to fill a vacancy with a proven commodity. My parents thought a "real job," as opposed to a year of service, was better for me.

However, I had to decide. And, I made the correct decision.

The common sense career success coach point here is simple. Successful people look deep inside themselves to discover their purpose and direction in life. They listen to, even solicit, advice from people they respect and trust. But when it comes to creating their personal mission and vision, they follow the advice in Tweet 6 in *Success Tweets*: "Make sure that your personal mission and vision are what you want – not what someone else wants for you." It's your life and your career. You have to live it. That's why you have to choose your personal mission and vision based on what's right for you – not what other people think is right for you. Other people, particularly those close to you, have your best interests at heart. That's why you should listen to what they have to say; but you need to make the final decision on your personal mission by yourself. That's the first step in taking personal responsibility for your life and career success.

Success Tweet 7

Figure out what you really want to do. Work you love will make it easier to create the life and career success you want and deserve.

In this post, I'd like to tell you a story about a young woman who has figured out what she wants to do and is really going after it.

Morgan O'Reilly is my niece. I love her dearly. Ever since I can remember, Morgan has been interested in houses and decorating. I remember her visiting Cathy and me when she was about 12. She wanted to explore Denver's neighborhoods; she was very interested in the different types of houses and how prices varied from neighborhood to neighborhood. I remember telling her that she should get into real estate.

Morgan graduated from high school and enrolled at Florida State where she studied fashion merchandising. After graduation she got a job as an assistant buyer with a large and profitable retailing chain. She got a couple of promotions and was doing quite well. She was moving up the ladder there.

But she wasn't happy. Not only did she not love her work, she came to dislike it.

She decided that she needed to change careers. She thought about what she really loves, and it turned out to be houses and decorating. She concluded that real estate was a good fit for her. Unfortunately, real estate is a tough 100% commission business. That's the reason why Morgan didn't get into it right out of college.

But this time, she decided that real estate was the right career for her. She discussed it with her husband Aaron, and together they decided that they could forgo her salary for several months. She interviewed and got a job with Keller Williams, a large national real estate firm. She took a certification exam prep course and nailed the practice exam. In fact, she got a hundred – excuse this uncle's bragging. She passed the Florida state licensing exam – they don't give scores to people who pass, so she doesn't know how well she did. I'm sure she passed by a wide margin.

When Morgan resigned her job with the retailer, they offered her a promotion. She didn't even think twice about turning it down. She is starting her career in real estate. She isn't looking back.

As a career success coach – and her uncle – I say, "Good for you, Morgan. You've found a career you love, and you're putting all of your heart and soul into it. I'm proud of you."

Morgan is working in the Jacksonville Beach, FL area. If you, or anyone you know is interested in buying property there, get in touch with her at moreilly@comcast.net. Tell her I sent you.

The common sense career success coach point is simple. Remember Tweet 7 in *Success Tweets* when you are thinking about your life's purpose and work. "Figure out what you really want to do. Work you love will make it easier to create the life and career success you want and deserve." Work you love doesn't seem like work. It is enjoyable and fun. Morgan O'Reilly, my niece, recently made a career change. She went from being a buyer with a large national retailer to a career in real estate. She didn't like retailing. She loves real estate – especially matching buyers and houses. Since she made this move within the month, it's too early to tell how well she'll do. However, from her enthusiasm, and perfect score on the licensing exam practice test, I'm sure she's going to kick some serious butt.

Success Tweet 8

Don't focus just on making money. If you do, you'll be asking too little of yourself. Focus on how you can be useful in this world.

I loved the 1972 movie, *Cabaret* (I can't believe it was that long ago). If you haven't seen *Cabaret*, rent the DVD. It's a funny and sad movie at the same time. I bring up *Cabaret* here because one of the dance routines in it popped into my mind when I typed Tweet 8 just now. It features Joel Grey and Liza Minnelli and is called "Money Makes the World Go 'Round."

Yes, money does make the world go 'round. We all need money. It is difficult to live with little or no money. But I suggest that choosing a career solely on the basis of the money you can make is not a good idea.

John D. Rockefeller, once the richest man in the USA, said, "If your only goal is to become rich, you'll never achieve it."

This is great common sense career success advice. Your goals in life should be more than just making money. Your goals should spring from your purpose in life, your passion. This isn't to say that you should choose a career in which you can make little or no money. Choose your life's work based on what you love to do, and you'll find a way to make money. The old saying, "Do what you love, and the money will follow," is true.

Michelle Schubnel is a coach to coaches. She runs a program called Coach and Grow R.I.C.H. Her R.I.C.H. acronym applies here:

R   Rewarded

I   Inspired

C   Confident

H   Happy

I think this is a great way to think about making money and being useful in this world. You are rich when you are: rewarded for your contributions; inspired by what you do;

confident as a professional; and happy with the way you spend your time. Let's talk about each of these.

Rewarded – We all deserve to be appropriately compensated for the work we do and the value we bring to others. This means that you shouldn't feel bad about making money, only that making money shouldn't be your sole goal in life. Some might say that the current financial crisis is the result of some people who valued making money at the expense of others. Do your job, get good at it and the money will follow.

Inspired – You can find inspiration in the work you do every day. If you're a realtor like my niece, Morgan, you can be inspired when you help a person or a couple find the home of their dreams. If you're a pharmaceutical sales rep, you can be inspired by the fact that you're helping doctors understand how the medicines your company makes can save lives. My dad was a steel worker for 37 years. He found inspiration in the buildings and bridges he helped build. I find inspiration every time someone leaves a comment on this blog or tells me that one of my tweets made a difference in their life.

Confident – Doing something you love, doing it well and being useful in this world will build your confidence. Your confidence grows as your skill level grows and you begin to make bigger contributions at work and in the world. A world of confident people would be a wonderful place to live. Confident people see the world from a win-win perspective.

Happy – When are you happiest? I'm willing to bet it's when you accomplish something – or help someone else accomplish something – not when you get your pay check. When you do something you love everyday you can't help but be happy. I am happiest when I finish a book. Writing a book takes a lot of time and effort. And, I'm a perfectionist. I want to make sure my books are the best I can make them, so I put in a lot of time and effort making sure they're just right. And, you know what? I'm really happy when I first hold a copy of one of my books in my hand. At that moment, I know the work was worth it. I'm happy when I help others succeed too. I love the moments when I can see the light go on in one of my career success coach client's eyes. I love it when I help other people get it.

I saw a young woman wearing a T shirt the other day that made a profound point. On the front it said, "Wealth is not the opposite of poverty." On the back it said, "Enough is the opposite of poverty." This message goes to the heart of the message in Tweet 8. Successful people know what "enough" is for them and their family. They are happy with enough. They pursue a life and career that fulfills them. They know that being rich is more than having a lot of money.

If you read this blog with any regularity, you know that my mom passed away a little over a year ago. She was one for schmaltzy cards. I'm not. But several years ago, she sent me a card on my birthday. I cut out the message and taped it to my printer. I look at it several times a day…

"That man is a success who is happy with himself and gives happiness to others; who makes the world a better place simply by being a part of it."

My mother believed this about me. I do my best to live up to it every day.

The common sense career success coach point here is simple. Successful people see money as the byproduct of their work – not as their sole reason for working. They follow the advice in Tweet 8 in *Success Tweets*. "Don't focus just on making money. If you do, you'll be asking too little of yourself. Focus on how you can be useful in this world." Successful people know that being rich doesn't mean you have tons and tons of money. They know that being rich means that you are: Rewarded for your contributions; Inspired by what you do; Confident in your skills, and Happy with the way you spend your days.

Success Tweet 9

Happiness doesn't come from getting more things. It comes from finding a worthy purpose and pursuing it.

I'd like to begin with three quotes. The first is from T.E. Lawrence – you know, the Lawrence of Arabia guy.

"All men dream, but not equally. Those who dream by night in the dusty recesses of their minds wake in the day to find that it was vanity. But the dreamers of the day are dangerous men, for they may act on their dreams with open eyes, to make it possible."

The second is from my favorite playwright, George Bernard Shaw.

"This is the true joy in life, being used for a purpose recognized by yourself as a mighty one; being thoroughly worn out before you are thrown on the scrap heap; being a force of nature instead of a feverish, selfish little clod of ailments and grievances complaining that the world will not devote itself to making you happy."

The third is from Oscar Wilde.

"To live is the rarest thing in the world. Most people exist, that is all."

I dream by day, and I hope you do too. I want to be thoroughly worn out before I'm thrown on the scrap heap. I refuse to be a selfish little clod of ailments complaining about the world. And I choose to live – completely and fully. My purpose in life helps me do this.

As you know, I'm a career success coach. My purpose is to help other people create the life and career success they want and deserve. That's why I am a career success coach. To me this is a worthy purpose. More important, it's a purpose that makes me happy.

As I'm writing this, I keep seeing a tweet by the mythical Frank Tyger that has been re-tweeted at least 10 times in the past hour. "Doing what you like is freedom. Liking what you do is happiness."

All of this goes back to Tweet 9 in *Success Tweets*. "Things don't make you happy. Happiness comes from doing something of value." Success Tweet 4 says, "The mightier

32

your purpose, the more likely you are to succeed. It will give you a strong foundation when the winds of change shift."

If you want to create a mighty life purpose, it's a good idea to write a life purpose statement. However, many people tell me that they have tried to write a life purpose statement with little success.

Steve Pavlina offers a common sense, four-step approach to finding your life purpose. I really like these four simple steps:

1. Take out a blank sheet of paper or open up a word processor where you can type (I prefer the latter because it's faster).

2. Head it, "What is my true purpose in life?"

3. Write an answer (any answer) that pops into your head. It doesn't have to be a complete sentence. A short phrase is fine.

4. Repeat step 3 until you write the answer that makes you cry. This is your purpose.

That's it. It doesn't matter if you're a counselor or an engineer or a bodybuilder. To some people this exercise will make perfect sense. To others it will seem utterly stupid. Usually it takes 15-20 minutes to clear your head of all the clutter and the social conditioning about what you think your purpose in life is. The false answers will come from your mind and your memories. But when the true answer finally arrives, it will feel like it's coming to you from a different source entirely.

I love Steve's simple common sense approach to finding your life purpose. As a career success coach, I suggest you try it if you don't have a clear statement of your life's purpose.

However, once you find your life purpose, you have to live it every day. This blog is one way that I live my purpose every day. I post five days a week. That means that five days a week I write 800 to 1,200 words on career and life success and post it here. My daily success quotes are another way I live my purpose every day. If you want to receive these daily quotes, go to www.BudBilanich.com. Enter your name and email address in the box at the top right of the page.

My books are another way I live my life purpose every day. I write books to help me clarify my thinking on life and career success – and to help others apply my career success coach thoughts to create their life and career success.

What is your purpose in life? I hope it's not getting more things. I hope it has something that is bigger than you; something that benefits others and all of us in general. I hope it's mighty.

Once you have determined your life purpose, ask yourself what you do to live it every day. Then start doing that every day. Doing something every day that reinforces your life purpose is the best way to creating a happy life and career success.

The common sense career success coach point here is simple. Successful people identify their purpose in life and then pursue it with passion. They follow the advice in Tweet 9 in *Success Tweets*. "Happiness doesn't come from getting more things. It comes from finding a worthy purpose and pursuing it." Follow Steve Pavlina's advice to develop your life purpose. Ask yourself, "What is my true purpose in life?" Keep listing answers until you find one that makes you cry. Once you get to this point, dry your tears and begin doing something every day to live that purpose. The old saying, "Whoever dies with the most toys wins," is just flat not true. As George Bernard Shaw says, success comes to those who are "used for a purpose recognized by yourself as a mighty one; being thoroughly worn out before you are thrown on the scrap heap; being a force of nature." I choose to be a force of nature, not a collector of things and toys. I hope you do too.

Success Tweet 10

Emerson says, "Good luck is another name for tenacity of purpose." Find your purpose and pursue it tenaciously.

Today, I want to focus on tenacity. Tenacious people commit to three things. First, they take personal responsibility for their success. They know that they are responsible for their own life and career success. They are willing to do the things necessary to succeed. Second, tenacious people set high goals – and then do whatever it takes to achieve them. Third, tenacious people know that stuff happens as they go through life. They realize they will encounter many problems and setbacks. Tenacious people choose to react positively to the negative stuff that happens and move forward toward their goals.

I live in Denver; the weather here is very changeable. On December 21 2009, the first day of winter, we had 60-degree weather. That night the weather announcer on TV reminded us that we had snow on the last day of summer.

This got me thinking about the unpredictability of life. As I frequently say to my career success coach clients, stuff will happen as you go through life – good stuff, bad stuff, happy stuff, sad stuff, encouraging stuff, frustrating stuff. However, it's not the stuff that happens that's important, it's how you react to it. You cannot control the people and events in your life. You can control how you react to the people and events in your life.

I choose to react positively to the people and events in my life – especially the bad stuff, sad stuff and frustrating stuff that happens to me. I choose to tenaciously follow my purpose and dreams. And I urge you to do the same if you want to create the life and career success you want and deserve.

I know this isn't always easy. In fact, it's seldom easy. But the harder you find it to react positively to negative people and events, the more important it is for you to do so. Don't blame people or circumstances when things go wrong. Instead, choose to be tenacious and learn the lesson behind every less than successful relationship or event in your life.

When you look for the lesson behind problems, setbacks and failures you are being tenacious; you are taking responsibility for your life and career success. Find the lessons in the bad stuff that happens and then do something to put those lessons to work. Commit to taking responsibility for yourself, your life and your career success. Put yourself in the driver's seat. Don't let events and people stop you from achieving your goals. Be persistent. Be tenacious.

As I write this, I'm reminded of the famous quote on persistence by Calvin Coolidge…

> "Nothing in the world can take the place of persistence. Talent will not; nothing is more common than unsuccessful men with talent. Genius will not; unrewarded genius is almost a proverb. Education will not; the world is full of educated failures. Persistence and determination alone are omnipotent."

The common sense career success coach point here is simple. Successful people commit to taking personal responsibility for their life and career success. They heed the advice in Tweet 10 in Success Tweets: "Emerson says, 'Good luck is another name for tenacity of purpose.' Find your purpose and pursue it tenaciously." Only you can make you a success. You have to take personal responsibility for creating the life and career success you want and deserve. Tenacity and persistence are the hallmarks of people who are committed to taking personal responsibility for their life and career success. Tenacious and persistent people keep going, even in – no, especially in – the face of difficulties and problems. Promise yourself that you will commit to taking personal responsibility for your life and career success. Be persistent. Be tenacious. Keep at it, and you will reach your goals.

Success Tweet 11

Create a vivid mental image of yourself as a success. This vivid image will keep you motivated and moving forward when things get tough.

Dr. Martin Luther King is one of my personal heroes. He helped lead our nation out of the dehumanizing segregation policies that flourished in the post-civil war period. I believe that he, more than any other single person, was responsible for the passage of the Civil Rights Act of 1964. Today a black man is president of the United States. This would have been unthinkable on August 28, 1963, the day Dr. King delivered his famous speech, "I Have a Dream."

I bring up Dr. King and the "I Have a Dream" speech because it is the embodiment of a vivid mental image of success. Read the words below and see how they so clearly describe Dr. King's vivid mental image of success, for himself and the nation.

> "And so even though we face the difficulties of today and tomorrow, I still have a dream. It is a dream deeply rooted in the American dream.
>
> "I have a dream that one day this nation will rise up and live out the true meaning of its creed: 'We hold these truths to be self-evident, that all men are created equal.'
>
> "I have a dream that one day on the red hills of Georgia, the sons of former slaves and the sons of former slave owners will be able to sit down together at the table of brotherhood.
>
> "I have a dream that one day even the state of Mississippi, a state sweltering with the heat of injustice, sweltering with the heat of oppression, will be transformed into an oasis of freedom and justice.
>
> "I have a dream that my four little children will one day live in a nation where they will not be judged by the color of their skin but by the content of their character.
>
> "I have a *dream* today!

"I have a dream that one day, down in Alabama, with its vicious racists, with its governor having his lips dripping with the words of 'interposition' and 'nullification' – one day right there in Alabama, little black boys and black girls will be able to join hands with little white boys and white girls as sisters and brothers.

"I have a *dream* today!

"I have a dream that one day every valley shall be exalted, and every hill and mountain shall be made low, the rough places will be made plain, and the crooked places will be made straight; and the glory of the Lord shall be revealed and all flesh shall see it together."

Those are powerful words and a powerful vivid mental image. They kept Dr. King moving forward through the dark days in Selma all the way to the passage of the Civil Rights Act of 1964.

I urge all of my career success coach clients to develop a vivid mental image of themselves as a career success. What is your vivid mental image of your career success? Can you articulate it as clearly and vividly as Dr. King?

The common sense career success coach point in this discussion of Dr. King's "I Have a Dream" speech is simple. Successful people clarify their purpose and direction for their life and career. Few people have demonstrated such a clear sense of purpose and direction for their lives as Dr. Martin Luther King. His famous "I Have a Dream" speech is one of the best examples of a clear, vivid mental image of not only personal success, but success for us as a society. "I have a dream… that little black boys and black girls will be able to join hands with little white boys and white girls as sisters and brothers." The dream is alive – although we still need to keep working on it. You need to work on creating a vivid mental image of yourself as a career success. The more vivid the image the better. As Tweet 11 in Success Tweets says, your vivid mental image of yourself as a success "will keep you motivated and moving forward when things get tough."

Success Tweet 12

Visualization is powerful. The more vivid the image you have of your success, the more likely you are to succeed.

As a career success coach, I suggest that once you define what career success means to you personally, you need to develop a clear mental picture of your career success. This image should be as vivid as you can you make it. Try to create your career success vivid image in 3-D.

As I mentioned in my discussion of Success Tweet 2, when I was 25, I conjured up a vivid image of myself as a success coach, motivational speaker, management consultant and author. I worked in my home office – where I wrote and developed the programs I delivered at client locations. This office had a floor-to-ceiling wall of books that I could use for easy reference. It also had a state of the art IBM Selectric typewriter and a big, clunky telephone. PCs and the Internet were science fiction in 1975.

I also saw myself having one to one discussions with senior leaders in a variety of organizations, conducting training and team-building sessions in conference rooms at their locations. Amazingly, many of the people in the sessions were smoking. I had very vivid images of standing in front of large audiences at sales meetings doing talks. I saw myself signing a book I had written at a bookstore. I also saw myself on airplanes, traveling to my speaking, coaching and consulting gigs.

All of these vivid images came true. My office is much as I had imagined it – except it has two PCs and a cell phone, not a Selectric typewriter and clunky phone. The wall of books is there – overflowing. I've written 11 of the books on the shelf. People don't smoke in my training and team-building sessions anymore and I use PowerPoint instead of handwritten flip charts, but the big stuff is the same as I've imagined it. I've spoken to audiences all over North America, in Latin America, Europe and Asia. I am a million-mile flyer with Continental Air Lines.

I'm living my career success dream – in large part because I dared to dream it all those years ago.

What's your career success dream? Have you created a vivid mental image of it?

I suggest that you take some time for yourself. Ask and answer these three questions:

- Where do I want to be 10, 20 and 30 years from now?

- What will it look like and feel like when I'm there?

- What will my life be like?

Ask and answer these and any other questions that will help you develop a clear, vivid mental image of your career success. This is not day-dreaming. It is real work. You are designing your future in your mind.

Keep this mental picture of your career success with you as you go about your day-to-day business. Every once in a while, ask yourself if what you did that day brought you any closer to your mental image of career success. If the answer is no, make sure that you take at least one act the very next day to move closer to your vivid mental image of your career success. In this way, you'll be keeping your dream alive – and moving toward your goal.

The common sense career coach success point here is simple. Successful people define what success means to them. Then they develop a compelling and clear mental image of their success. They heed the advice in Tweet 12 in Success Tweets: "Visualization is powerful. The more vivid the image you have of your success, the more likely you are to succeed." They use their vivid mental image to help keep their dreams alive and to keep moving forward to what they want in their lives and careers. Creating a vivid mental image of your success is not day-dreaming. It's real work – it's the work of designing your future, so you can take the steps necessary to create it.

Success Tweet 13

Your vivid mental image is a blueprint. It is a plan for success, but you still have to do the work to make it a reality.

I probably should amend the tweet to say, "Your vivid mental image is a goal. You need to create a plan (a blueprint) to make this goal a reality – and then do the work." Regardless, the career success coach message here is simple. You have to do the work to achieve your goals. It's up to you. You're the one who has to do the work.

My current vivid image of my career success is one in which I work primarily from home as an Internet marketer.

I have a plan to make this vivid mental image come true. To implement this plan I need to manage my time well. Most of the really important work I do requires large chunks of unbroken time. I create large chunks of time for working on big projects and important activities – like writing books, blogging and creating products.

The same is true for you. You have to figure out what's important to you and then create chunks of time to do what's important. Besides my career success goals, my health is important to me; so I allocate 30 to 60 minutes a day for exercise. I'm going for a bike ride as soon as I finish writing this post. I have a friend who reads inspirational literature for at least 15 minutes each night before he goes to sleep. He says that this helps him begin each day inspired and ready to move forward toward his goals.

The important point here is to plan your days in advance. Schedule specific fixed time periods for particularly important activities and tasks. Make appointments with yourself and then discipline yourself to keep them. Set aside 30-, 60- and 90-minute time segments in which you will work on and complete important tasks that move you toward your vivid mental image of success.

Stephen Covey tells us that successful people find the time to focus on the important, but not urgent tasks. If you're not careful, your day will get taken up with urgent (sometimes important and sometimes unimportant) tasks. If this happens, you will be keeping your head above water, but not gaining any ground. You won't be moving toward your vivid mental image of your success.

Writing and posting this blog is a good example of one of the chunks of time I carve out for myself. My blog is an important, but not urgent activity for me. If you're a regular reader, you know that I post every day, Monday through Friday. I post on a different topic each day. This structure helps me when it comes to composing my posts. Right now, I've added even more structure. I am doing a series of blog posts that further explain the advice in Success Tweets. This is the 13th post in the series. I will keep going until I have done a blog post on all 141 tweets – there is a bonus tweet in the book. If you want a free copy of the eBook version, go to www.SuccessTweets.com.

I usually write my posts two or three days ahead. At a minimum, I write blog posts the night before I post them. It takes me 30 to 45 minutes to write a blog post. My discipline in writing a day before I post means that I don't feel under the gun to write something every morning. I think it results in better quality posts, and moves me toward my vivid mental image of success.

I post my blogs first thing every day. If I have a very early meeting, or will be traveling early, I post the night before. It takes me about 30 minutes to post this blog, as I post it in several locations. www.BudBilanich.com is the main page for this blog. However, I also post to several other sites.

All of this takes time and discipline. The time I spend writing and posting every day is a very important part of maintaining my Internet presence. My Internet presence is the cornerstone of my marketing efforts. I carve out large chunks of time to do the important, but not urgent task of building and maintaining my Internet presence. I have disciplined myself to set aside 60 to 90 minutes per day for writing and posting my blogs.

I also carve out time to comment on five blog posts, written by other bloggers, every day. This also helps with my Internet presence and takes about an hour a day. I have identified a number of blogs I read regularly and on which I comment. It takes about seven to ten minutes to compose a thoughtful comment for each post.

In the past, I have had good intentions of doing this, but the urgent tasks that come up every day have made this a hit and miss proposition. Recently, I decided that I will take one hour at the end of every day to read and comment on other blogs. I will do this before I end my business for the day.

The common sense career success coach point here is simple. From a time perspective, you get the biggest bang for the buck from the activities that are important to your success, but are not urgent. Unfortunately, important but not urgent tasks often don't get done because of all of the urgent tasks that come up during any given day. Tweet 13 in Success Tweets says, "Your vivid mental image is a blueprint. It is a plan for success, but you still have to do the work to make it a reality." One way to get started doing the work is to schedule time to work on the important but not urgent tasks that will result in achieving your vivid mental image of your career success. My best career success coach advice is to keep your commitment to yourself and your career success by planning your work and working your plan.

Success Tweet 14

Don't visualize the pain of failure, visualize the euphoria of success.

I think it goes without saying that positive visualization is more productive than negative visualization. You don't need a career success coach to tell you that.

"What ifs" can become a form of negative visualization. You know what I mean. "What if I try to do this, and I fail?" That's visualizing the pain of failure, not the euphoria of success.

Positive visualization will help you create the life and career success you want and deserve. Take it from a career success coach; creating a vivid mental image of you as a career success is the first step in becoming a career success. As the tweet says, focus on the euphoria of success.

You get this; it's the law of attraction at work. If you visualize yourself as a failure, you will attract failure. If you visualize yourself as a career success, you will attract career success.

'Nuff said about that.

I'd like to spend some time discussing the importance of failure – specifically how learning from failure can help you create the life and career success you want and deserve.

The late Ted Williams is famous for having a season batting average of .411. That means that out of every 1,000 times at bat, he got a hit 411 times. This is considered by baseball fans as one of the greatest records ever and unlikely to ever be broken. I met Ted Williams once. By a strange turn of events, we were staying in the same corporate suite at the same time. Ted Williams lived baseball. He told me that he learned from every at bat – whether or not he got a hit. He said that he wanted to get a hit every time he came to bat. When he didn't, he said he analyzed the situation to see what he could learn.

Ted Williams failed over half the time in his record-setting year. And he learned that failure is inevitable if you are trying for greatness. Failure is just a bump in the road to success.

Many people don't even set out on the road to success because they fear that they may fail and not reach their destination. I was speaking with one of my career success coach clients today. She told me that she had found a great job with Google – one that was a perfect match for her qualifications. But she didn't even apply because she was afraid she wouldn't get the job. By not applying, she guaranteed that she wouldn't get the job.

To put this story in the context of Tweet 14 in Success Tweets, she visualized the pain of failure, not the euphoria of getting a job with one of the best companies in the world.

Fear works in a funny way. When you embrace the fact that you will fail on your journey to life and career success, you'll find that you have nothing to fear anymore. When this happens you'll keep your eyes open, pick yourself up, learn from the failure, and move on.

As I tell my career success coach clients, "Failure is never failure unless you fail to learn something from it."

I choose to call the bumps in the road that I experience learning experiences, not failures. When things don't work out for you, ask yourself, "What can I learn from this?" Even the smallest learning makes the experience worth it.

Treat failure not as an end but as a beginning. As Mike Ditka, the famous football coach, says, "Failure is rarely fatal." This is true. Treat failures as learning experiences; pick yourself up, make some adjustments and be on your way. There are always opportunities for new beginnings. Don't quit in the middle of a problem; failure happens only when you quit. Don't give up. Visualize the euphoria of success when you are tempted to quit.

The common sense career success coach point here is simple. Successful people don't quit. They treat failures as mere setbacks on the road to career success. They heed the advice in Tweet 14 in Success Tweets: "Don't visualize the pain of failure. Visualize the euphoria of success." If you visualize yourself as a failure, you will attract failure. If you visualize yourself as a career success, you will attract career success. This doesn't mean that the road will always be smooth. But this career success coach will tell you that the road will always be smoother when you have a vivid mental image of your success awaiting you at the end. Treat failure as the learning opportunity it is. Give yourself a minute or two to be frustrated. Find the learning in the failure. Then use this learning to move forward to the life and career success that you have visualized for yourself.

Success Tweet 15

Napoleon Hill on visualization: "What the mind can conceive and believe it can achieve." What is your vision for your future?

I am a big Chinese food fan. I sometimes find inspiration for blog posts in fortune cookies. It's been a while since I did a fortune cookie post. But, as luck would have it, last night my fortune cookie read, "Advancement will come with hard work." I agree. This post is about doing the work necessary to make the vision of your career success a reality.

While you need to visualize your life and career success, your vision is for naught if you don't have the will and determination to work hard at making it a reality. There's a quote that I've seen attributed to many American football coaches, "Nobody ever drowned in his own sweat." You have to be willing to work hard if you're going to succeed.

Yes, you need to work smart, not just hard, but hard work is the best way to create the career and life success you want and deserve. Fortune Magazine says it succinctly: "There is no substitute for hard work." Bobby Fischer became a chess grandmaster at age 16. However, he had nine years of hard work and intense study to get to that place. Few of us are willing to work that hard at that early of an age.

The success literature is full of quotes on hard work. Take a look...

> "I do not know anyone who has gotten to the top without hard <u>work</u>. That is the recipe. It will not always get you to the top, but it will get you pretty near." <u>Margaret Thatcher</u>

> "I'm a great believer in luck and I find the harder I work, the more I have of it." <u>Thomas Jefferson</u>

> "Love conquers all, but if love doesn't do it, try hard work." <u>Unknown</u>

"If the power to do hard work is not a skill, it's the best possible substitute for it." James A. Garfield

"When you live for a strong purpose, then hard work isn't an option. It's a necessity." Steve Pavlina

"There is no substitute for hard work." Thomas Edison

"The daily grind of hard work gets a person polished." Unknown

"Unless you are willing to drench yourself in your work beyond the capacity of the average man, you are just not cut out for positions at the top." J.C. Penney

"Hard work is the key to success, so work diligently on any project you undertake. If you truly want to be successful, be prepared to give up your leisure time and work past 5 PM and on weekends." Charles Lazarus

"I learned the value of hard work by working hard." Margaret M. Fitzpatrick

"Hard work has made it easy. That is my secret. That is why I win." Nadia Comaneci

"Hard work certainly goes a long way. These days a lot of people work hard, so you have to make sure you work even harder and really dedicate yourself to what you are doing and setting out to achieve." Lakshmi Mittal

"Striving for success without hard work is like trying to harvest where you haven't planted." David Bly

Here's a story my friend Andy O'Bryan tells about his success journey...

The year was 2004.

I had left my high-paying marketing director position and was trying to get traction with a fledgling home business. To pay the bills I was cold calling from 9-5 for $400 a week.

From 7 pm to 1 am every night I was interviewing. Authors, speakers, coaches, trainers, gurus, icons, industry leaders. For a while I was doing 6 or 7 interviews a week.

Life lessons, business advice, sales training, inspiration, just an amazing amount of content came out of these sessions.

The calls were recorded and the mp3's were put up on a website: http://www.AudioMotivation.com.

Co-founder Josh Hinds and I grew this site to over 1,500 paying members and 800 affiliates. There are over 100 interviews in there. It was a very challenging but extremely rewarding time of my life.

Andy now has a very successful home-based business. But he put in the time and hard work it took to make it so.

The common sense career success coach point here is simple. Successful people heed the advice in Tweet 15 in Success Tweets: "Napoleon Hill on visualization: 'What the mind can conceive and believe it can achieve.' What is your vision for your future?" Achieve is the key word here. And achieve goes hand-in-hand with hard work. Successful people not only create a vivid mental image of their success. They put in the hard work necessary for realizing that vision. There are no two ways about it. If you want to create a successful life and career, you need to put in the time and effort necessary to succeed. Sometimes this means working longer hours than others. I have found that a well-focused extra hour a week can yield big results.

Success Tweet 16

Use affirmations to realize your vision of your success. Affirmations are statements about the future stated in the present tense.

Self-confidence is an important key to life and career success. This career success coach has learned that self-confidence is an upward spiral. Self-confidence leads to career success, which leads to increased self-confidence, which leads to higher levels of career success, and so on.

You might be saying, "That's great, but how do I become self-confident if I'm new in my job or if I haven't had a lot of success to bolster my self-confidence?" There's an old saying that applies here: "Fake it till you make it." In other words, act as if you are a career success already. This will help you succeed. Your success will help you build your self-confidence.

How do you "fake it, till you make it?" As Tweet 16 in Success Tweets says, begin with affirmations. If you're in a new job, tell yourself something like, "I have the skills and desire to succeed in this job," several times a day. If you repeat this to yourself often enough, you will begin to believe it. This will help you perform at the level necessary in order to actually succeed in your job.

Affirmations are positive self talk. The idea behind affirmations is simple. When you think of the things to which you aspire, like becoming a career success, and then tell yourself that you are a career success, you will believe that you can become a career success. More important, you will be more likely to do the work it takes to make your career success aspirations come true.

As I mentioned in my discussion of Success Tweet 2, I follow my own career success coach advice. A couple of years ago, I wrote a book called Star Power, Common Sense Ideas for Career and Life Success. I used a star to depict this model. I urged readers to think of themselves as a star and to aspire to becoming a career and life star. I like the star metaphor. Daily, I repeat the following affirmation to myself: "Bud Bilanich is a star."

I've done a lot of working in making this affirmation a reality – redoing my website, developing better promotional materials, speaking, writing books, blogging.

I've also done something a little unusual. A few years ago, right after Star Power was published, I went to the "Name a Star" website and named a star after myself. Now I can say, "Bud Bilanich is a star" and really believe it, because Bud Bilanich really is a star.

Bud Bilanich the star is Catalog Number TYC 868-1011-1 in the constellation Leo. Bud Bilanich has a Visual Magnitude indicator of 11.2. Right Ascension is 11h 58m 21s. Declination is 11degrees, 43,'18."

I don't have a clue what all of these things mean, except the constellation Leo, which I chose because my birthday is August 14. But I do know one thing. Bud Bilanich is a star!

How's that for an affirmation?

Affirmations work. I have become a minor star in the career success coach world.

You don't need to go to the lengths I did to make your personal affirmations work either. Just decide what you want, visualize yourself as having it. Tell yourself you have it. Repeat that affirmation several times a day. Then do whatever it takes to make your affirmation come true.

Affirmations alone, however, are not enough to guarantee your career success. You have to do the work. Spend the time necessary to accomplish your goals. Volunteer for projects that will get you noticed. Become an expert on your company, its competitors, and your industry. In other words, bust your butt, and you will succeed.

The common sense point here is simple. Successful people are self-confident. If you want to become self-confident, you need to become an optimist, face your fears, and hang around with self-confident people. Your self-confidence will improve as you begin to become a life and career success. The self-confidence => career success => self-confidence cycle is an upward spiral. You have to enter the cycle somewhere. You might not have a strong track record as you begin your career, move into a new job, or start a business. Therefore, you have to "fake it till you make it" by "acting as if" you are a career success." Find ways to bolster your self-confidence until you have some real successes on which you can build. Tweet 16 in Success Tweets says, "Use affirmations to realize your vision of your success. Affirmations are statements about the future stated in the present tense." Use this career success coach advice. Affirmations are a great tool for helping you "fake it till you make it."

Success Tweet 17

Clarify your personal values. You values are your anchor. They ground you. They center you. They keep you focused on what's important.

Your personal values are important for a number of reasons. They can help you determine the types of people with whom you want to spend your valuable time. They can help you determine which company you want to join. They can help you make decisions in ambiguous situations. This career success coach is a big believer in the power of personal values.

Here is what I value. These values guide my life. They ground me and center me. They keep me focused on what's important.

Common Sense. Ralph Waldo Emerson once said, "nothing so astonishes men as common sense and plain dealing." I agree. I help my career success coach clients figure out the common sense solution to creating the life and career success they want and deserve, and then to do the work it takes to apply their common sense.

Simplify the complex. I believe that all too often people make things more complex than they really are. I help my career success coach clients simplify the complex, and develop and implement common sense solutions to their problems and issues.

Optimism. I believe that optimism is essential for anyone to grow and flourish. I live by the words in The Optimist Creed. I share these words with my career success coach clients. If you would like a copy, go to http://budbilanich.com/optimist.

Human potential. I believe we all can accomplish great things. I help my career success coach clients use applied common sense to achieve their full potential.

Value. My career success coach clients pay hard-earned money for my services. I provide them with extraordinary value-added services in order to justify their faith in me.

Trust. My career success coach clients trust me. They openly discuss their hopes, fears, problems and opportunities with me. This trust is sacred. I will not violate it.

Individuality. All of my career success coach clients are unique individuals. I honor this uniqueness. I don't sell one-size-fits-all coaching services. I am diligent about gaining a complete understanding of each individual's unique needs as I begin working with him or her.

Hard work. There are no shortcuts. I am willing to put in the time and effort necessary to succeed. I share this message with my career success coach clients. I encourage them to be true to themselves by being diligent in pursuing their career success goals and dreams.

The Power of 1. One person can make a difference. I do the work I do, because I believe I can make a difference – in the lives of my career success coach clients, and in the world.

Those are my values. What are yours?

The common sense career success coach point here is simple. Successful people live their lives by a set of well-defined personal values. They follow the advice in Tweet 17 in Success Tweets: Clarify your personal values. Your values are your anchor. They ground you. They center you. They keep you focused on what's important. If you haven't taken the time to clarify your personal values, you need to do so – the sooner the better. This is some of the best career advice I can give you. Clarifying your personal values will help you deal with the ambiguity and complexity the world throws at you.

Success Tweet 18

You've got to stand for something, or you'll fall for anything. Your values help you make decisions in ambiguous situations.

If you know your rock and roll, you know that the first sentence in today's tweet is the title of a John Mellencamp song – one of my favorites. And it's true. You, me, all of us, need to stand for something if we're going to create the life and career success we want and deserve. Your personal values are what you stand for.

In the Tweet 17 post, I shared my personal values: common sense, simplicity, optimism, human potential, value, trust, individuality, hard work, the power of 1. These values are the foundation on which I have built my life and career. They guide my decision making. I turn to them when I need help figuring out what to do. They have served me well.

In April of 1988, I was facing a major life and career decision – stay in a good, secure, albeit somewhat unsatisfying job with a top-notch corporation, or strike out on my own as an independent career success coach, speaker and consultant. I looked to my values. Optimism, human potential and hard work jumped out at me. I am an optimist. I believe in human potential, including mine. I have always been a hard worker.

Reflecting on my values – especially these three – made the decision easy. An optimist, someone who believes in human potential, and a hard worker would take the chance and start a small business – which is what I did. I became The Common Sense Guy over 22 years ago and have never looked back. My values guided me through the decision-making process.

Here's another example. As I began my work as a career success coach, I found that many of my clients were overwhelmed by the complexity of creating the life and career success they wanted. They were looking for simple answers to complex questions. I created my 4 C's of Success Model to help provide these answers. By studying successful people, I was able to create a simple, straightforward, common sense model that showed my career success coach clients how to create life and career success…

1. Clarify your purpose and direction in life and your career.
2. Commit to taking personal responsibility for your life and career success.
3. Build unshakeable self-confidence.

4. Get competent in four important areas: creating positive personal impact, outstanding performance, dynamic communication, and relationship building.

I've used this simple model to help hundreds of people create the life and career success they want and deserve. Success Tweets is organized around it. Tweet 18 is one way to clarify the purpose and direction for your life and career. My personal values, of common sense and simplifying the complex, helped me figure out a simple, but comprehensive model of life and career success. I use this model in my work as a career success coach.

I am a career success coach in large part because of my commitment to my personal value of the power of 1. I believe that one person can change the world. That's why I work so hard to help the people in my life see that they can become a life and career success. My personal value of giving value comes into play here as well. I always provide my career success coach clients with more than I have to. I give away a lot of my books. In this way, people have a reminder of the things we've talked about to which they can refer over and over again. I have a goal of giving away 10,000 copies of the eBook version of Success Tweets. If you want a copy, go to www.SuccessTweets.com. Feel free to send your friends there, too.

The career success coach common sense point here is simple. Successful people clarify their purpose and direction in life. Your personal values are an important part of your personal clarity of purpose and direction. Tweet 18 in Success Tweets says, "You've got to stand for something, or you'll fall for anything. Your values help you make decisions in ambiguous situations." Once you've clarified your personal values, you need to live them. Using your values to guide your decision making is a great way to live them on a day-to-day basis. Your values will help you stand for something – so you don't fall for anything. Just ask John Mellencamp.

Success Tweet 19

Your personal values are things that you hold near and dear; things on which you absolutely will not compromise.

Kevin Eikenberry is a friend of mine, and a leadership expert. I subscribe to his blog. The other day he did a post in which he talked about the importance of a firm and steady foundation. He used the Bible parable about the wise man who built his house upon the rock, and the careless man who built his house on sand. When the rains and winds came, the wise man's house stayed strong; the other man's was washed away.

Kevin went on to say…

> "The story speaks to building on a firm and steady foundation. The parallel for us as leaders is to build our leadership habits, values and beliefs on solid unshakable principles. It is easy to read a book or article and be excited about a new technique, approach or method. Most of these are sound and valuable. But ultimately they will hold the greatest value for you when they are integrated into the foundation of your leadership house – and the techniques, methods and approaches are understood based on their underlying and unassailable principles."

Your personal values are your career success foundation. As Kevin says, they should be solid, unshakeable principals, things that guide your life and your decision making. They should be fad-proof; ideas on which you can rely in the long run.

A couple of days ago, I did a post in which I identified my personal values: common sense, simplicity, optimism, human potential, value, trust, individuality, hard work, the power of 1. These values are the foundation on which I have built my life and career. They guide my decision making. I turn to them when I need help figuring out what to do. They have served me well. And, I will not compromise on them.

Let me give you an example. Back in December I was approached by an HR executive at one of my corporate clients. He asked if I would be willing to provide some coaching for one of the leaders at the operation for which he is responsible. Of course, I said yes.

I submitted a proposal outlining how I would approach this specific coaching project. Then, over the next few months, I answered a lot of questions about my approach to the coaching, how much it would cost, etc. I sent the HR exec several of my books gratis. I really thought I had the gig sown up. Last week he called me to tell me that while he would have preferred to use my services, his HR boss at corporate headquarters instructed him to use another coach who was doing some work in another part of the company.

If you've ever worked hard to make a sale and then lost it due to something completely out of your control, you know how I felt – frustrated. I was discussing this situation with a colleague. She said that she would have been very angry about this situation. I wasn't angry, stuff happens in business. I was a little frustrated, but I chose to let it go.

I value optimism. The Optimist Creed guides my behavior. Point 1 of The Optimist Creed says, "Promise yourself to be so strong that nothing can disturb your peace of mind." Point 4 says, "Promise yourself to look at the sunny side of everything and make your optimism come true." As I truly value optimism and this advice, I had to let go of the frustrating situation. Holding on to it would have created negative energy that would have impacted my work. I don't have time for negative energy. I'm an optimist. As Point 10 of The Optimist Creed says, I am "too large for worry, too noble for anger, too strong for fear, and too happy to permit the presence of trouble." I value optimism. Therefore, I let go of the situation and moved on.

By the way, I have created a frameable .pdf of The Optimist Creed. If you would like a free copy to frame and hang in your workspace, go to http://budbilanich.com/optimist/ to download it. I have given away over 1,000 copies of it to readers of this blog and my career success coach clients.

Here's another example. I value trust. I am a trustworthy person, and I assume that on the part of other people. That's why most often I do business on a handshake. I will sign a contract if it's absolutely necessary; some companies won't hire me without a signed contract. But I prefer my working relationships to be less formal. Some people say this is naïve. I think it is trusting. I'm not trying to convince you to do business on a handshake. I bring it up here to show you how my personal value of trust impacts my work every day.

I value hard work. It's in my genes. I am skeptical of and turned off by Internet offers to set up a business that requires little to no work. My belief is that the dictionary is the only place success comes before work. This doesn't mean that I am inefficient about what I do. That's not the case. I outsource a lot of my technical work because I'm not good at it. I don't want to become an html expert. On the other hand, I use my time to do the things I'm good at – like writing books and this blog, appearing as a guest on Internet and broadcast radio interviews, working with my career success coach clients. I work hard at doing the things that help me advance my business and career success. I believe the old adage, "the harder I work, the luckier I get."

The common sense point here is simple. Successful people use their personal values as a foundation. They will listen to new ideas, but don't change on a whim. They heed the advice in Tweet 19 in Success Tweets, "Your personal values are things that you hold near and dear; things on which you absolutely will not compromise." This means that you should think long and hard about your values. They should come from deep inside you. Once you clarify them, live them. Be true to yourself and your personal values. You'll find that your personal values are a foundation that will serve you well when things get tough and frustrating.

Success Tweet 20

Your values come from deep inside you. Spend the time necessary to discover them. Then hold fast to them. Honor them with your actions.

I love blogging. It gives me the opportunity to share my thoughts and ideas with people who can't afford my career success coach services. It also keeps me sharp. My thinking on life and career success has grown and developed because of this blog. I hope this is reflected in the quality of my posts. I think I give better career advice as a result of writing this blog.

There is a side benefit to blogging too. People send me free books in the hopes that I will review them. A while back, I received a copy of Masha Malka's latest book, The One Minute Coach. It's a great little book.

Masha has organized **The One Minute Coach** into bite-sized chunks. One three-paragraph chapter entitled, "What Does It Take to be Attractive?" makes a great point about being true to yourself...

> "Being attractive comes from having that magnetic power that pulls people towards you. A power that inspires them to talk to you and find out more about who are; a power that makes them want to be like you!"

She follows this up with five action steps. I love the fifth step...

> "Focus on who you are and not just what you look like. People fall in love with the essence of you – your energy, the sparkle in your eyes, your passion for living, your unconditional love, everything that makes you unique and special...people fall in love with your beautiful soul."

What is your essence, your beautiful soul? It lies in your personal values. Do you let your essence and values shine through? Or do you keep them both under wraps, thinking that you won't measure up in others' eyes if you let your true self show?

When I was in high school and reading **Hamlet**, we got to the point in the play where Hamlet is setting off to avenge his father. Polonius gives him some advice. We were reading the play out loud. I was reading just before Polonius' advice. Mrs. Yothers stopped me and said, "This is some of the best advice on life that you will ever get. Read slowly Bud, and the rest of you should listen closely."

I can't remember the entire verse anymore, but there was one line that has always stuck with me. "And above all else, to thine own self be true, and it must follow as the day the night, thou canst be false to no man."

When my nephew Matt Seaton was going off to college, his grandfather and my father-in-law, Roy Blackman, gave him a piece of advice written on a scrap of paper. It read "TTOSBT – figure it out and live by it."

Can you figure it out? Here's a hint: read the quote from Polonius.

The common sense career success coach point here is simple. We are all unique human beings. Each of us has wonderful traits. Our best traits come from deep inside ourselves, our personal values. We all need to have the confidence to let our wonders shine through. You create positive personal impact when you live by your values and let your essence shine through. Pay attention to the advice in Tweet 20 in Success Tweets: "Your values come from deep inside you. Spend the time necessary to discover them. Then hold fast to them. Honor them with your actions." Honor your values in the way you live your life. Let your values shine through the next time you are in a room full of strangers. You might be surprised at the way people respond to you.

Success Tweet 21

You're in charge! Commit to taking personal responsibility for creating the successful life and career you want and deserve.

The other day I saw a great quote from Margaret Thatcher…

> "Look at a day when you are supremely satisfied at the end. It's not a day when you lounge around doing nothing; it's when you've had everything to do, and you've done it."

Ole' Iron Maggie really nailed it with this one. I like this quote because it gets at the essence of Tweet 21 – committing to taking personal responsibility for your life and career. Commitment to taking personal responsibility is the second of the four pillars of my Career Success GPS System, and some of the most important career advice I offer my career success coach clients.

You demonstrate your commitment to your career success – to yourself and to the world – by doing three things. First, take personal responsibility for your career success. Only you can make you a career success. You must be willing to do the things necessary to succeed. Second, set high goals – and then do whatever it takes to achieve them. Third, stuff happens; as you go through life you will encounter many problems and setbacks. You need to react positively to the negative stuff and move forward toward your goals, dreams and career success.

Those days in which you have a lot to do, and you get it all done, are not only satisfying; they demonstrate your commitment to your career success, and they help strengthen that commitment. I'm writing this on a plane on Friday night. It's about 8:00 in the evening. I've been up since 5:00 because I needed to finish an important project for one client before I spent the day working with another. I've had a full, but very satisfying, day. And, as Ms. Thatcher points out, one in which I feel a sense of supreme satisfaction. I've demonstrated to myself that I'm willing to do the things necessary to succeed.

I had a bout with the flu this winter. It left me feeling weak and tired. I spent all of a Monday afternoon and a good part of the following Tuesday morning in bed. It couldn't be helped. I needed to get my strength back. By Tuesday afternoon, I was feeling physically better, but emotionally drained. I felt as if I hadn't moved forward toward my goals. I didn't get anything done for about 24 hours – and I hated it. Even though I was sick, I felt as if I had lounged around and done nothing for a day and a half.

I agree not only with Maggie Thatcher, but with George Bernard Shaw, my favorite playwright...

> "I want to be thoroughly used up when I die, for the harder I work the more I live. I rejoice in life for its own sake. Life is no 'brief candle' for me. It is a sort of splendid torch which I have got hold of for the moment, and I want to make it burn as brightly as possible before handing it on to future generations."

I know that I want my life to be a splendid torch that burns long and brightly. That's why I choose to commit to taking personal responsibility for my life and career success. This career success coach is here to tell you that reveling in hard work is the best way to create the life and career success you want and deserve.

The common sense career success coach point here is simple. Successful people commit to taking personal responsibility for creating the successful life and career they want and deserve. They follow the advice in Tweet 21 in Success Tweets. They set high goals – and do whatever it takes to accomplish them. They react positively to the people and events in their lives – especially the negative people and events. They relish the days when they have a lot to do, and then go on and do it. They get great satisfaction from working hard and seeing the results of their labor. When was the last day when you were truly busy? How did you feel at the end of it? If you're an achiever – someone who is committed to your life and career success – I bet you felt exhilarated and ready to go the next day. That's how I felt after a very long day last Friday.

Success Tweet 22

Set and achieve S.M.A.R.T. goals. S.M.A.R.T. goals are Specific, Measureable, Achievable, Relevant and Time Bound.

Outstanding performance begins with S.M.A.R.T. goals. These goals are Specific, Measurable, Achievable, Results Oriented, and Time Specified.

> **Specific** – Your goals should be targeted, not broad and general. They should be unambiguous and explicit.

> **Measurable** – You should be able to tell quickly and easily if you've met your goal. Develop a set of criteria that will be indicative of success or failure in meeting each of your goals.

> **Achievable** – Set goals that are challenging but not incredibly difficult to achieve. A challenging goal is motivating, an impossible one is demotivating.

> **Results Oriented** – Focus on results; avoid the activity trap. Your goals should focus on the results you want to achieve, not the activities you will undertake to get there. For example, "improved presentation skills" is a result; "participating in a presentation skills training program" is an activity. It's possible to complete activities and not achieve the desired result.

> **Time Specified** – Set deadlines for achieving your goals. Well-developed goals come with time limits.

Once you have developed a set of S.M.A.R.T. goals, you need to work them. Here are some ideas for accomplishing your goals and becoming an outstanding performer:

> **Write your goals.** People who take the time to write their goals accomplish them more frequently than people who don't.

Keep your goals with you – in your wallet, on a clipboard, on your screen saver. In this way, they'll be a constant reminder of what you are going to achieve.

List at least one reason you want to achieve each goal. These reasons will help you stay focused when you get tired and frustrated and begin asking yourself questions like, "Why am I working so hard on this?"

Share your goals with people with whom you are close. These folks can be a big help in achieving your goals. Goals become more real when you share them with others. Goals that you don't share are merely aspirations.

Talk about your goals at social and networking functions. The help you need to achieve one or more of your goals can come from some surprising places. You never know who might be the one person who can offer the assistance it takes for you to get over the top on one or more of your goals.

Focus on your goals several times a day. Ask yourself, "Is what I'm doing right now helping me achieve one of my goals?" If the answer is no, stop what you're doing and do something that will help you reach your goals.

Stay balanced by creating goals in all areas of your life: career, business, personal, family, hobbies, health. These goals will help guide you to where you want to go.

Have congruent goals. Make sure your goals are congruent with one another. Conflicting goals create undue stress. If you have a work or career goal that is going to take up 60 to 80 hours a week of your time, it will be pretty difficult to realize a goal of running a marathon. You simply won't have time to train.

Consider the sacrifices – what you might have to forego or give up in order to reach your goals. This could be things like family or hobby time. Ask yourself questions like, "Is this goal important enough for me to give up time with my kids or my weekly yoga class?"

The common sense career success coach point here is simple. Successful people follow the advice in Tweet 22 in Success Tweets. "Set and achieve S.M.A.R.T. goals. S.M.A.R.T. goals are Specific, Measureable, Achievable, Relevant and Time Bound." Once you set S.M.A.R.T. goals, work them. Focus on them. Do whatever it takes to achieve them. Setting and achieving S.M.A.R.T. goals is some of my best career advice.

Success Tweet 23

Goals are important. You can't get what you want if you don't know where you're going.

If you want to succeed, you must commit to three things. First, you must take personal responsibility for your success. Only you can make you a success. You need to be willing to do the things necessary to succeed. Second, you must set high goals – and then do whatever it takes to achieve them. Third, stuff happens; as you go through life you will encounter many problems and setbacks. You need to react positively to the negative stuff and move forward toward your goals.

The other day, I came across a succinct statement on goal setting and goal achievement from Denis Waitley…

> "The secret to productive goal setting is in establishing clearly defined goals, writing them down and then focusing on them several times a day with words, pictures and emotions as if we've already achieved them."

I really like what Denis has to say. Let's break it down.

1. Your goals need to be clear.
2. Your goals need to be written.
3. You need to focus on your goals several times a day.
4. You need to visualize yourself achieving your goals.

Clear goals follow the S.M.A.R.T. formula. They are Specific, Measureable, Achievable, Relevant and Time Bound. Do your goals pass the S.M.A.R.T. test? If you've written them, it should be pretty easy to review them to see.

Here's a goal that one of my friends shared with me recently.

To become a millionaire, selling products on the Internet.

Let's see how well it stacks up to the S.M.A.R.T. test.

Specific? Reasonably so. This guy wants to become a millionaire by selling products on the Internet. This goal would be more specific if he had specified the product or type of product he wants to sell, and if he is going to develop the product himself, or resell others' products.

Measurable? Overall yes, if he defines being a millionaire as having a net worth of over a million dollars.

Achievable? Probably. He's a smart guy who has the desire. And, he is committed to this goal. I think he can achieve it if he works hard and smart.

Relevant? For him, yes. The guy defines success in monetary terms, so becoming a millionaire is certainly a relevant goal for him.

Time Bound? No. He hasn't set a date by when his net worth will reach one million dollars.

Not bad for a first try. Here's how I would make this goal more S.M.A.R.T…

> To build a net worth of $1,000,000 by the time I am 40 by being an Internet super affiliate marketer, reselling products in the self-help field.

Specific? Very. Net worth of $1,000,000; Internet affiliate marketer; reselling self-help products.

Measurable? Yes. He can check his net worth on his 40th birthday.

Achievable? Likely, given some hard work and tenacity.

Relevant? Yes. Money is how he defines success.

Time Bound? Yes. His 40th birthday is a hard deadline.

This career success coach suggests that you take some time to review your goals. Make them S.M.A.R.T. S.M.A.R.T. goals are written and clear – the first two recommendations from Denis Waitley when it comes to accomplishing your goals.

The common sense career success coach point here is simple. Successful people set and achieve high goals. They understand the power of Tweet 23 in Success Tweets. "Goals are important. You can't get what you want if you don't know where you're going." Written goals are the first step when it comes to life and career success. Sharpening your goals until they are clear and concise is the second step. If you don't have written goals for your life, and for this year, write some tonight. Then check them against the S.M.A.R.T. criteria. Make sure your goals are Specific, Measureable, Achievable, Relevant and Time Bound. If you take just these two steps you'll be well ahead in the career success game.

Success Tweet 24

Focus on your goals several times a day. Spend your valuable time on the things that will help you achieve them.

Stephen Covey lays out the most elegantly simple approach to time management that I've ever seen. He says that you can group all tasks into one of four categories:

- Not Important and Not Urgent
- Not Important and Urgent
- Important and Urgent
- Important and Not Urgent

Urgent tasks are deadline based. They are usually imposed by someone other than you. The sooner the task needs to be completed, the more urgent it is. Importance is independent of urgency. Important tasks are those that you need to complete to achieve your goals.

For me, writing this blog is an important and urgent task. I have committed to posting every day, Monday through Friday. That makes it urgent. Also, this blog is my primary marketing vehicle. That makes it important. Life would be great if every task with which we are faced were this simple.

Not important and not urgent tasks are easy to forgo. If they are neither important, nor urgent, I simply ignore them.

On the other hand, most of us are bombarded with tasks that are not important, but urgent. Often these tasks come from our boss. Just read "Dilbert" for a week to see what I mean. It is difficult to refuse many of these tasks. However, people who manage their time well have the ability to do so.

When I am faced with such a task, I always say, "I was planning on doing this today. I am happy to drop what I was doing and work on your request, but I want you to know that I will have to push back the completing of the other project." Sometimes, my bosses have said, "That's fine." On other occasions, they have instructed me to focus on the urgent task that seems unimportant to me.

Here's an example. Many years ago, I was working for a large company. I was in the Training and Development Department. I was working on designing the curriculum for a sales manager workshop. My bosses' boss came to me and said, "We have some important visitors from Japan here today. I would like you to join them for lunch." I was zoned in on the training design. I didn't want to spend two and a half hours at lunch with guests. So I told him that I was working on the sales manager curriculum design and asked to be excused from the lunch. He told me that it was important for us to be good hosts and that I should make time for the lunch – so I did. Urgent, but not important won out that day. And the reality of everyday life in most companies is that it often will.

However, rather than bemoan this fact, I'd like to focus on where you get the most bang for your time buck – important, but not urgent tasks.

Here's an example. Writing books is very important to me. My books help me establish credibility with my current and prospective clients. However, writing a book is a time-consuming activity. If I'm not careful and budget my time well, it is easy to let my book writing slip – because for me writing a book is an important but not urgent task. I need to keep getting my thoughts out there – but I also have a business to run.

If you've never done it, when you run a small business, you are faced with a series of important and urgent tasks. But you have to make the time for the important, but not urgent tasks. Because, if you don't, important but not urgent tasks have a way of becoming urgent – and still important.

Once I finish one book, I immediately begin on another. As a matter of fact, I have four book projects going right now – all are with coauthors, which can take more time than writing a book on my own. Cathy and several of my friends have said, "Give it a break, you just finished one, enjoy it. Don't get started on another book so soon." My response is that I want to keep the momentum I've gained – and I know that writing a book is an important but not urgent task that is all too easy to put off.

While you have to do important and urgent tasks, and sometimes can't avoid not important but urgent tasks, your career success will depend on finding the time to focus on the important but not urgent tasks.

The common sense career success coach point here is simple. Successful people follow the career advice in Tweet 24 in Success Tweets: "Focus on your goals several times a day. Spend your valuable time on the things that will help you achieve them." All work can be divided into one of four categories: Not Important and Not Urgent, Not Important and Urgent, Important and Urgent, Important and Not Urgent. Make time for the important, but not urgent tasks. That's where you'll get the most out of your most precious and non-renewable resource – your time. And that's where you'll begin achieving your goals. Remember this career advice. Sometimes you'll be forced into doing not important but urgent tasks. Dispense with them as expeditiously as possible. Make sure you keep up with your important and urgent tasks. But always make time for the important but not urgent tasks.

Success Tweet 25

List the reasons you set for each goal you set for yourself. These reasons will come in handy when you get tired and frustrated.

A couple of days ago, I mentioned Denis Waitley's ideas on goal achievement.

1. Your goals need to be clear.
2. Your goals need to be written.
3. You need to focus on your goals several times a day.
4. You need to visualize yourself achieving your goals.

Listing the reasons for your goals can help you with visualization. This is turn will help you when you get tired and frustrated. Tweet 14 says, "Don't visualize the pain of failure, visualize the euphoria of success." Achieving a goal should be a euphoric experience. If not, you probably didn't set a high enough goal.

If you want a job with a specific company, list the reasons why you want to work for that company, then visualize yourself showing up at work the first day and entering your new office. If you want a promotion, list the reasons you want it and then visualize yourself reading the congratulatory emails from your friends when they read the announcement of your promotion. If you want to start your own business, list the reasons for starting a business and then visualize yourself depositing your first check. If you want to marry the woman (or man) of your dreams, list the reasons you want to marry that particular person and then visualize yourself on your wedding day and honeymoon.

Listing the reasons for each of your goals and then creating a vivid mental image of the euphoria you'll feel when you accomplish them is a great way to keep you going when you are struggling with a goal.

I used to work for Marathon Oil Company. My job with Marathon was my first business job. Prior to that, I had been working in government. I met my future Marathon boss at an ASTD convention in Atlanta. He invited me to company headquarters to interview. I arrived there the night before I was scheduled to have a full day of interviews. I had the names and titles of the people with whom I would interview. I had one big reason for wanting this job – it was my ticket to a career in business, a stepping stone to creating my own business one day.

That night, before I went to bed, I visualized myself on my first day of work there. I also visualized (and rehearsed) what I would say to each of the people with whom I would interview the next day. This visualization and rehearsal helped me relax during the interviews. I kept the image of me on my first day at work for Marathon in mind as I interviewed. I got the job. I was euphoric.

Many of the naysayers in my life told me that since I had worked in government for five years after college I would be unlikely to get a job in business. I proved them wrong – because of my very important reason for wanting the job, my visualization of my success and because of my preparation. I knew more about Marathon Oil Company than many of the people who interviewed me.

These days I visualize myself as a successful Internet entrepreneur. I work in my home office, creating new information products that I sell on line. I see big numbers in my PayPal account. My reason is simple. I want to spend more time at home, with Cathy and doing all of the things I like to do in beautiful Colorado. I want to spend less time on planes and in hotels.

What are your reasons for each of your goals that will lead to your career success? Are they really important to you? Do you have a clear vision of you achieving these goals? Are these mental images sharp, clear and vivid – or are they fuzzy and out of focus? If it's the latter, sharpen them up. Create a really vivid mental image of you achieving each of the goals you've set for yourself. Use the reasons for setting these goals in the first place as a place to start. As I've mentioned in other blog posts and in several of my career success coach books, visualization isn't daydreaming. It's important work that will help you become the life and career success you deserve to be.

The common sense career success coach point is simple. Successful people follow the career advice in Tweet 25 in Success Tweets: "List the reasons you set for each goal you set for yourself. These reasons will come in handy when you get tired and frustrated." As a career success coach, I'm here to tell you that you will get frustrated as you pursue your goals. Your reasons for each goal will help you better visualize the euphoria of achieving it. If you can vividly imagine the euphoria associated with achieving your life and career goals, you'll be well on your way to achieving them. Visualization makes it easier to do the work when things are not going well. The reasons for each of your goals help you create clear and vivid images of you as a success.

Success Tweet 26

Keep your goals with you – in your wallet, or on your screen saver. They will be a constant reminder of what you will achieve.

Notice the last two words in the tweet – "will achieve." I didn't say, "hope to achieve," or "want to achieve," or worse yet, "try to achieve." I said, "will achieve." "Will achieve" is a positive, proactive statement that reinforces your visualization of your career success. As the tweet suggests, keeping your goals close at hand is a constant reminder of what you will achieve. Thinking in terms of "will achieve" rather than "hope to achieve," want to achieve," or "try to achieve" is a solid piece of career advice.

The other day, I saw a quote from John Wooden, legendary college basketball coach, and the author of several books on life and career success. This career success coach has them all in his library. Coach Wooden's success pyramid is a truly comprehensive look at how to become the life and career success you deserve to be.

Here is the quote…

> "I am not as good as I ought to be. I am not as good as I want to be. I am not as good as I'm going to be. But I am thankful that I am better than I used to be."

Notice that Coach Wooden uses positive affirmative language when he says, "I am not as good as I'm going to be." Even at 99 years old, he was still growing.

Keeping your goals with you is a great way to help you become as good as you're going to be. For one thing, keeping your goals nearby makes it easy for you to reflect on them several times a day – see the post I did on this. For another, keeping your goals with you makes them part of you.

I keep my goals in my wallet. They're easily accessible. I pull them out and look at them so often I usually have to print a second copy midyear. The originals tend to get creased, dirty and threadbare from so much folding and unfolding. Having my goals in my wallet in my right front pants pocket every day makes them seem more real to me. Reviewing them a couple of times a day motivates me to do the work I need to do to accomplish them.

As I often am when I write these blog posts, I'm on a plane. I just wrote all of this week's posts. Then I took a minute to stretch and review my goals. One of those goals is to create a membership site using Success Tweets and these blog posts as part of the content. The sooner I write all 140 blog posts, the sooner I'll be able to put up my membership site. The sooner the membership site goes up, the sooner I'll be helping more people take advantage of my career success coach thoughts and ideas. Just reviewing my goals gave me the energy to keep writing, instead of reading for the last hour of the flight.

See how this works? First of all, be thankful for being better than you were; believe that you will be better than you are. Use your goals – the things you will achieve – to inspire you to do the work necessary to become better than you are, and to become the life and career success you deserve to be. Pretty good career advice, if I do say so myself.

The common sense career success coach point here is simple. Successful people set and achieve high goals. Goals are your promise to yourself that you will become better than you are. If you follow the advice in Tweet 26 in Success Tweets – "Keep your goals with you – in your wallet, or on your screen saver. They will be a constant reminder of what you will achieve" – you will be more likely to achieve your goals, become better than you are, and create the life and career success you want and deserve. I keep my goals in my wallet, and look at them at least a couple of times a day. Try this career success coach advice. You'll be surprised at how much you can accomplish.

Success Tweet 27

Create goals in all areas of your life: career, personal, business, family, hobbies, health and fitness. Make sure they are congruent.

Since I am self employed, my career and business goals overlap. I have personal goals that overlap with my health and fitness. Biking and reading are my hobbies. I have goals for them too. My most important goal is to be a loving and supportive husband.

My career and business goals focus on helping others succeed, getting my career success coach message out in as many different ways as I possibly can, and making enough money to let me travel less and work from home more.

I have lost quite a bit of weight in recent years. My personal and health goals focus on maintaining that weight loss and losing even more. I have a long-term goal of doing a metric century bike ride (62 miles) in 2011. I have another goal to reread several of Tolstoy's works this year.

I have goals for our marriage as well. My marriage goals intersect with my business and career goals. The more time I spend at home, the more time I have to devote to our relationship.

See how this works?

What are the important parts of your life? Do you have goals in each of them? Are these goals congruent? Even though I am a career success coach, I urge you to spend time thinking about both your life and career success. Create goals in all parts of your life. Make sure these goals are congruent. You'll be happier – and more likely to achieve the career success you deserve – this way.

The common sense career success coach point here is simple. Successful people are well rounded. They set and achieve goals in all facets of their lives. What are the important parts of your life? Do you have goals for each of them? If not, create some. Follow the advice in Tweet 27 in Success Tweets: "Create goals in all areas of your life: career, personal, business, family, hobbies, health and fitness. Make sure they are congruent." Pay particular attention to being congruent. Your goals need to complement one another. If they don't, you'll find yourself trying to juggle competing priorities. This is difficult at best, and often leads to failure on several fronts. Congruent goals on the other hand will complement one another and lead to your life and career success.

Success Tweet 28

Write your goals. Share them with others. You are more likely to achieve goals that you write and share.

Accountability is the key career advice here. When you write your goals and share them with others you are choosing accountability.

Writing your goals demonstrates your accountability to yourself. Written goals are real and tangible. Goals that you keep in your head most often are fuzzy and poorly defined, little more than wishes.

Taking the time to write your goals, and then making them S.M.A.R.T. (see my recent post) puts some rigor into the goal setting process. You end up with a set of well-defined goals on which you can build your career success.

Sharing your goals with others close to you is another way of choosing accountability. When you share your goals, you are making a public statement about what you are going to accomplish. This makes you more likely to do the work necessary to achieve them.

Let me give you an example. I have made a big effort to improve my level of health and fitness in recent years. A few years ago, I set a weight loss goal. I shared this goal with several of my friends, especially those who are committed to their own health and fitness.

One of these people is one of my clients. I was visiting his office one day. There was a big platter of oatmeal raisin cookies left over from a meeting sitting in an open area near his office. As we passed the cookies, I took one. I was beginning to take a bite when he turned to me and said, "Do you really want that?"

In the moment, I really did. But in the greater scheme of things and given my health and fitness goal, I really didn't want to be eating cookies in the middle of the afternoon. I tossed the cookie into the trash.

Sharing my health and fitness goal with this guy helped me achieve it. By asking me a simple question, "Do you really want that?" he helped me make progress toward my goal. He helped me fight the temptation to do something that ran counter to achieving my goal. But remember, he never would have asked me the question if I had not first shared my health and fitness goal with him. This is one of the basic ideas behind the Weight Watchers program. This works for goals in all areas of your life and career.

Here's another example. I was having a conversation with Doug Westmoreland, king of motivational videos. He and I were talking about email list building. I mentioned that I have a goal of growing my subscriber list. Doug asked a few questions, made a few suggestions and then said something really profound. "Bud, you're a great guy, you give lots of value to your subscribers. It's about time that you begin offering them the opportunity to reciprocate by making products available for sale in your electronic correspondence with them."

Doug's comment was really helpful. He got me to rethink how I communicate with my subscribers. I never would have received this great advice if I hadn't shared one of my goals with him.

The common sense career success coach point here is simple. Successful people set and achieve high goals. They follow the advice in Tweet 28 in Success Tweets. "Write your goals. Share them with others. You are more likely to achieve goals that you write and share." I have found that writing your goals and sharing them with others are two of the best ways to ensure that you achieve them. Both of these simple actions increase your personal accountability for achieving your goals. When you write your goals, they become more real for you. When you share them, you invite others to help you achieve them. You build a support network that can keep you on track and moving forward in creating the career success you deserve.

Success Tweet 29

Aim high. Set and achieve high goals – month after month, and year after year. Do whatever it takes to achieve your goals.

This post is more about goal achievement than goal setting. You know that you need to set goals in all parts of your life. You know you need to set S.M.A.R.T. goals. You know that you need to break your goals into manageable milestones. You know that you need to keep your goals with you. You know that you need to write your goals and share them with others. All of this is a great start. However, it's just the start.

Successful people do whatever it takes to achieve their goals. This takes commitment and tenacity. It means working towards your goals when you are tired. It means not giving up in the face of problems and setbacks. It means doing what needs to be done, not what you want to do, or feel like doing.

This reminds me of one of my favorite quotes from Malcolm Forbes...

"Diamonds are nothing more than chunks of coal that stuck to their jobs."

It takes thousands of years and tremendous amounts of pressure to turn coal into diamonds. While you don't need to spend thousands of years creating the successful life and career you want and deserve, you do have to stick with it. If you give up every time you run into a problem, setback, or roadblock, you'll never become a diamond. If you can't take the pressure, you'll never become a diamond. You have to stick to it and bear up under the pressure. It doesn't take a career success coach to tell you that you need to be persistent if you're going to achieve your goals.

I am a fan of Lindsey Vonn, an Olympic gold medal-winning alpine skier who makes her home in Vail; so she's a local as far as I'm concerned. She is the most successful American woman skier in World Cup history.

She's 26 years old and has been skiing for 24 of those years. She moved away from home and her family at a young age to pursue her dream of being a world class skier. She started skiing competitively at seven and competing internationally when she was nine. She is devoted to her sport.

Check out what Lindsay Vonn says about going for your goals...

> "When you fall down, just get up again. If you fall, get up stronger, hungrier, more ambitious. Setbacks help you concentrate. When success falls into your lap, you lose sight of your goals."

She fell hard earlier this year and had a terrible bone bruise on her arm. She didn't miss an event. She had a terrible injury just prior to the Olympics and still won the gold medal in the downhill – the most prestigious skiing event – in the 2010 Winter Games.

I tell my career success coach clients that Lindsey Vonn is someone who can be likened to a lump of coal that has turned into a diamond because she's stuck to her job. Remember her story the next time you feel like giving up on your goals and your dreams.

The common sense career success coach point here is simple. Successful people commit to taking personal responsibility for their lives and careers. They follow the career advice in Tweet 29 in Success Tweets. "Aim high. Set and achieve high goals – month after month, and year after year. Do whatever it takes to achieve your goals." You can begin achieving your career success goals by taking personal responsibility for your life and career success. Do whatever it takes to succeed. Stick with it when the pressure gets strong. Do whatever it takes to achieve the life and career success goals you set for yourself. Respond positively to the negative people and events in your life. Remember what Malcolm Forbes has to say about success: "Diamonds are nothing more than chunks of coal that stuck to their jobs." Become a diamond. Stick with it. Set high goals, achieve them. Repeat. Repeat. Repeat.

Success Tweet 30

Success is a journey, not a destination. When you accomplish one goal, reach higher and set a new one.

You've probably heard of Maslow's Hierarchy of Needs – it's a staple in undergraduate social psychology. In case you haven't, or need a refresher, here is a quick recap.

In 1943, Dr. Abraham Maslow wrote a paper called, "A Theory of Human Motivation" in which he described his ideas about what motivates humans. He suggested that human beings have a series of needs which we strive to meet and that the best way to motivate someone is to appeal to the need most relevant to him or her at a given time. He arranged these needs in a pyramid.

Physiological or survival needs like breathing, food, water and sleep are at the base of the pyramid. Dr. Maslow suggested that until these basic survival needs are met, human beings will not be motivated by any other needs.

Safety and security needs are the next up on the pyramid. Dr. Maslow suggests that once people feel that they will survive today, they will be motivated by the need to survive tomorrow, the next day and in the long term.

Love and belonging needs are next. Dr. Maslow suggests that once human beings experience a reasonable level of security, their needs turn to developing friendship and family relations.

Esteem needs are next. Once people feel secure and loved, Dr. Maslow says that they seek gratification that comes from achievement, self respect and the respect of others.

Self actualization needs are at the top of the pyramid. Dr. Maslow often described self actualization as "being all that one can be." And therefore, one can never be truly self actualized. Dr. Maslow suggested that self actualization is the pursuit of perfection. In other words, once you accomplish something that you previously thought of as the pinnacle, you will find that there is more that you can accomplish. This is in keeping with Tweet 30 which suggests that becoming self actualized is a process in which you set new and higher goals whenever you accomplish one of your goals.

That's why I say that success is a journey, not a destination. Successful people see themselves as works in progress. Successful people are never finished becoming all that they can be. If you want the life and career success you deserve, you need to think of yourself this way.

I'm not suggesting that you take no time to celebrate your successes and look back at them with pride. I am saying however, that if you want to build long-term career success, you will use your successes as springboards to bigger and better things.

Set new goals. Develop plans for achieving these new goals. Work your plans. And then do it again. Think of yourself as someone who is "becoming" not as someone who is "complete." Successful people realize that there are always new challenges and opportunities. Some of the best career advice I ever received was from an early mentor who told me to see beyond the horizon, to keep actively looking for new ways to learn, grow and succeed.

The common sense career success coach point here is simple. Successful people never stop learning and growing. They follow the advice in Tweet 30 in Success Tweets. "Success is a journey, not a destination. When you accomplish one goal, reach higher and set a new one." This is the idea embodied in the concept of self actualization; you can never be all that you can be because there will always be new challenges ahead. Setting and achieving ever increasingly difficult goals is the best way to live a fulfilling life and to create the career success you deserve. Keep learning, keep growing, keep achieving, and you will succeed beyond your wildest dreams.

Success Tweet 31

Plan how you will achieve your goals. Then do whatever you have to do, not want or feel like doing, to achieve them.

Your goals won't get done just because you've written them. Common sense career advice says that you have to work your goals. There are two steps here. First, plan how you will achieve each of your goals. Second, work your plan. You can have all of the good intentions in the world, but if you don't plan how you will achieve your goals and then work your plan, you will not achieve the life and career success you want and deserve.

Gary Ryan Blair, The Goals Guy, and author of a great little book called "Everything Counts" makes an important point about the importance of working your goals…

> "Good intentions, while honorable, are of little use when you let weeks, months, and years of potential and possibility slip by."

Gary has a weekly ritual of reflecting, reviewing and updating his goals. He said that this ritual has allowed him to continue to grow and make significant performance gains for twelve straight years without missing a beat.

Check it out.

Every Sunday night, or Monday morning, isolate one goal and ask yourself the following five questions:

1. What are my current year-to-date results in relation to this goal?

2. What has gone right so far this year? Why? Identify strengths and strategies to repeat.

3. What has gone wrong so far this year? Why? Identify weaknesses and strategies to drop.

4. What corrective actions will I immediately implement to remain on target?

5. What will I commit to doing this week to ensure that I will meet or achieve this goal?

I love this exercise. I have committed to doing it every Monday morning. I began today. As a career success coach, I encourage you to do the same. Give this exercise the time and attention it deserves, and as Gary says, "you will have positioned yourself for having a breakthrough week."

Tweet 31 in Success Tweets provides some no nonsense career success coach advice. It says "do whatever you have to do, not want or feel like doing, to achieve them." Gary Ryan Blair, the Goals Guy, provides a great exercise to help you stay on target and move ahead toward achieving your goals. Even if you don't feel like reviewing one of your goals every week, I suggest you do it. This is common sense career advice. The more you focus on your goals, the more likely you are to achieve them.

There is a Japanese proverb that I like and is appropriate here...

Vision without action is a daydream. Action without vision is a nightmare.

No matter how big, your goals, plans, thoughts and dreams will never become a reality until you act on them. You have to commit to taking personal responsibility for achieving your goals and for creating the life and career success you want and deserve. And action is the single most important word when it comes to demonstrating your commitment.

On the other hand, action without vision truly is a nightmare. You'll never get where you want to go if you don't have a clear idea of exactly what you want to achieve. That's why you have to set goals. Your goals are your vision for the career success you will create.

Goals give you direction and focus. Action makes your goals a reality.

The common sense career success coach point here is simple. Successful people follow the career advice in Tweet 31 in Success Tweets. "Plan how you will achieve your goals. Then do whatever you have to do, not want or feel like doing, to achieve them." Goals are the foundation of your success. You need to do two things to achieve your goals. First, create a plan. Second, implement your plan; do whatever you have to do to achieve your goals. Gary Ryan Blair, The Goals Guy, suggests focusing on one of your goals every week. Figure out how well you're doing on this one goal. Then commit to doing the things necessary to move you closer to achieving it. If you rotate through your goals, one week at a time, you'll be moving in the right direction. You'll be on the road to creating the life and career success you want and deserve. This technique works. Take it from a career success coach who uses it.

Success Tweet 32

Stuff happens as you go about creating a successful life and career. Choose to respond positively to the negative stuff that happens.

It's simple, really. Success is all up to you, and me, and anyone else who wants it. We all have to take personal responsibility for our own success. I am the only one who can make me a career success. You are the only one who can make you a career success.

Stuff happens: good stuff, bad stuff, frustrating stuff, unexpected stuff. Successful people respond to the stuff that happens in a positive way. Humans are the only animals with free will. That means we – you and me – get to decide how we react to every situation that comes up. That's why taking personal responsibility for yourself and choosing to respond positively to the negative stuff that happens to you is so important.

Personal responsibility means recognizing that you are responsible for your life and the choices you make. It means that you realize that while other people and events have an impact on your life, these people and events don't shape your life. When you accept personal responsibility for your life, you own up to the fact that how you react to people and events is what's important. And you can choose how to react to every person you meet and everything that happens to you.

The concept of personal responsibility is found in most writings on success. Stephen Covey's first habit in *The 7 Habits of Highly Effective People* is, "Be proactive." I have a little book called "Daily Reflections for Highly Effective People," also by Stephen Covey. It is one of the most-read books that I have. I like it because it provides a little snippet of advice from *The 7 Habits of Highly Effective People* every day.

The daily reflection for September 24 goes directly to the advice in this tweet, and it gets to the heart of personal responsibility and life and career success.

> "It's not really what happens to us, but our response to what happens to us that hurts us. Of course, things can hurt physically or economically and can cause sorrow. But our character, our basic identity, does not have to be hurt at all. In fact, our most difficult experiences become the crucibles that forge our

character and develop the internal powers, the freedom to handle difficult circumstances in the future and to inspire others to do so as well."

Dr. Covey provides some great career advice here. We can't always choose what happens to us, but we can choose how we react to both the positive and negative experiences we have as we go through life. Successful people choose to make lemonade out of lemons. Unsuccessful people choose to complain about the bitter, tart taste of the lemons they are handed.

I know the "lemons into lemonade" line is a cliché. However, clichés become clichés because they have an underlying truth. The important point is that human beings are blessed with free will. As such, we can choose what we do and how we react to the world around us. We can choose a positive, productive path, or we can choose a path of self pity and inaction – and hurt only ourselves in the end.

The 7 Habits advice for September 25 carries on in the same vein...

> "Proactive people can carry their own weather with them. Whether it rains or shines makes no difference to them. They are value driven; and if their value is to produce good quality work, it isn't a function of whether the weather is conducive to it or not."

I love the concept of carrying your own weather with you. Choosing to react positively to the negative people and events in your life is the best way to carry your weather – and to take personal responsibility for your life and career success.

The common sense career success coach point here is clear. Successful people know that they can choose how they respond to everyone they meet and everything that happens to them. They know that "the devil made me do it" is never an accurate statement. They also know that no one can "make" them mad. In short, they follow the advice in Tweet 32 in Success Tweets. "Stuff happens as you go about creating a successful life and career. Choose to respond positively to the negative stuff that happens." If you want to create the career success you deserve, remember Stephen Covey's advice. Carry your weather with you. In this way, whether it rains or shines on the outside, it will be sunny on the inside. Choose to react positively to the negative people you meet, and the negative things that happen to you. When you do, you'll find that you'll have less negative things happening and fewer negative people entering your life.

Success Tweet 33

Take personal responsibility for your success. No one is going to do it for you. Adopt the motto, "If it's to be, it's up to me."

When you take personal responsibility, you eliminate blame, stop complaining, and stop being a victim. You take charge of your life. You demonstrate your commitment to taking personal responsibility for your career success by responding positively to the people and events and events in your life – especially when they are less than positive. I frequently offer this advice to my career success coach clients.

I had an opportunity to test myself on this one a couple of months ago. I got up very early to post my blog. When I got to my office, my computer was frozen. I could move the cursor, but could not actually open a document – or do anything else for that matter.

I was the first guy in line when the Geek Squad opened at 8:30. My buddy Nate was there. I showed him the machine and explained the problem. He found a minor virus, deleted a few files and said I was good to go. I went home, and the machine worked – for about a half hour. I went back to the Geek Squad and Nate worked on the problem for the second time.

When I got back to my office, I was able to post the blog and to get my daily podcast up on the net. Then it happened again. Completely frozen, unable to raise the volume to listen to the podcast, close the podcast application, or open any other program.

I called Nate and told him I would bring the machine in for a full diagnostic – and pay the 24-hour service premium. I got back in my car, drove to the Geek Squad and dropped off the computer.

I had been meaning to read a couple of novels I had picked up the week before. I figured my computer problems presented an excellent opportunity to spend that afternoon and the following day doing just that. However, in the middle of all this, I realized that I was being presented with a challenge to see if I could walk my talk when it comes to reacting positively to the negative events in my life. Reading novels instead of working would not be demonstrating my commitment to taking personal responsibility for my career success – even if no one else knew I'd blown off a day and a half.

I knew that I couldn't do everything I wanted to do with my backup computer. But there were things I could do. I chose to figure out what I could accomplish without the use of my main machine and set out doing it. I could still write blog posts. I could still continue developing learning modules for the Career Success GPS System. That's what I did those days. And that's my career success coach advice to you – when you run into problems, don't complain about what you can't do, figure out what you can do and then do it.

The common sense career success coach point here is simple. Successful people commit to taking personal responsibility for their lives and careers. They choose to respond positively to the people and events in their lives – especially the negative people and the unexpected and uncontrollable problems. They keep moving forward. They don't get distracted in their quest to create the successful life and career they want and deserve. They follow the career advice in Tweet 33 in Success Tweets. "Take personal responsibility for your success. No one is going to do it for you. Adopt the motto, 'If it's to be, it's up to me'." Have you committed to taking personal responsibility for your career success? How do you react when life throws those inevitable curve balls your way? Do you choose to move forward, finding ways around life's little problems? As a career success coach, I hope so, because that's the choice that will put you on the path to career success.

Success Tweet 34

Treat failures as the tuition you pay to succeed. If you have a setback, choose to react positively and learn something,

Failure truly is the tuition you pay for success. Katina Solomon at OnLineCollege.org has created a list of "50 Famously Successful People Who Failed at First." These people come from all walks of life. But they shared one characteristic in common – the commitment to their own career success. Katina has graciously allowed me to post her list here...

50 Famously Successful People Who Failed at First

Not everyone who's on top today got there with success after success. More often than not, those whom history best remembers were faced with numerous obstacles that forced them to work harder and show more determination than others. Next time you're feeling down about your career failures, keep these fifty famous people in mind. Remind yourself that sometimes failure is the tuition you pay for your career success.

Business Gurus

These businessmen and the companies they founded are today known around the world, but as these stories show, their beginnings weren't always smooth.

1. **Henry Ford:** While Ford is today known for his innovative assembly line and American-made cars, he wasn't an instant success. In fact, his early businesses failed and left him broke five times before he founded the successful Ford Motor Company.
2. **R. H. Macy:** Most people are familiar with this large department store chain, but Macy didn't always have it easy. Macy started seven failed businesses before finally hitting big with his store in New York City.
3. **F. W. Woolworth:** Some may not know this name today, but Woolworth was once one of the biggest names in department stores in the U.S. Before starting his own business, young Woolworth worked at a dry goods store and was not allowed to wait on customers because his boss said he lacked the sense needed to do so.

4. **Soichiro Honda:** The billion-dollar business that is Honda began with a series of failures and fortunate turns of luck. Honda was turned down by Toyota Motor Corporation for a job after interviewing for a job as an engineer, leaving him jobless for quite some time. He started making scooters of his own at home, and spurred on by his neighbors, finally started his own business.

5. **Akio Morita:** You may not have heard of Morita but you've undoubtedly heard of his company, Sony. Sony's first product was a rice cooker that unfortunately didn't cook rice so much as burn it, selling less than 100 units. This first setback didn't stop Morita and his partners as they pushed forward to create a multi-billion-dollar company.

6. **Bill Gates:** Gates didn't seem like a shoe-in for success after dropping out of Harvard and starting a failed first business with Microsoft co-founder Paul Allen called Traf-O-Data. While this early idea didn't work, Gates' later work did, creating the global empire that is Microsoft.

7. **Harland David Sanders:** Perhaps better known as Colonel Sanders of Kentucky Fried Chicken fame, Sanders had a hard time selling his chicken at first. In fact, his famous secret chicken recipe was rejected 1,009 times before a restaurant accepted it.

8. **Walt Disney:** Today Disney rakes in billions from merchandise, movies and theme parks around the world, but Walt Disney himself had a bit of a rough start. He was fired by a newspaper editor because, "he lacked imagination and had no good ideas." After that, Disney started a number of businesses that didn't last too long and ended with bankruptcy and failure. He kept plugging along, however, and eventually found a recipe for success that worked.

Scientists and Thinkers

These people are often regarded as some of the greatest minds of our century, but they often had to face great obstacles, the ridicule of their peers and the animosity of society.

9. **Albert Einstein:** Most of us take Einstein's name as synonymous with genius, but he didn't always show such promise. Einstein did not speak until he was four and did not read until he was seven, causing his teachers and parents to think he was mentally handicapped, slow and anti-social. Eventually, he was expelled from school and was refused admittance to the Zurich Polytechnic School. It might have taken him a bit longer, but most people would agree that he caught on pretty well in the end, winning the Nobel Prize and changing the face of modern physics.

10. **Charles Darwin:** In his early years, Darwin gave up on having a medical career and was often chastised by his father for being lazy and too dreamy. Darwin himself wrote, "I was considered by all my masters and my father, a very ordinary boy, rather below the common standard of intellect." Perhaps they judged too soon, as Darwin today is well-known for his scientific studies.

11. **Robert Goddard:** Goddard today is hailed for his research and experimentation with liquid-fueled rockets, but during his lifetime his ideas were often rejected and mocked by his scientific peers who thought they were outrageous and impossible. Today, rockets and space travel don't seem far-fetched at all, due largely in part to the work of this scientist who worked against the feelings of the time.

12. **Isaac Newton:** Newton was undoubtedly a genius when it came to math, but he had some failings early on. He never did particularly well in school and when put in charge of running the family farm, he failed miserably, so poorly in fact that an uncle took charge and sent him off to Cambridge where he finally blossomed into the scholar we know today.

13. **Socrates:** Despite leaving no written records behind, Socrates is regarded as one of the greatest philosophers of the Classical era. Because of his new ideas, in his own time he was called "an immoral corrupter of youth" and was sentenced to death. Socrates didn't let this stop him and kept right on, teaching up until he was forced to poison himself.

14. **Robert Sternberg:** This big name in psychology received a C in his first college introductory psychology class with his teacher telling him that, "there was already a famous Sternberg in psychology and it was obvious there would not be another." Sternberg showed him, however, graduating from Stanford with exceptional distinction in psychology, summa cum laude, and Phi Beta Kappa and eventually becoming the President of the American Psychological Association.

Inventors

These inventors changed the face of the modern world, but not without a few failed prototypes along the way.

15. **Thomas Edison:** In his early years, teachers told Edison he was "too stupid to learn anything." Work was no better, as he was fired from his first two jobs for not being productive enough. Even as an inventor, Edison made 1,000 unsuccessful attempts at inventing the light bulb. Of course, all those unsuccessful attempts finally resulted in the design that worked.

16. **Orville and Wilbur Wright:** These brothers battled depression and family illness before starting the bicycle shop that would lead them to experimenting with flight. After numerous attempts at creating flying machines, several years of hard work, and tons of failed prototypes, the brothers finally created a plane that could get airborne and stay there.

Public Figures

From politicians to talk show hosts, these figures had a few failures before they came out on top.

17. **Winston Churchill:** This Nobel Prize-winning, twice-elected Prime Minister of the United Kingdom wasn't always as well regarded as he is today. Churchill struggled in school and failed the sixth grade. After school, he faced many years of political failures, as he was defeated in every election for public office until he finally became the Prime Minister at the ripe old age of 62.
18. **Abraham Lincoln:** While today he is remembered as one of the greatest leaders of our nation, Lincoln's life wasn't so easy. In his youth he went to war a captain and returned a private (if you're not familiar with military ranks, just know that private is as low as it goes). Lincoln didn't stop failing there, however. He started numerous failed businesses and was defeated in numerous runs he made for public office.
19. **Oprah Winfrey:** Most people know Oprah as one of the most iconic faces on TV, as well as one of the richest and most successful women in the world. Oprah faced a hard road to get to that position, however, enduring a rough and often abusive childhood as well as numerous career setbacks, including being fired from her job as a television reporter because she was "unfit for TV."
20. **Harry S. Truman:** This WWI vet, Senator, Vice President and eventual President eventually found success in his life, but not without a few missteps along the way. Truman started a store that sold silk shirts and other clothing–seemingly a success at first–only to go bankrupt a few years later.
21. **Dick Cheney:** This recent Vice President and businessman made his way to the White House but managed to flunk out of Yale University, not once, but twice. Former President George W. Bush joked with Cheney about this fact, stating, "So now we know –if you graduate from Yale, you become President. If you drop out, you get to be Vice President."

Hollywood Types

These faces ought to be familiar from the big screen, but these actors, actresses and directors saw their fair share of rejection and failure before they made it big.

22. **Jerry Seinfeld:** Just about everybody knows who Seinfeld is, but the first time the young comedian walked on stage at a comedy club, he looked out at the audience, froze and was eventually jeered and booed off of the stage. Seinfeld knew he could do it, so he went back the next night, completed his set to laughter and applause, and the rest is history.

23. **Fred Astaire:** In his first screen test, the testing director of MGM noted that Astaire, "Can't act. Can't sing. Slightly bald. Can dance a little." Astaire went on to become an incredibly successful actor, singer and dancer and kept that note in his Beverly Hills home to remind him of where he came from.

24. **Sidney Poitier:** After his first audition, Poitier was told by the casting director, "Why don't you stop wasting people's time and go out and become a dishwasher or something?" Poitier vowed to show him that he could make it, going on to win an Oscar and become one of the most well-regarded actors in the business.

25. **Jeanne Moreau:** As a young actress just starting out, this French actress was told by a casting director that she was simply not pretty enough to make it in films. He couldn't have been more wrong as Moreau when on to star in nearly 100 films and win numerous awards for her performances.

26. **Charlie Chaplin:** It's hard to imagine film without the iconic Charlie Chaplin, but his act was initially rejected by Hollywood studio chiefs because they felt it was a little too nonsensical to ever sell.

27. **Lucille Ball:** During her career, Ball had thirteen Emmy nominations and four wins, also earning the Lifetime Achievement Award from the Kennedy Center Honors. Before starring in *I Love Lucy,* Ball was widely regarded as a failed actress and a B-movie star. Even her drama instructors didn't feel she could make it, telling her to try another profession. She, of course, proved them all wrong.

28. **Harrison Ford:** In his first film, Ford was told by the movie execs that he simply didn't have what it takes to be a star. Today, with numerous hits under his belt, iconic portrayals of characters like Han Solo and Indiana Jones, and a career that stretches decades, Ford can proudly show that he does, in fact, have what it takes.

29. **Marilyn Monroe:** While Monroe's star burned out early, she did have a period of great success in her life. Despite a rough upbringing and being told by modeling agents that she should instead consider being a secretary, Monroe became a pin-up, model and actress that still strikes a chord with people today.

30. **Oliver Stone:** This Oscar-winning filmmaker began his first novel while at Yale, a project that eventually caused him to fail out of school. This would turn out to be a poor decision as the text was rejected by publishers and was not published until 1998, at which time it was not well-received. After dropping out of school, Stone moved to Vietnam to teach English, later enlisting in the Army and fighting in the war, a battle that earned him two Purple Hearts and helped him find the inspiration for his later works that often center around war.

Writers and Artists

We've all heard about starving artists and struggling writers, but these stories show that sometimes all that work really does pay off with success in the long run.

31. **Vincent Van Gogh:** During his lifetime, Van Gogh sold only one painting, and this was to a friend and only for a very small amount of money. While Van Gogh was never a success during his life, he plugged on with painting, sometimes starving to complete his over 800 known works. Today, they bring in hundreds of millions.

32. **Emily Dickinson:** Recluse and poet Emily Dickinson is a commonly read and loved writer. Yet in her lifetime she was all but ignored, having fewer than a dozen poems published out of her almost 1,800 completed works.

33. **Theodor Seuss Giesel:** Today nearly every child has read *The Cat in the Hat* or *Green Eggs and Ham*, yet 27 different publishers rejected Dr. Seuss's first book *To Think That I Saw It on Mulberry Street*.

34. **Charles Schultz:** Schultz's Peanuts comic strip has had enduring fame, yet this cartoonist had every cartoon he submitted rejected by his high school yearbook staff. Even after high school, Schultz didn't have it easy, applying and being rejected for a position working with Walt Disney.

35. **Steven Spielberg:** While today Spielberg's name is synonymous with big budget, he was rejected from the University of Southern California School of Theater, Film and Television three times. He eventually attended school at another location, only to drop out to become a director before finishing. Thirty-five years after starting his degree, Spielberg returned to school in 2002 to finally complete his work and earn his BA.

36. **Stephen King:** The first book by this author, the iconic thriller *Carrie,* received 30 rejections, finally causing King to give up and throw it in the trash. His wife fished it out and encouraged him to resubmit it, and the rest is history, with King now having hundreds of books published and the distinction of being one of the best-selling authors of all time.

37. **Zane Grey:** Incredibly popular in the early 20th century, this adventure book writer began his career as a dentist, something he quickly began to hate. So, he began to write, only to see rejection after rejection for his works, being told eventually that he had no business being a writer and should give up. It took him years, but at 40, Zane finally got his first work published, leaving him with almost 90 books to his name and selling over 50 million copies worldwide.

38. **J. K. Rowling:** Rowling may be rolling in a lot of Harry Potter dough today, but before she wrote the series of novels she was nearly penniless, severely depressed, divorced, trying to raise a child on her own while attending school and writing a novel. Rowling went from depending on welfare to survive to being one of the richest women in the world in a span of only five years through her hard work and determination.

39. **Monet:** Today Monet's work sells for millions of dollars and hangs in some of the most prestigious institutions in the world. Yet during his own time, it was mocked and rejected by the artistic elite, the Paris Salon. Monet kept at his Impressionist style, which caught on and in many ways was a starting point for some major changes to art that ushered in the modern era.

40. **Jack London:** This well-known American author wasn't always such a success. While he would go on to publish popular novels like *White Fang* and *The Call of the Wild*, his first story received six hundred rejection slips before finally being accepted.

41. **Louisa May Alcott:** Most people are familiar with Alcott's most famous work, *Little Women*. Yet Alcott faced a bit of a battle to get her work out there and was encouraged to find work as a servant by her family to make ends meet. It was her letters back home during her experience as a nurse in the Civil War that gave her the first big break she needed.

Musicians

While their music is some of the best selling, best loved and most popular around the world today, these musicians show that it takes a whole lot of determination to achieve success.

42. **Wolfgang Amadeus Mozart:** Mozart began composing at the age of five, writing over 600 pieces of music that today are lauded as some of the best ever created. Yet during his lifetime, Mozart didn't have such an easy time, and was often restless, leading to his dismissal from a position as a court musician in Salzburg. He struggled to keep the support of the aristocracy and died with little to his name.

43. **Elvis Presley:** As one of the best-selling artists of all time, Elvis has become a household name even years after his death. But back in 1954, Elvis was still a nobody, and Jimmy Denny, manager of the Grand Ole Opry, fired Elvis Presley after just one performance, telling him, "You ain't going nowhere, son. You ought to go back to driving a truck."

44. **Igor Stravinsky:** In 1913 when Stravinsky debuted his now famous *Rite of Spring*, audiences rioted, running the composer out of town. Yet it was this very work that changed the way composers in the 19th century thought about music and cemented his place in musical history.

45. **The Beatles:** Few people can deny the lasting power of this super group, still popular with listeners around the world today. Yet when they were just starting out, a recording company told them no. They were told, "we don't like their sound, and guitar music is on the way out," two things the rest of the world couldn't have disagreed with more.

46. **Ludwig van Beethoven:** In his formative years, young Beethoven was incredibly awkward on the violin and was often so busy working on his own compositions that he neglected to practice. Despite his love of composing, his teachers felt he was hopeless at it and would never succeed with the violin or in composing. Beethoven kept plugging along, however, and composed some of the best-loved symphonies of all time–five of them while he was completely deaf.

Athletes

While some athletes rocket to fame, others endure a path fraught with a little more adversity, like those listed here.

47. **Michael Jordan:** Most people wouldn't believe that a man often lauded as the best basketball player of all time was actually cut from his high school basketball team. Luckily, Jordan didn't let this setback stop him from playing the game and he has stated, "I have missed more than 9,000 shots in my career. I have lost almost 300 games. On 26 occasions I have been entrusted to take the game winning shot, and I missed. I have failed over and over and over again in my life. And that is why I succeed."

48. **Stan Smith:** This tennis player was rejected from even being a lowly ball boy for a Davis Cup tennis match because event organizers felt he was too clumsy and uncoordinated. Smith went on to prove them wrong, showcasing his not-so-clumsy skills by winning Wimbledon, the U. S. Open and eight Davis Cups.

49. **Babe Ruth:** You probably know Babe Ruth because of his home run record (714 during his career), but along with all those home runs came a pretty hefty

amount of strikeouts as well (1,330 in all). In fact, for decades he held the record for strikeouts. When asked about this he simply said, "Every strike brings me closer to the next home run."

50. **Tom Landry:** As the coach of the Dallas Cowboys, Landry brought the team two Super Bowl victories, five NFC Championship victories and holds the record for the most career wins. He also has the distinction of having one of the worst first seasons on record (winning no games) and winning five or fewer over the next four seasons.

The common sense career success coach point here is simple. Successful people commit to taking personal responsibility for their career success. They set high goals and do whatever it takes to achieve them. They also react positively to the people and events in their lives – especially the negative people and events. They follow the career advice in Tweet 34 in Success Tweets. "Treat failure as the tuition you pay to succeed. If you have a setback, choose to react positively and learn something." In this post, I told the stories of 50 well-known people who ended up being wildly successful and well known because they learned from their mistakes and failures. Use this career advice; let these successful people be an example and inspiration for you the next time you feel up because you've failed.

Success Tweet 35

Persistent people keep going; especially in the face of difficulties. Keep at it and you will accomplish your goals.

John Miller is a friend of mine. He is also the author of a great little book called "QBQ! The Question Behind the Question." John says that all too often we ask the wrong questions when we run into problems. These questions focus on other people. They seek to find who to blame for our troubles and difficulties. John suggests that you (and I) should ask the question behind the question – the question that empowers us and helps us take charge of our life and career success.

John is on to something here. His question behind the question concept is great career advice. QBQs, as John calls them, help us become persistent and keep going in the face of difficulties.

At the end of the book, John provides "a great list of lousy questions," along with a QBQ that he suggests will help you move toward your life and career success. Check them out…

Lousy Customer Service Questions

- When will shipping start getting orders out on time?
- Why do our customers expect so much of us?
- Why don't customers follow the instructions?

Customer Service QBQ

- How can I best serve our customers?

Lousy Sales Questions

- Why are our prices so high?
- When will our products become more competitive?
- Why won't customers call me back?
- When will marketing give us better sales aids?
- Why can't manufacturing make what we sell?

Sales QBQs

- What can I do today to become a more effective sales person?
- How can I add value for my customers?

Lousy Marketing Questions

- When will salespeople deliver our programs?
- Why won't salespeople take the time to learn our new products?

Marketing QBQs

- What can I do to understand sales reps' issues and concerns?
- How can I learn more about what our customers want and need?

Lousy Manufacturing Questions

- Why can't salespeople stay within our capabilities?
- When will they learn to sell according to our specifications?

Manufacturing QBQ

- How can I better understand the challenges our salespeople face?

Lousy Individual Contributor Questions

- Why do we have to go through all this change?
- When will I get the training I need?
- Why don't I get paid more?
- Who is going to clarify my role and responsibilities?
- When is management going to get their act together?
- Who will set our vision?

Individual Contributor QBQs

- What can I do to be more productive?
- How can I adapt to our changing environment?
- What can I do to develop myself?

Lousy Management and Leadership Questions

- Why doesn't the younger generation want to work hard?
- When am I going to find good people?
- Why aren't my people motivated?
- Who made that mistake?
- Why don't people come in on time?
- Who dropped the ball?
- When are they going to catch the vision?
- Who will care as much as I do?
- When will the market turn around?
- Who do I have to do everything myself?

Management and Leadership QBQs

- How can I be a more effective coach?
- What can I do to better understand each person on my team?
- How can I be a better leader?
- What can I do to show I care?
- How can I communicate better?
- How can I do a better job of delegating?

The common sense career success coach point here is simple. Successful people are persistent. They follow the career advice in Tweet 35 in Success Tweets. "Persistent people keep going; especially in the face of difficulties. Keep at it and you will accomplish your goals." Successful people don't search for blame. They ask what my friend John Miller calls "the question behind the question," or a QBQ. They search for what they can do to overcome the problems and difficulties that are getting in the way of their career success. Questions behind the question focus on what you can do to solve problems and handle difficulties. They begin with the words "how" and "what". They contain the word "I;" and they focus on action. Here is my best career success coach QBQ: "What can I do to create my own success?" Ask and answer this question and you'll be well on your way to the life and career success you want and deserve.

Success Tweet 36

Don't be afraid to fail. You fail only if you don't learn something from the experience. Treat every failure as an opportunity to grow.

Fear is the enemy of self-confidence – and career success. Most people fear failure, criticism and rejection. It's only normal. We all want to feel good about ourselves. Failure, criticism and rejection are not pleasant experiences. They lower our self-esteem and make us feel bad about ourselves, so we often avoid doing things that we think might lead to failure, criticism or rejection. However, if you want to create the life and career success you want and deserve, you have to have the courage to do things that might result in failure, criticism or rejection.

Failure, criticism and rejection provide you with the opportunity to grow and develop – to succeed. You can't take failure, criticism and rejection personally. Failure, criticism and rejection are outcomes. They are a result of things you have done. They are not who you are. We all make mistakes and fail. We all do things that cause others to criticize or reject us. This doesn't mean that we are failures. It means that we have made some poor choices and done some not-so-smart things.

Failure, criticism and rejection provide the opportunity to start over – hopefully a little smarter. Buckminster Fuller once said, "Whatever humans have learned had to be learned as a consequence of trial and error experience. Humans have learned only through mistakes."

That's why fear is the enemy of self-confidence and career success. Take it from a career success coach. If your fear of failure, criticism and rejection paralyzes you to the point where you aren't willing to take calculated risks, you'll never learn anything or accomplish any of your goals.

Don't be too hard on yourself when you fail, or when others criticize or reject you. My best career advice is to put your energy into figuring out why you failed and then do something different. Here are four career success coach questions to ask yourself the next time you fail, or get criticized or rejected.

1. Why did I fail? Why did I get criticized or rejected? What did I do to cause the failure, criticism or rejection?

2. What could I have done to prevent the failure, criticism or rejection?
3. What have I learned from this situation?
4. What will I do differently the next time?

If you do this, you'll be using failure, criticism and rejection to your advantage. In **Think and Grow Rich,** Napoleon Hill says, "Every adversity, every failure and every heartache carries with it the seed of an equivalent or greater benefit." I know it's hard to see the benefit or opportunity in failure, criticism and rejection. But it's there – you just have to look hard enough. But it all begins by facing your fear and acting. The less you fear failure, the more career success you'll create.

I am proud of my niece, Brett. A little over a year ago, she left a good job in Florida and moved to San Diego. She had no job lined up in San Diego when she moved. Some members of the family thought she was silly to leave a good job to move across the country with no job. I thought that she demonstrated amazing optimism and courage in making such a long move in such a difficult economy. Brett wasn't afraid to fail. Seventeen days after she arrived in San Diego she landed a job as an account manager for an athletic apparel manufacturer. She has since received two promotions. I'm proud of Brett. She didn't let her fear of failure, criticism, or rejection stop her from pursuing her dreams.

The common sense career success coach point here is simple. Successful people are self-confident. Self-confident people face their fears and act. They follow the advice in Tweet 36 in Success Tweets. "Don't be afraid to fail. You fail only if you don't learn something from the experience. Treat every failure as an opportunity to grow." Our most common fears are failure, criticism, and rejection. Follow this career advice. Choose to find – and use – the learning opportunity in your failures and you will become more self-confident and successful. It's sad but true – failure, criticism and rejection are often the price you pay for becoming a career success. Facing your fear of failure, criticism and rejection, and acting will pay big dividends when it comes to your life and career success.

Success Tweet 37

It's not what happens to you, but how you react to it. Don't dwell on the negative, use it as a springboard to action and creativity.

Successful people have a habit of focusing on the positive and putting the negative out of their minds. Positive habits like this are an important key to career success. Habits are like muscles. The more you use them, the stronger they get. Dan Robey is the King of Positive Habits. His eBook, "The Power of Positive Habits," is one of my go-to books when I need to give myself a little boost. You can get a copy at www.ThePowerOfPositiveHabits.com.

Dan's book is based on the idea of cognitive restructuring. According to Dan, cognitive restructuring is learning to identify your personal cycle of negative thoughts, habits, and routines and replacing them with positive thoughts, habits, and routines that will provide you with lifelong benefits.

Today, I'd like to discuss an important positive habit – proactively managing your stress. When I was a kid about a million years ago, there was a popular song. I believe it was a show tune. A couple of the lines went like this...

> You've got to ac – cen – tu – ate the positive, and
> e — lim — in – ate the negative

I don't know the show. If you do, please leave a comment letting us know. I'll give a free copy of the eBook version of Straight Talk for Success to everybody who knows the name of the show and shares it in a comment.

Anyway, I was thinking about that song the other day because I came across a new book on stress management by Evelyn Brooks, called ***Forget Your Troubles: Enjoy Your Life Today***.

Evelyn suggests that you get S.M.A.R.T. about managing stress...

- S   Smash the negative.
- M   Maximize the positive.

- A Act.
- R Relax.
- T Target your next action.

Sounds a lot like the advice in the song. As they say, "there's nothing new under the sun." And, more importantly, as a career success coach, I agree. It doesn't matter if you "accentuate the positive and eliminate the negative," "smash the negative and maximize the positive," or do a bit of "cognitive restructuring," you'll be on your way to managing your stress and becoming a life and career success.

Stuff happens as you go through life; positive stuff, negative stuff, happy stuff, sad stuff, frustrating stuff. The important thing is not what happens, but how you react to it. In other words, smash your negative thoughts; replace them with positive ones. Don't dwell on the negative, use it as a springboard to action and creativity. Maximize the positive in your life by creating positive habits and routines. When something goes well, take the time to celebrate. You deserve it. And, small celebrations when you succeed are a positive habit that will put you in a positive frame of mind, which in turn, will help you create more life and career successes.

I have given away almost 1,000 copies of the eBook version of Success Tweets. I mention this because I'm celebrating. I want to get the positive message in Success Tweets into the hands of as many people as I can. I'm accentuating the positive, or if you prefer, maximizing the positive. You might say that 1,000 people choosing to receive a free eBook is not a reason for a huge celebration; but I do – and I'm following my own career success advice by doing some cognitive restructuring – creating a habit of celebrating small successes. Celebrating small wins is a great positive habit for me. It will help me manage my stress and not get overwhelmed by the negatives that will invariably creep into my life. I'm sticking to it.

The common sense career success coach point here is simple. Successful people follow the advice in Tweet 37 in Success Tweets. "It's not what happens to you, but how you react to it. Don't dwell on the negative, use it as a springboard to action and creativity." Get competent. Create positive personal impact. Become an outstanding performer and a dynamic communicator. Build strong relationships with the important people in your life. Positive habits will help you do all of these. Smash the negatives in your life and create positive thoughts, habits and routines. Use the negatives that come your way as learning experiences, and positive thoughts, habits and routines to create small victories. Treat these small victories as a reason for celebration. Celebrating small victories is a good way to keep things in perspective and build the resilience necessary for dealing with the tough times – and for ac – cen – tu – ating the positive, and e – lim – in – ating the negative. Take it from a career success coach, positive habits are powerful and will help you become the life and career success you deserve to be.

Success Tweet 38

Don't let a slow day get you down. If you come back empty handed in your quest for success, get up the next day and keep working.

As a career success coach, I'm always looking for ways to get my common sense message about life and career success across to my clients, people who read my blog and listen to my podcasts. That's why I was struck by a passage in Tracy Chevalier's new book, *Remarkable Creatures*. If you don't know Tracy Chevalier, you should. For my money she is one of the best novelists writing today. Her first book, *Girl With a Pearl Earring*, was made into a movie starring Scarlett Johansson.

In *Remarkable Creatures,* she tells the story of two women fossil hunters in early 19th-century England. Her protagonists are a middle-aged spinster and a young girl. Both are committed fossil hunters. Here is how Elizabeth Philpot, the spinster, describes committed fossil hunters…

> "Hunters spend hour after hour, day after day, out in all weather, our faces sunburnt, our hair tangled by the wind, our eyes in a permanent squint, our nails ragged and our fingertips torn, our hands chapped. Our boots are trimmed with mud and stained with seawater. Our clothes are filthy by the end of the day. Often we find nothing, but we are patient and hardworking and not put off by coming back empty handed… Those serious about fossils know their search is never over. There will always be more specimens to discover and study, for, as with people, each fossil is unique. There can never be too many."

I love this passage. It describes – in wonderful prose – my thoughts and beliefs on the importance of knowing your purpose in life and committing to taking personal responsibility for living it. "Often we find nothing, but we are patient and hardworking and not put off by coming back empty handed." That's exactly what I'm talking about when I tell my career success coaching clients, "Stuff happens. The stuff that happens, good or bad, isn't what's important. What is important is how you react to it."

Follow this career advice. Be patient and hardworking. Don't be put off by a day in which you come back empty handed. Choose to believe that your hard work will pay off in the end. Commit to taking personal responsibility for living your life's purpose – whether it be fossil hunting, selling, building things, or helping others.

People who commit to taking personal responsibility for creating the successful lives and careers they want and deserve know that their personal quest is never over – there will always be more to do, more to accomplish.

I mentioned Abraham Maslow's hierarchy of human needs in a post a while back. It's been almost 40 years since I first heard of it. If you're not familiar with it, Dr. Maslow suggested that all human beings have a series of needs that they strive to satisfy. He arranged these needs in a pyramid. According to his theory, safety is the first and most basic human need. It is at the bottom of the pyramid. We all strive to remain safe in an uncertain world – we all want to live another day. Security is next. Once we are reasonably sure that we will survive this moment and this day, our needs move to developing a sense of security, one in which we feel that our lives and quality of our lives will remain constant. Affiliation is next. Once we feel safe and secure, we search for meaningful relationships in our lives. Recognition is next. Once we feel safe, secure and valued by others, we crave recognition—in the form of praise, promotions, more money. Self actualization is at the top of the pyramid. Dr. Maslow says that after our safety, security, affiliation and recognition needs are satisfied, we turn our attention to what he calls "self actualization," a state of being all that we can be.

Dr. Maslow suggests that we human beings can never be completely self actualized because as soon as we reach one goal, we realize that there is always something more that we can achieve. Once Bill Gates became one of the world's wealthiest men, he realized that he could be doing more to help others. So he created his foundation. Once I created and ran a successful consulting practice, I realized that I could do more to share my knowledge about career success with a wider audience. That's why I started blogging and writing books.

And speaking through a spinster fossil hunter, Tracy Chevalier says, "There will always be more specimens to discover and study, for, as with people, each fossil is unique. There can never be too many." Indeed; there will always be more to do, more to accomplish – if only you clarify your life's purpose and then commit to taking personal responsibility for it.

The common sense career success coach point here is simple. Successful people are clear on their purpose and direction in life. They commit to taking personal responsibility for living their life purpose. If you want to achieve career success, you need to do the same. Clarify what you want from your life and career. Then commit to doing whatever it takes to get it. Follow the career advice in Tweet 38 in Success Tweets. "Don't let a slow day get you down. If you come back empty handed in your quest for success, get up the next day and keep working." Set high goals. React positively to the setbacks, problems and negative people and events in your life. Keep at it. Don't let a day when you come back empty handed in your quest for career success get you down. Get up the next day with optimism in your heart and keep working toward the mighty purpose you've set for yourself.

Success Tweet 39

While other people and events have an impact on our life, they don't shape it. You get to choose how you react to people and events.

As I was getting ready to write this post, an email from my friends at Heart Math popped up in my inbox. It had a quote from Viktor Frankl...

> "Between stimulus and response, there is a space. In that space lies our freedom and power to choose our response. In our response lies our growth and freedom."

Victor Frankl survived the Nazi death camps in WWII. He lost his wife, mother and father in those camps. His experience with the Nazis led him to conclude that even in the most absurd, painful and dehumanized situation, life has potential meaning. Therefore, even suffering is meaningful. He chronicled his experiences in the camps and what he learned from them in his famous book, "Man's Search for Meaning." In 1991, the US Library of Congress designated it as one of the ten most influential books in the United States. It has sold over 10 million copies and been translated into 24 languages.

One of his famous quotes always brings tears to my eyes...

> "We who lived in concentration camps can remember the men who walked through the huts comforting others, giving away their last piece of bread. They may have been few in number, but they offer sufficient proof that everything can be taken from a man but one thing: the last of the human freedoms—to choose one's attitude in any given set of circumstances, to choose one's own way."

Speaking of attitude, the June 2010 issue of SUCCESS Magazine has a great article by John Maxwell called, "Attitude Is the Difference Maker." John says, "Attitude isn't everything, but it's the main difference maker."

As you can see from the Viktor Frankl quote above, choosing your attitude is choosing your own way. As a human being, you get to choose how you respond to the people and events in your life. You can choose to have a positive, optimistic attitude and respond to difficult people and events in a constructive manner. Or, you can choose to have a negative attitude and respond to difficult people and events in a self-destructive manner. Your attitude is the difference maker between a successful, rewarding life and career, and an unsuccessful and unfulfilling life and career.

Take it from a career success coach. You get to choose how you respond to every person you meet and everything that happens to you. Your moment of choice comes in between the stimulus and your response. This can be a small space, but it is a space that exists. Your attitude has a big impact on what you choose in these moments of choice.

John Maxwell says, "Your attitude makes a difference in how you face challenges. Successful people don't have fewer problems than unsuccessful people – they just have a different mindset." That bears repeating – "Successful people don't have fewer problems than unsuccessful people – they just have a different mindset."

We all have our problems and challenges. The difference between successful people and unsuccessful people is simple. Successful people choose to respond to problems in a positive manner. They choose a positive, proactive approach. They choose to take personal responsibility for themselves, their actions and their life and career success. They choose to see problems as challenges – and they meet the challenges they encounter.

"Choose" is the important word here. We human beings have free will. We can choose how we respond to the things that happen to us. We can choose our attitude. Successful people choose to respond positively to the negative people and events in their lives. Successful people choose to have a positive attitude.

John Maxwell quotes Chuck Swindoll on the "Power of Attitude"…

> "The longer I live, the more I realize the impact of attitude on life. Attitude, to me, is more important than education, than money, than circumstance, than failures, than successes, than what other people, think, say or do. It is more important than appearance, giftedness or scale. It will make or break a company, a church, a home. The remarkable thing is we have a choice every day regarding the attitude we embrace for that day. We cannot change the past. We cannot change the fact that people act in a certain way. We cannot change

the inevitable. The only thing we can do is play on the one string we have, and that is our attitude. I am convinced that life is 10% what happens to me and 90% how I react to it; and so it is with you. We are in charge of our attitude."

Or as Viktor Frankl says...

"Life ultimately means taking the responsibility to find the right answer to its problems and to fulfill the tasks which it constantly sets for each individual."

The common sense career success coach point here is simple. Your attitude is the difference maker. A positive attitude leads to positive results and career success. A negative attitude leads to negative results. The good thing is that you can choose your attitude. Remember the career advice and wisdom in Tweet 39 in Success Tweets. "While other people and events have an impact on our life, they don't shape it. You get to choose how you react to people and events." Use the free will that God has given you to create your life and career success. Choose a positive attitude. Choose to respond positively to the negative people and events in your life. Remember what Viktor Frankl, a holocaust survivor, teaches us: "Between stimulus and response, there is a space. In that space lies our freedom and power to choose our response. In our response lies our growth and freedom." Empower yourself to make the right choices, the positive choices, when you encounter negative people and events.

Success Tweet 40

Vision without action is a daydream. No matter how big your plans and dreams, they'll never become reality until you act on them.

As a career success coach, I'm always looking for new and different ways to get across my common sense ideas on life and career success. I found some great ideas and great career advice in a Denver elementary school a couple of months ago. I was invited to see the Go For It! Institute's program in action at a school in Denver. If you don't know about the Go For It! Institute, you should. The Institute teaches kids the value of things like positive attitude, believing in themselves, positive habits, goal setting and persistence.

Their work is based on ideas created by Judy Zerafa. Judy has created seven keys to success for young students. Check them out...

> **KEY 1: I Have a Positive Attitude!** Learn what attitude is; what aspects of your life are controlled or directed by your attitude; how to determine your attitude at any given moment; specific strategies to make a positive attitude a permanent habit in your life. I wrote about the importance of attitude in yesterday's post.

> **KEY 2: I Believe in Myself!** Understand the nature of human potential through a simple process of identifying your personal talents and abilities; developing academic strengths and personal interests to create personal fulfillment and economic opportunities for your future.

> **KEY 3: I Build Positive Habits!** Understand the process of how habits are created; learn to identify and remove self-defeating habits; create habits that will make all aspects of your life easier and more successful. I wrote about the power of positive habits in a recent post.

> **KEY 4: I Make Wise Choices!** Learn the dramatic relationship between any current circumstances in your life and the choices that created these; develop a personal proactive plan for desired outcomes through conscious, wise choices.

> **KEY 5: I Set and Achieve Goals!** Recognize the difference between a wish and a goal; make a commitment, plan and take action; recognize completion.

KEY 6: I Use My Creative Imagination! Extend your physical ability to accelerate problem solving and goal achievement in all areas of your life.

KEY 7: I Am Persistent! Track progress; develop the focus and determination required to succeed; create an attitude of gratitude as the access to fulfilling your dreams, link the Seven Keys to Success together in everyday life.

The Go For It! Institute is in business to bring these keys to young people and their parents. But as a career success coach, I think they are important ideas for anyone interested in creating life and career success. The Go For It! Institute's Seven Keys to Success bear a remarkable similarity to the ideas behind one of my four keys for career success: commitment to taking personal responsibility for your life and career success.

Since we're at Tweet 40, it makes sense to do a quick overview of my four keys to life and career success, the "4Cs:" Clarity, Commitment, Confidence, and Competence." Here they are in a little more detail...

- Clarity of purpose and direction
- A sincere commitment to taking personal responsibility for your life and career
- Unshakeable self-confidence
- Competence in four key areas:
    - Creating positive personal impact
    - Outstanding performance
    - Dynamic communication
    - Relationship building

When I visited the school, I watched a class of fourth graders work with the Seven Keys to Success. It was great to see these little guys and gals put their own spin on things like having a positive attitude, setting and achieving goals and being persistent. I wish I had someone work with me on these principles when I was that young.

Judy Zerafa developed the Seven Keys to Success on which the Go For It! Institute's program is based after interviewing 35 Horatio Alger Award winners. I think they are a brilliantly simple success formula. She is taking her positive message to kids and parents in an attempt at starting the success cycle early in life.

The common sense career success coach point here is simple. Successful people are self-confident and are committed to taking personal responsibility for their lives and careers. They follow the career advice in Tweet 40 in Success Tweets. "Vision without action is a daydream. No matter how big your plans and dreams, they'll never become reality until you act on them." The Go For It! Institute's Seven Keys to Success are all about taking personal responsibility for acting on your plans and dreams. You will succeed if you have a positive attitude, believe in yourself, build positive habits, make wise choices, set and achieve goals, use your imagination and persist. The last of these seven keys is the important one here: Persist. Keep working toward your goals and dreams, and you will become a career success. It's only common sense. I'm glad I was introduced to the Go For It! Institute and the great work they are doing with kids. I think their message applies to all of us. If you incorporate their seven keys into your life, you'll be well on your way to creating the life and career success you want and deserve.

Success Tweet 41

Focus on what you are becoming. This helps you believe in yourself and builds your confidence. Confidence is important to your success.

I love the idea of "becoming." It's really a positive concept. And it's similar to a couple of the ideas in The Optimist Creed. The sixth point of The Optimist Creed says, "Forget the mistakes of the past and press on to the greater achievements of the future." The ninth point says, "Give so much time to the improvement of yourself that you have no time to criticize others."

Tweet 41 in Success Tweets and points six and nine in The Optimist Creed reinforce one of my career success coach points – success is a journey, not a destination. Keep moving forward in your life and you'll succeed.

I'm going to be 60 this year and I keep learning, growing and moving forward. To celebrate my 60th birthday, I will be releasing three new books and a home study course on life and career success this year. I am becoming a better career success coach because of my writing and my blogging. But I'm nothing compared to Peter Drucker. He wrote 39 books in his long and distinguished life and career – two thirds of them were written after he was 65 years old.

"Becoming" is not a function of age. It's a function of your willingness to look ahead and see the opportunities life brings your way – and then to act on them. Take it from a career success coach. When you focus on what you are becoming, you will be building the life and career success you want and deserve. Keep becoming and you will succeed. I guarantee it.

I like the idea of "becoming" so much because it gets at the idea that all of us can always become something more, no matter our age, or our previous successes or failures. There is always more to do, more to accomplish, a way to become more remarkable.

Becoming and thinking go hand in hand. Your thoughts determine what you will become. It's true –you become what you think about most. That means that the quantity and quality of the life and career success you will achieve will be in direct proportion to the size of your thoughts. If you allow your mind to be dominated by trivial matters, your achievements are likely to be unimportant.

If you discipline yourself to think about things important to your life and career success, you will achieve great things. Take my career advice; keep up with what's new in your field and with what's going on in the world. Create a list of good ideas that you can use anytime you are searching for a creative solution to a problem. Remember, people with small minds think and talk about other people. People with medium-sized minds think and talk about things. People with great minds think and talk about ideas.

The common sense career success coach point here is simple. Build your life and career success by focusing on what you are becoming. Career success is a journey, not a destination. Treat it that way. Use the career advice in Tweet 41 in Success Tweets. "Focus on what you are becoming. This helps you believe in yourself and builds your confidence. Confidence is important to your success." Commit to taking personal responsibility for your life and career. Set high goals; then do whatever it takes to meet or exceed them. React positively to the setbacks, problems and negative people and events in your life. Keep at it. Don't let a day when you come back empty handed in your quest for building a remarkable life and career get you down. Get up the next day with optimism in your heart, focused on what you are becoming and keep working.

If you would like a copy of The Optimist Creed to frame and hang in your office, go to http://budbilanich.com/optimist and enter your name and email address.

Success Tweet 42

Choose optimism. It builds your confidence. Believe that today will be better than yesterday, and that tomorrow will be better yet.

I'm a big believer in the power of optimism. I think it is the foundation of all self-confidence. You can't be self-confident if you're not optimistic. And, optimism is a choice. I get up every day believing that good things will happen – and then I go about making them happen.

When I was a kid, I participated in the local Optimist International chapter's oratory contest. I won my section, and finished third in the state. The topic that year was "Optimism, Youth's Greatest Asset." That's hard enough for a ninth grader to say (think Joe Pesci in "My Cousin Vinnie"), let alone write and deliver a ten-minute talk.

Optimist International is a great service organization. They help kids build self-confidence and become more optimistic. The Optimist Creed defines them. It's powerful stuff. Take a look…

The Optimist Creed

Promise Yourself:

- To be so strong that nothing can disturb your peace of mind.
- To talk health, happiness and prosperity to every person you meet.
- To make all your friends feel that there is something in them.
- To look at the sunny side of everything and make your optimism come true.
- To think only of the best, to work only for the best, and to expect only the best.
- To be just as enthusiastic about the success of others as you are about your own.
- To forget the mistakes of the past and press on to the greater achievements of the future.
- To wear a cheerful countenance at all times and give every living creature you meet a smile.
- To give so much time to the improvement of yourself that you have no time to criticize others.
- To be too large for worry, too noble for anger, too strong for fear, and too happy to permit the presence of trouble.

I love The Optimist Creed. I have it framed and hanging in my office, just above my desk. I have made a .pdf of The Optimist Creed that is suitable for framing. If you want a copy, just go to http://budbilanich.com/optimist.

One thing that you'll notice about The Optimist Creed is that it is proactive. It asks you to promise yourself to do ten things that will help you create the life and career success that you want and deserve. It suggests that optimism is related to action – action you can take to become more optimistic and to build your career success. I think it is some of the best career advice I've come across. I do my best to live the 10 points in The Optimist Creed every day. You should too.

I especially like the fourth point – promise yourself to look at the sunny side of everything and make your optimism come true. This point goes directly to the idea of committing to taking personal responsibility for your life and career success. I know it's difficult to look at the sunny side of things when you're mired in a problem or are dealing with a failure. However, if you look for what you can learn from problems and failures, you'll be looking at the sunny side. More important, you'll be on your way to making your optimism come true.

Christopher Reeve is no longer with us, but he exemplified the idea of looking at the sunny side of things. Even though he was paralyzed from the neck down after a riding accident, he devoted himself to finding a cure for spinal cord injuries. I love the way his optimism comes across in this quote...

> "So many of our dreams at first seem impossible, then they seem improbable, and then, when we summon the will, they soon become inevitable."

Christopher Reeve looked at the sunny side of his injury and did what he could to make his optimism come true. His foundation carries on the work he started.

The common sense career success coach point here is simple. Successful people are self-confident. Self-confident people are optimists. They follow the career advice in Tweet 42 in Success Tweets. "Choose optimism. It builds your confidence. Believe that today will be better than yesterday, and that tomorrow will be better yet." The Optimist Creed is a great guide to becoming more optimistic and self-confident. Its proactive approach to life is a great guide to creating the life and career success you want and deserve. Remember the old saying, "Whether you're an optimist, or a pessimist you'll be proven right." I choose optimism, and suggest you do too.

Success Tweet 43

Optimism is contagious. Become a positive, optimistic person. Surround yourself with positive people. They will build your confidence.

The FIFA Soccer World Cup is being contested in South Africa as I write this. But in this post, I'd like to focus on another World Cup, the 1995 Rugby World Cup, also played in South Africa. This was the first time the South Africa Springboks were allowed to compete. They had been banned from competing in previous Rugby World Cups because of the racist policies of the apartheid government.

But 1995 was different. Nelson Mandela, a black man, was the President of South Africa. The apartheid era was over. And the Springboks were invited not only to play in the World Cup, but to host it. The 2009 movie, *Invictus*, chronicled that story.

I'm a retired rugby player. I played my first game in 1968 at Penn State and my last in 2010 on my 60th birthday for the Colorado Ole' Pokes. I'm active in youth rugby and olde boys rugby here in Colorado. I love the game, so I couldn't wait to see the movie *Invictus*.

Invictus is the story of the South African victory in the 1995 Rugby World Cup. That victory is credited for healing many of the wounds caused by the apartheid years. Nelson Mandela consciously chose to support the Springboks – long seen as a symbol of white oppression in South Africa and hated by most of the country's black population – as a rallying cry for national unity and putting aside the hatred of the dehumanizing apartheid policy of the white South African government. The team did not disappoint. They won the World Cup in a memorable match against New Zealand, then the best rugby side in the world.

Morgan Freeman plays Mandela in the film. Matt Damon plays Springbok Captain, Francois Pienaar. I loved the movie – it was right up my alley – about two things I love to discuss: politics and sports. It was a bonus that it was about my favorite sport, rugby football. I actually saw that famous 1995 match on video two days after it happened. As I watched it, I commented that Pienaar was a mad man on the pitch that day. He willed the South African team to victory.

Cathy made my Christmas by giving me a copy of the book, *Invictus* – originally published as *Playing the Enemy*. Until I saw the movie and read the book, I had no idea that Mandela befriended Pienaar and convinced him that the 1995 Rugby World Cup was more than a game; it was a chance to help unify a deeply divided country. Mandela was an optimist. So was Pienaar. South Africa was not the rugby power they had been prior to being shunned because of apartheid. However, this unlikely pair fed on each other's optimism, resulting in a huge sporting upset.

Nelson Mandela was supremely self-confident and an optimist. He believed that he could heal the wounds of oppression and unite a country through tolerance. He also believed that sport – especially rugby – could play a big part in helping him achieve his goal.

There is an interesting quote on pages 252 and 253 of *Invictus*...

> "His (Mandela's) secret weapon was that he assumed not only that he would like the people he met; he assumed also that they would like him. That vast self-confidence of his coupled with that frank confidence he had in others made for a combination that was as irresistible as it was disarming.

> "It was a weapon so powerful that it brought about a new kind of revolution... Conceiving of his revolution not primarily as the destruction of apartheid but, more enduringly, as the unification and reconciliation of all South Africans, Mandela broke the mold."

It took a supremely self-confident man to believe that he could erase years of hatred by embracing, rather than destroying his enemy. It took a supremely self-confident group of South African rugby players to believe that they could beat the best rugby side in the world. Both Nelson Mandela and the Springboks proved the value of self-confidence that day in 1995. While unifying the country and winning the Rugby World Cup took a lot of hard work, both were accomplished by building on the foundation of self-confidence and optimism.

Mandela and Pienaar were the embodiment of Helen Keller's famous quote on optimism and self-confidence, "Optimism is the faith that leads to achievement. Nothing can be done without hope and confidence."

If you like sports and/or politics, rent *Invictus*. If you're really interested in the subject matter, pick up a copy of the book and read it. Trust me, you will be inspired – not only by the story, but by how optimism is contagious, and surrounding yourself with optimistic, confident people will build your self-confidence and help you create the life and career success you want and deserve.

The common sense career success coach point here is simple. Successful people follow the career advice in Tweet 43 in Success Tweets. "Optimism is contagious. Become a positive, optimistic person. Surround yourself with positive people. They will build your confidence." Successful people are self-confident and optimistic. They face their fears and act. They surround themselves with positive people. The story told in the movie and book *Invictus* demonstrates the power of self-confidence and optimism. Nelson Mandela's supreme self-confidence allowed him to unify a nation when most thought that it was headed for a bloody civil war. Francois Pienaar and the Springbok rugby side believed that they could defeat the best team in the world and win the Rugby World Cup for South Africa. They did, when all of the experts predicted they would lose in a big way. What's your big hairy audacious goal for your life and career? Do you have the confidence that you will achieve it? If you do, you are well on your way to success.

Success Tweet 44

Be an optimist. Believe that things will turn out well. When they don't, don't sulk. Learn what you can, use it next time.

There are two important pieces of career advice about optimism and life and career success in this tweet. First, optimists believe things will turn out well. Second, optimists see failure and defeat as temporary. They treat them as learning opportunities.

Have you seen the movie, *Remember the Titans*? It's a sports movie about an improbable situation based on a true story. Denzel Washington stars as the coach of the T. C. Williams High School Titans. Williams was a newly integrated high school in Alexandria, Virginia, in 1971. Denzel's character, Coach Herman Boone, was a black man chosen to be the head coach over a very popular coach who had been the head coach at the high school prior to it being integrated.

The team had a lot of good athletes. They were undefeated as they entered the State Championship game. Things didn't go well in the first half. In the locker room at half time, Denzel makes a speech in which he congratulates the team on coming so far in such a short period of time. He tells them that win or lose he is proud of them. It seems as if he has given up. It sounds like a speech losing coaches give to teams after a game – not at half time.

One of the players speaks up. He challenges the coach. He says something like, "We were perfect when this game started. We're still perfect until it's over. I, for one, want to finish this game like we started it – perfect." This impassioned speech rallies the team, and they win the game. It's a feel-good movie about a group of young men who learned how to pull together regardless of their differences.

And it makes the first point about optimists. Even when the coach seemed ready to give up, one player wouldn't. He was an optimist. He believed they would win. His optimism was contagious. The team rallied and won. I don't know if things went down exactly that way in that locker room, but that scene reinforces the power of believing things will turn out well.

If you don't believe you can win, if you don't believe you can create a successful life and career, you won't. If you do believe, if you're an optimist, you're on the right path to winning and life and career success.

But believing is not enough. It will set you up for success, but you will still find times when you fail. That's where the second piece of career advice in Tweet 44 comes in. Don't sulk when you fail or lose. Treat every failure and loss as a learning experience. Use failures and losses as stepping stones to creating the life and career success you want and deserve.

I was frustrated early in my career. I saw other people getting promotions for which I thought I was better qualified. My first job in business was in the training department of a large oil company. I worked hard, did a good job – and kept getting passed over for promotion. The reasons were vague – "you've only been here a little while," "the hiring manager thought the other person was a better fit," "you need to polish up some of those rough edges."

So I found another job; this time with a chemical company. I worked hard, did a good job, got good performance reviews – and no promotions. I was frustrated. In my heart of hearts, I knew I was as good as or better than people who were moving ahead while I was standing still.

I decided that maybe more school would be the answer. I quit my job, and enrolled in a PhD program in Adult Education and Organizational Behavior at Harvard. Once I got there, I realized that the same thing happens in academia as happens in business. The hardest workers and best performers don't always get rewarded and promoted.

I decided that I had an opportunity to use my situation – and my frustration – as a lab. I didn't sulk. I chose to learn from my frustrations and failures. After all, I was at Harvard. I was surrounded by high performers – people who had achieved a lot at an early age, and seemed destined to achieve even more. I decided that maybe I should pay some attention to these folks.

I got one of those marble-covered notebooks and made a list of all the people I admired at Harvard. Then I made a list of all the people in the companies where I had worked who got the promotions I didn't. I made another list of the people I knew whom I considered to be positive role models. I didn't stop there. I started reading biographies of successful people. I created a page for each person. I wrote down the characteristics that I observed in these people. When I was finished, I had a notebook full of the characteristics I observed in successful people.

It was a long list. So I did kind of a human regression analysis on it. I started looking for patterns and groups of behaviors. When it was all said and done, I found four distinct characteristics that the successful people I had studied had in common.

They all:

- Had a clearly defined purpose and direction for their lives.
- Were committed to succeeding. They faced obstacles and overcame them.
- Were self-confident. They knew they were going to succeed and continue to succeed as they went through life.
- Shared some basic competencies. They knew how to present themselves in a favorable light. Other people were attracted to them and wanted to be around them. They were high performers. They were great communicators. They were good at building relationships.

If you've been paying attention, you've probably figured out that these are the ideas I cover in Success Tweets and what I've been blogging about for the past month.

Once I finished my degree, I took a job with a very large pharmaceutical company in New York. I started applying the lessons I'd learned from observing successful people – and I began getting promotions and good assignments. I became the confidant of several senior executives and I began coaching up-and-comers in the company – teaching them the basic principles I had discovered by writing my observations in that marble covered notebook.

I also kept refining my ideas – making them easier for others to understand and apply. You never learn something as well as when you teach it. I became the most sought-after internal coach in that company.

In 1988, I was faced with a decision: accept a big promotion to Vice President, or strike out on my own. I decided that I have an entrepreneurial bent and chose the latter. I opened up a small consulting, coaching and speaking business. The idea was to reach even more people with what I knew about creating a successful life and career.

I tell this story not to pat myself on the back, but to illustrate the second point in today's tweet: When things don't turn out as you hope, don't sulk. Learn what you can, use it next time.

The common sense success coach point here is simple. Successful people are self-confident and optimistic. Optimism means believing that things will turn out well, and more important, when they don't, using the experience to learn and grow and do better next time. Follow the career advice in Tweet 44 in Success Tweets. "Be an optimist. Believe that things will turn out well. When they don't, don't sulk. Learn what you can, use it next time." I'm big on optimism. My optimism has helped me create the career and life success I wanted. Your optimism can do the same for you.

Success Tweet 45

Everyone is afraid sometime. Self-confident people face their fears and act. Look your fears in the eye and do something.

Fear is the enemy of self-confidence. Self-confident people face their fears and act. Procrastination is the manifestation of fear. When I find myself procrastinating, I stop and ask myself "What are you afraid of here, Bud?"

Usually, the answer is on the 12 most common fears on the list below. Which of these stop you from moving forward? What are you doing about them?

1. Fear of failure – This type of fear has its roots in the misconception that everything you do has to be 100% successful.
2. Fear of success – This type of fear is based on the idea that success is likely to mean more responsibility and attention, coupled with pressure to continue to perform at a high level.
3. Fear of being judged – This type of fear comes from the need for approval that most people develop in childhood.
4. Fear of emotional pain – This type of fear is rooted in wanting to avoid potential negative consequences of your actions.
5. Fear of embarrassment – This type of fear is a result of empowering others to judge you when you demonstrate that you're only human by making mistakes and having lapses of judgment.
6. Fear of being abandoned or being alone – This type of fear is related to rejection and low self-esteem.
7. Fear of rejection – This type of fear comes from personalizing what others do and say.
8. Fear of expressing your true feelings – This type of fear holds you back from engaging in open, honest dialogue with the people in your life.
9. Fear of intimacy – This type of fear manifests itself by an unwillingness to let others get too close, lest they discover the "real you."

10. Fear of the unknown – This type of fear manifests itself as needless worry about all of the bad things that could happen if you decide to make a change in your life.
11. Fear of loss – This type of fear is related to the potential pain associated with no longer having something or someone of emotional significance to you.
12. Fear of death – The ultimate fear of the unknown. What will happen once our spirits leave our bodies?

By identifying your fear, you are more than half way to conquering it. In the next post, I will present my four-step plan for dealing with fear.

But in the meantime, remember this. Action is the antidote to fear. In most cases, you'll choose wisely and your fears won't be realized. In the cases when you choose poorly, you'll find that failure isn't as catastrophic as you imagined. Successful people learn from their failures. By taking action on your fears, you win on both counts. You win if you make a good decision and things work out. You even win if you make a bad decision and things go poorly, because you have an opportunity to learn from your decision and the subsequent problems you faced.

The common sense point here is simple. Successful people are self-confident. Self-confident people face their fears and act. They follow the career advice in Tweet 45 in Success Tweets. "Everyone is afraid sometime. Self-confident people face their fears and act. Look your fears in the eye and do something." Procrastination is the physical manifestation of fear. When you find yourself procrastinating, figure out what scares you about the situation. Is it fear of failure? Is it fear of success? Is it fear of rejection? Is it fear of being embarrassed? Is it fear of the unknown? Once you've figured out why you are afraid, do three things: admit your fear to yourself; embrace your fear; take action. Action is the antidote to fear.

Success Tweet 46

Four steps for dealing with fear that can sabotage your success: identify it, admit it, accept it, do something about it.

Fear is normal. Fear is common. Fear is human. However, fear is a career success killer. We're all afraid sometime. Successful people face their fears and act. I've learned a few things about fear over the years.

Fear breeds indifference. Indifference breeds self doubt and worry. Often, it's easier to go with the flow and do nothing than attempt to do something of which you're afraid. When you say to yourself, "It's OK, it doesn't really matter anyway," ask the next question – "What am I afraid of here?" Identifying your fear is the first step in dealing with it.

Self-doubt is a form of negative self-talk. Our words can become self-fulfilling prophecies. Positive self-talk leads to success. Negative self-talk leads to fear and failure. If you catch yourself saying things like, "I can't do this; I'll never be successful; I'll never get out of this mess," then you never will. If you say things like, "I can do this; I have what it takes to succeed; I can solve this problem," then you will.

Worry and excessive caution will paralyze you. Some people spend so much time worrying about the bad things that *could* or *might* happen that they never take action and actually do something to prove that good things happen too. Worrying too much can bring you and your life to a screeching halt.

A boat that never leaves the harbor is pretty safe. However, it is not doing what it is meant to be doing. The same is true for people. If you never take a risk, you'll never know what you are capable of accomplishing.

Here are my tips for doing battle with your fears.

1) **Identify what you fear**. Figure out why you're afraid. Is it fear of failure? Is it fear of making the wrong decision? Is it fear of a lost opportunity?

Are you afraid that you aren't up to task? Once you identify the reason behind your fear, you are well on the way to overcoming it.

2) **Admit what you fear**. It's OK to be afraid. You wouldn't be human if you were never afraid. A common definition of courage is the ability to feel fear and still do what you need to do, regardless. In 1988, I faced a very frightening decision. Should I stay in a comfortable but ultimately unsatisfying job with a large corporation, or should I start my own business? I was afraid of failing. Failing meant that I would lose my savings and have to start over again, looking for a job in another corporation. However, once I identified and admitted my fear, I was able to take the next step – acceptance.

3) **Accept what you fear**. Accepting your fears is important, because it shows that you know you're human. Once I accepted that I was afraid of failing, I was able to start my business and succeed. In fact, I embraced my fear of failure. It made me work harder; it pushed me to work the long hours and learn the entrepreneurship lessons necessary to be successful as a self-employed coach, consultant and speaker.

4) **Take action**. Action cures fear. It is the most important of these four steps. Do something! The worst thing that can happen is that you'll find it was the wrong thing to do – and you will have eliminated at least one thing from your list of possible actions.

The common sense career success coach point here is simple. Successful people follow the career advice in Tweet 46 in Success Tweets. "Four steps for dealing with fear that can sabotage your success: identify it, admit it, accept it, do something about it." Action is the antidote to fear. In most cases, you'll make good decisions and your fears won't be realized. In the cases when you choose poorly, you'll find that failure isn't as catastrophic as you imagined. Successful people learn from their failures. By taking action on your fears, you win on both counts. You win if you make a good decision and things work out. You even win if you make a bad decision and things go poorly, because you have an opportunity to learn from your decision and the subsequent problems you faced.

Success Tweet 47

Act. Feel the fear and do it anyway. That's the definition of courage, and a great way to build your self-confidence.

I subscribe to Sharon Melnick's online newsletter. In a recent post, she made several interesting points about confidence.

- Confidence will help you be flexible. You will consider all alternatives and options.

- Confidence will help you follow through on ideas that you might otherwise talk yourself out of.

- Confidence will help you be persistent – and hold on to your vision for your life.

She's right. Confidence is the foundation of all success. Without it, you will have a difficult time succeeding. To build your self-confidence, you have to be optimistic, face your fears and surround yourself with positive people.

Fear is a great confidence and success killer. Elbert Hubbard, the author of "A Message to Garcia" (http://budbilanich.com/garcia), one of the best essays on personal responsibility ever written, has some great things to say about facing your fears.

> "The greatest mistake you can make is continually fearing that you will make one."

Read that again. Those 14 words are powerful! They are some fundamental career advice.

If you let your fear of making a mistake stop you from taking action, you will never take any action and your fear will ruin your life and any chance of creating the career success you want and deserve.

In 1988 I was ready to start my career success coach and speaking business. I was afraid. I was worried that I wouldn't succeed. I had always worked for large companies. I wasn't sure I knew exactly what to do to run a successful career success coach business. Nevertheless, I looked my fear in the eye, quit my job and moved forward. Twenty-two years later, I'm still at it. My fears were unfounded – but they were real. I'm glad I faced them and acted.

Fear is persistent. It doesn't go away. It will wait for one of your weak moments and then it will strike. If you let it get the best of you, you'll never move forward.

Fear most often manifests itself in procrastination. When I find myself procrastinating, I always ask myself, "What are you afraid of here, Bud?" Identifying what I fear always help me defeat it. Once I identify what I am afraid of, I can take positive steps to move forward through my fear and on to success.

Make a list of your doubts and fears. Decide what you can do to overcome them. Then act. Take at least one positive action – no matter how small – every day to overcome your doubts and fears. Even if these actions don't work out as well as you hope, you will be on the road to overcoming your fears and creating the life and career success you want and deserve.

Remember, procrastination feeds fear, and action cures it. The choice is up to you. I choose action. My best career advice says you should, too.

The common sense career success coach point here is simple. Successful people are self-confident. Self-confident people don't let their fears get in the way of their success. They follow the career advice in Tweet 47 in Success Tweets. "Act. Feel the fear and do it anyway. That's the definition of courage, and a great way to build your self-confidence." Identify your fears, and then do what you need to do to move past them. Action is the great antidote to fear. It puts inertia on your side. Once you are moving forward, you are likely to continue moving forward. It's the first step that is the hardest – and scariest. If you want to beat your fears, you need to take the first step – act, and then keep on going.

Success Tweet 48

Procrastination is the physical manifestation of fear and is a confidence killer. Act; especially when you're afraid.

As I've mentioned in previous posts on Success Tweets 45, 46 and 47, fear is the enemy of self-confidence and success. Fear often manifests itself as procrastination. Most people fear failure, criticism and rejection. It's only normal. We all want to feel good about ourselves. Failure, criticism and rejection are not pleasant experiences. They lower our self-esteem and make us feel bad about ourselves, so we often avoid doing things that we think might lead to failure, criticism or rejection. As a career success coach, I advise my clients to have the courage to do things that might result in failure, criticism or rejection.

Failure, criticism and rejection provide you with the opportunity to grow and develop – to become a life and career success. You can't take failure, criticism and rejection personally. Failure, criticism and rejection are outcomes. They are a result of things you have done. They are not who you are.

Remember this career advice. We all make mistakes and fail on occasion. We all do things that cause others to criticize or reject us. This doesn't mean that we are failures as people. It means that we have made some poor choices and have done some dumb things.

Failure, criticism and rejection provide the opportunity to start over – hopefully a little smarter. Buckminster Fuller once said, "Whatever humans have learned had to be learned as a consequence of trial and error experience. Humans have learned only through mistakes." That's great career advice. I agree with it wholeheartedly.

Fear leads to procrastination. That's why putting off things you want to do, and need to do can really hurt your self-confidence and career success. If your fear of failure, criticism, and rejection paralyzes you to the point where you aren't willing to take calculated risks, you'll never learn anything or accomplish any of your goals.

Don't be afraid to fail, or too hard on yourself when you fail – or when others criticize or reject you. Instead, put your energy into figuring out why you failed and then do something different. Here are my four career success coach questions to ask yourself the next time you fail, or get criticized or rejected.

1. Why did I fail? Why did I get criticized or rejected? What did I do to cause the failure, criticism or rejection?

2. What could I have done to prevent the failure, criticism or rejection?

3. What have I learned from this situation?

4. What will I do differently the next time?

If you do this, you'll be better able to face your fears and act; and you'll be using failure, criticism and rejection to your advantage. In *Think and Grow Rich*, Napoleon Hill says...

"Every adversity, every failure, and every heartache carries with it the seed of an equivalent or greater benefit."

I know it's hard to see the benefit or opportunity in failure, criticism and rejection. But it's there – you just have to look hard enough. But it all begins by facing your fear and acting; by conquering procrastination.

The common sense career success coach point here is simple. Successful people are self-confident. Self-confident people face their fears and act. They follow the career advice in Tweet 48 in Success Tweets. "Procrastination is the physical manifestation of fear and is a confidence killer. Act; especially when you're afraid." Our most common fears are failure, criticism and rejection. However, if you choose to find and use the learning opportunity in failure, criticism and rejection you will not only become more self-confident, you will become more successful. It's sad but true – failure, criticism and rejection are the price you pay for becoming a personal and professional success. Beating procrastination by facing your fear of failure, criticism and rejection and acting will pay big dividends – and help you create the life and career success you want and deserve.

Success Tweet 49

Surround yourself with positive people. Hold them close. They will give you energy and help you create the success you want and deserve.

Successful people surround themselves with positive people – people who are both positive by nature, and positive about their life and career success. Positive people are optimistic; and as I've discussed in the post on Tweet 44, optimism is the first step in building your self-confidence and life and career success.

Positive people help you feel good about yourself, because they feel good about themselves – and life in general. They help you build your self-esteem because they have a strong sense of self-esteem. Positive people are there when you begin to doubt yourself. They are not threatened by you or your success. They realize that self-esteem is not a fixed pie. There is an unlimited amount of it to go around, so positive people are always giving it away. Here's a bit of career advice. Build your self-confidence and jumpstart your life and career success by spending your time with upbeat, positive people.

Not too long ago, I did a talk for a local real estate company. This was at the height of the subprime mortgage crisis, not a good time to be in the real estate business. As people entered the room and saw me, most came over and asked if I were the speaker, and introduced themselves. This was great, because it helped put me at ease. Once I knew people's names, it was easier to feel relaxed and enjoy doing my talk.

As the moderator kicked off the session, she recognized several people in attendance, all of whom got a nice round of applause for their accomplishments. When she introduced me, the audience also applauded. During my talk, I could see people taking notes and nodding their heads as I spoke. All of this made it easier for me to connect with them as an audience and do a better job on my talk. My self-confidence was buoyed by the positive energy I observed prior to and during my talk.

I'm a professional speaker. I do lots of speeches. And I get a little nervous before each one. I welcome these nerves, because I know they are my body's way of telling me that

I am up for the presentation. I worry when I'm not a little nervous, as that is an indicator that I might be a little flat during the talk.

However, because the people at the real estate company introduced themselves to me prior to my talk, I knew that this was a positive audience. I still had the positive butterflies, but my nerves were in check and my self-confidence high because of the positive energy in the room.

When I got to the part in my talk about surrounding yourself with positive people, everyone in the audience nodded. They got it – they knew exactly what I was talking about. After the talk, a few people came up to me to discuss that very point. They said that being in the company of positive people was one of the most important aspects of their success.

This is a small example, but a telling one. To succeed in sales, you have to be self-confident. By its very nature, selling involves a lot of setbacks and rejection. It takes a self-confident person to make the sixth call after not getting anywhere on the previous five. Successful salespeople face and deal with their fears of rejection. And they seek out positive people to help them stay motivated to keep doing what it takes to succeed.

This is important in other aspects of life as well. The people around you have an amazing impact on your view of life. When you surround yourself with negative or cynical people, you become negative and cynical. On the other hand, when you surround yourself with positive, self-confident people, you become positive and self-confident.

The choice is yours. I choose to surround myself with positive people. Not only do they help my self-confidence, they are more fun to be around.

The common sense career success coach point here is simple. No one can go it alone. Follow the career advice in Tweet 49 in Success Tweets. "Surround yourself with positive people. Hold them close. They will give you energy and help you create the success you want and deserve." Positive people are great. They feel good about themselves and life in general. They are enthusiastic – and their enthusiasm is contagious. When you surround yourself with positive people, you'll become more positive and enthusiastic. And, you'll be on your way to creating the life and career success you want and deserve. Who are the most positive people you know? Get to know them better, spend more time with them.

Success Tweet 50

Jettison the negative people in your life. They are energy black holes. They will suck you dry, but only if you let them.

Positive people are optimistic. Negative people tend to be pessimists. I was leading a workshop on career and life success the other day and I mentioned that self-confidence is the hinge on which life and career success swings, and that optimism is the most important ingredient in the self-confidence mix. On the other hand, pessimism can cause the success hinge to rust and become difficult to swing. That's why some of my best career advice is to hold tight to the positive people in your life and run – as fast as you can – from the negative ones.

For me, optimism begins with the ten points of The Optimist Creed. I have given away a couple thousand copies of The Optimist Creed. If you would like one, just go to http://budbilanich.com/optimist.

Let's take a look at the difference between positive, optimistic people and negative, pessimistic people.

- Positive, optimistic people tend to see problems, failures and setbacks as temporary.

- Negative, pessimistic people tend to see problems, failures and setbacks as permanent – almost their destiny.

- Positive, optimistic people see problems, failures and setbacks as isolated occurrences.

- Negative, pessimistic people see problems, failures and setbacks as omnipresent – things from which you can't escape.

- Positive, optimistic people don't take problems, failures and setbacks personally.

- Negative, pessimistic people personalize problems, failures and setbacks.

If you read this blog with any regularity, you know that I am an incurable optimist. I see problems, failures and setbacks not only as temporary, but as opportunities to learn and grow. I expect things to go well. When I run into problems, failures and setbacks, I'm always a little surprised because I don't expect them. I do, however, plan for them. Finally, I never take a problem, failure or setback personally. I'm a human being. Sometimes I make great decisions. Sometimes I make poor ones. My self-worth is not threatened by the occasional problem, failure or setback.

And, I choose to hang around with positive, not negative people.

I'm a big fan of Mark Twain. One of my favorite quotes of his gets at the heart of surrounding yourself with positive people and jettisoning the negative people in your life…

> "Keep away from people who try to belittle your ambitions. Small people always do that, but the really great make you feel that you, too, can become great."

Negative people are a drag on your goals and your ambitions. They are quick to tell you what you can't do, offer little encouragement, and hate to see you prove them wrong by succeeding. Hold these kinds of people at arm's length. Don't spend time with them. Instead, invest in friendships with positive, upbeat people; the kind of people who not only don't belittle your ambitions, but do what they can to help you make them a reality.

Cynics are negative people. They are also dangerous, because they are seductive. They always have something witty to say about others – usually others' shortcomings. At first, they seem to be funny and amusing. But spend time with cynics, and you'll find that they have little joy in life except in pointing out and reveling in others' problems and failures.

Ambrose Bierce may well be the world's biggest cynic. I often see quotes attributed to him on line. In the early 20th century, he published a book called *The Devil's Dictionary*. Even I admit that some of his definitions are pretty funny. However, I get tired and frustrated after reading more than one or two. Here are a couple of quotes from *The Devil's Dictionary*…

"Optimism: The doctrine that everything is beautiful, including what is ugly, everything good, especially the bad, and everything right that is wrong... It is hereditary, but fortunately not contagious."

"Calamities: Two kinds – misfortunes to ourselves, and good fortune to others."

No wonder ole' Ambrose was called "Bitter Bierce" by his contemporaries. First, he bashes optimism, then he suggests that human beings see the good fortune of others as a personal calamity.

Here are a couple of other entries in *The Devil's Dictionary*...

"Politeness: The most acceptable hypocrisy."

"Perseverance: A lowly virtue whereby mediocrity achieves an inglorious success."

Do you know any people like Ambrose Bierce? If you do, my best career advice is to hold them at arm's length. While you may find them to be witty and entertaining at first, they will drag you down in the long run. They will not help you create the life and career success you want and deserve.

Point 6 of The Optimist Creed says...

"Promise yourself to be just as enthusiastic about the success of others as you are of your own."

This is 180 degrees from what Ambrose has to say. Successful, self-confident people aren't jealous or upset by the success of others. They are genuinely pleased when they see others succeed. They see the success of others as an inspiration. They use it to motivate themselves to achieve bigger and better successes. Negative people choose to see others' successes as a personal affront. Take it from a career success coach, these kinds of people will not help you create the life and career success you want and deserve.

The No Asshole Rule: *Building a Civilized Workplace and Surviving One That Isn't,* a book by Robert Sutton of Stanford University, does a great job of defining negative people – or "assholes" as he calls them. The first chapter is called "What Assholes Do and Why

You Know So Many." On page 10, he lists "The Dirty Dozen: Common Everyday Actions That Assholes Use." Check it out.

1. Personal insults.
2. Invading another's personal territory.
3. Uninvited physical contact.
4. Verbal and non-verbal threats and intimidation.
5. Sarcastic jokes and teasing used as insult delivery systems.
6. Withering email flames.
7. Status slaps intended to humiliate victims.
8. Public shaming or status degradation rituals.
9. Rude interruptions.
10. Two-faced attacks.
11. Dirty looks.
12. Treating people as if they are invisible.

If you've spent any time in a large organization, or even a small one, you've probably been on the receiving end of many of these asshole behaviors. Truth be told, you've probably been on the giving end of many of these asshole behaviors as well. I don't like to admit it, but I have been both the victim and perpetrator of some of these behaviors.

Dr. Sutton explains why a "no asshole rule" helps create a healthy, vibrant workplace…

> "Allowing a few creeps to make themselves at home in your company is dangerous. The truth is that assholes breed like rabbits. Their poison quickly infects others. Even worse, if you let them make hiring decisions, they will start cloning themselves."

He's writing for leaders, encouraging them to create what he calls "asshole-free workplaces."

I suggest that you create an "asshole-free life." Don't let negative people, assholes if you will, into your life. Hold them at arm's length. In my career success coach talks, I amend his quote. I tell people…

"Allowing a few creeps to make themselves at home in your life is dangerous. Their poison will quickly infect you. Assholes try to clone themselves. Spend too much time with them and you run the risk of becoming one."

The common sense career success coach point here is clear. Successful, self-confident people don't let negative people into their lives. They follow the career advice in Tweet 50 in Success Tweets. "Jettison the negative people in your life. They are energy black holes. They will suck you dry, but only if you let them." Avoid cynics. They are jealous and petty, unhappy when others succeed. As Dr. Sutton of Stanford suggests, avoid assholes – people who are rude, insulting, sarcastic and two-faced. They will only drag you down. Make a conscious choice to spend time with positive, optimistic people. Avoid negative, pessimistic ones.

Success Tweet 51

Find a mentor. Mentors are positive people who will help you find the lessons in your experience and use them to move forward.

This is a long post, because mentors are an important source of career advice. The term "mentor" comes from The Odyssey. Odysseus entrusted the care of his son, Telemachus, to Mentor when he set out to fight the Trojan War. The best mentors will help you learn and grow by sharing their knowledge and wisdom with you. In this way, you can benefit from their experience without having to suffer the consequences of gaining that experience firsthand.

Mentors are positive people by definition. It takes a positive person to give of himself or herself to help another learn, grow and succeed.

I have been fortunate to have had several mentors in my life and career. All of them shared several characteristics. They all…

- Were willing to share their wisdom, knowledge, skills and expertise.
- Had a positive outlook on life. They helped me through tough times and showed me how to find the opportunity in the difficulties I was facing.
- Were genuinely concerned about me and my success. In addition to being knowledgeable, they were empathic.
- Really knew what they were doing. I respected them for their knowledge and skills.
- Kept growing themselves. All of my mentors were curious and inquisitive. Sometimes the roles were reversed. They asked what I was reading, and then read the books themselves – so they could learn and we could discuss the ideas.
- Gave me direct, constructive feedback. They held me to high standards. They congratulated me when I met their expectations. They corrected me when I failed to do so – but in a manner where I learned what not to do the next time.
- Were respected by their colleagues. People who are highly regarded in their field or company make the best mentors.
- Sought out and valued the opinions of others. My best mentor always told me to listen most carefully to the people with whom I disagreed – in that way I might learn something. And, he was right.

As the old saying goes, a mentor is someone whose hindsight can become your foresight.

Do you want to find a mentor? Just look around you. Who are the people you admire and want to emulate? Watch what they do, and do the same. I've had several mentors who never even realized they were mentoring me.

I learned how to build a network of solid contacts by watching Maggie Watson. I learned the rules of business etiquette and dressing for success by watching Bill Rankin. I learned how to become a first-rate public speaker by watching Steve Roesler. I learned how to become a trusted advisor by watching Don Nelson. I learned how to carry myself with dignity in even the most difficult situations by watching JF and Carol Kiernan. I learned how to become a better conversationalist by watching Cathy, my wife.

The reverse is also true. I've learned plenty about what not to do to build self-esteem, give performance feedback and treat people with respect and dignity from observing a few of my managers over the years.

I've found that if you want to have an acknowledged mentoring relationship, all you have to do is ask. Go to the people you admire and tell them that you admire their judgment and would like to learn from them. Ask if you can impose on their time to get answers to questions you have. I have never had anyone turn me down when I've asked this way.

Just as it's important to find someone you respect to mentor you, it also important to mentor others. You don't have to be in a formal leadership position or have years and years of experience to mentor someone else. It's never too early to become a mentor. We all have something to give, and the sooner you begin giving, the better. If you're in college, you can mentor high school students. If you're a recent graduate, you can mentor others still in school.

I take great joy in mentoring other people. I love it when I can use my experience to help accelerate the growth of someone else. It takes the sting out of some of the negative consequences I've experienced because of poor judgment. I think to myself, "At least he or she won't have to go through that."

In his great book, *Love is the Killer App,* Tim Sanders tells the story of how he turned one of the people who worked for him from a "mad dog" into a "lovecat." The advice is simple: "Offer your wisdom freely… And always be human."

Tim is right on. Mentoring is a great way to become a lovecat by serving others. The more you serve others, the more confidence – and success – will come your way. Besides that, you'll grow by mentoring. As you reflect on your life experiences and distill them into some nuggets that you can share with others, your knowledge will become wisdom. In addition to being better able to help others learn and grow, you will be better able to take advantage of what you know. You never learn something so completely as when you teach it to another person.

Any mentoring relationship needs to focus on the person being mentored. While mentoring someone will most often be a satisfying experience for you, remember that it is not about you – it's about the other person. Accept him or her for who he or she is. Help him or her proceed at his or her own pace. The best mentoring relationships are guided by the person being mentored.

Mentoring should be a positive experience for both of you. That means that you need to avoid treating a person you are mentoring as incompetent or incapable. Rather, think of him or her as someone lacking in experience and who needs guidance. Don't criticize. Help the other person think through the consequences of his or her behavior and to identify more positive ways of handling difficult or troubling situations.

Hold the person you are mentoring responsible for his or her success. Give him or her small assignments. Don't let him or her off the hook if he or she fails to complete them. Be willing to give of yourself and your time, but make sure the other person is doing so, too.

Realize that the relationship will end. If you've done a good job, the person you are mentoring will need to move on at some point. It's all part of the cycle. It can be hard to let go, but feel good about seeing someone move on to bigger and better things – and another mentor.

I've created an acronym to define what it takes to become a good mentor. A good mentor...

M   Motivates you to accomplish more than you think you can.

E   Expects the best of you.

N   Never gives up on you or lets you give up on yourself.

T   Tells you the truth, even when it hurts.

O   Occasionally kicks your butt.

R   Really cares about you and your success.

Look for people with these qualities when you are searching for a mentor. Embody them yourself when you are mentoring others.

The common sense career success coach point here is simple. Mentors can help you create the life and career success you want and deserve. Success people follow the career advice in Tweet 51 in Success Tweets. "Find a mentor. Mentors are positive people who will help you find the lessons in your experiences and use them to move forward." You can enter into a formal mentoring relationship. Or you can just observe people you admire. They can mentor you without even realizing that they are doing so. And, it's never too early to become a mentor yourself. There is always someone who needs your career advice; someone who needs to know what you've already learned. Be a positive person. Help others achieve the life and career success they want and deserve.

Success Tweet 52

Identify the self-confident people you know. Pay attention to how they act and carry themselves. Watch what they do. Act like them.

I'm a basketball fan. I like high school, college and pro basketball. I especially enjoy the NCAA basketball tournament – March Madness, as it's called. In March of 2009, I did a blog post in which I told the story of tiny Siena College's upset of Ohio State in the NCAA tournament. Part of that story is worth repeating here...

> Siena is a small liberal arts college near Albany, New York. It has a total enrollment of about 3,000. Ohio State is one of the largest universities in the US. It has a total enrolment of over 60,000. I bet there are some dorms at Ohio State that have more residents than the total number of students enrolled at Siena.

None of that mattered last Friday night. Siena beat Ohio State 74 – 72. It took them two overtime periods to do it, but they did it. The Saints, as Siena's team is called, were losing by 11 points at one point in the second half. They demonstrated the power of optimism. They refused to quit. They believed in themselves. And they won a hard-fought victory.

This is a great story in and of itself. However, Ronald Moore's story is even better. Ronald is the Siena point guard. As the first overtime period was winding down, he found himself with the ball and Siena trailing by 3 points. At that point he was 0 for 4 in three-point shooting in the game. He shot and made a three-point basket that sent the game into a second overtime. Then he did it again! With 3.9 seconds remaining in the second overtime, and Siena losing by 1, Ronald made another three-point shot to win the game.

Ronald Moore made his last two three-point shot attempts after missing his first four. That takes some guts. He hadn't made a three-point shot in over 44 minutes of play, yet with the game on the line, he made not one, but two, three-pointers to win the game. Talk about facing your fears and acting. Ronald demonstrated the power of optimism by his willingness to take the shots he needed to win the game. Good for him – and for Siena.

Ronald Moore demonstrated supreme self-confidence in the Siena win in the 2009 NCAA basketball tournament. He was willing to take a three-point shot in overtime when he hadn't made one all game. If you want to create the life and career success you want and deserve, you need to follow Ronald's example. Take your best shot, even when things aren't going well. Look your fear in the eye and act.

Ronald Moore's and the 2009 Siena basketball team's story is nice, but you don't have to look for athletes to show you how to act in a self-confident manner. You can find self-confident people all around you.

I bet you know someone who is in sales. Watch him or her make several calls one day without a single sale – and then get up the next day and do it again. That's self-confidence.

You probably know someone who is in business for himself or herself. Watch him or her go about building his or her business. That's self-confidence.

Summer is budget time in many US corporations. If you work for one of them, you probably know some people who have to do budget presentations. Watch them as they prepare and present. That's self-confidence.

The common sense career success coach point here is simple. Successful, self-confident people follow the advice in Tweet 52 in Success Tweets. "Identify the self-confident people you know. Pay attention to how they act and carry themselves. Watch what they do. Act like them." Self-confident people are all around you. If you pay attention to what they do and how they act, you'll notice that they have several things in common. They are optimistic. They believe things will turn out well. They face their fears and act. They take the shot, make the sales call, start a business, make the presentation. They surround themselves with positive people. They work with mentors. They mentor others. Follow their lead, and you'll become self-confident too. Who are the self-confident people you know? What have you learned from them?

Success Tweet 53

Act as if you expect to be accepted and you will be. This will increase your confidence and help you make a strong personal impact.

"Acting as if" is great career advice on building your self-confidence. People respond to what you do and how you behave. So, if you act and look self-confident, people will treat you as someone who is self-confident. If you act as if you expect to be accepted – at work, by a customer or client, by a group you want to join – you will be likely to be accepted. It's all in how you carry and present yourself.

Self-confident people greet others with a firm handshake, look them in the eye, and smile. They offer their opinions confidently, and listen attentively to what others have to say.

Debra Benton is a friend of mine. Chapter two in her excellent book, *Executive Charisma*, is called "Expect and Give Acceptance to Maintain Esteem." She says...

> "As a human being walking this earth you have a right by birth to expect acceptance from everyone; and you have an obligation to give it to everyone. You can't expect it for yourself and not give it to others... If you don't expect acceptance, you won't get any... Ignore thoughts such as 'I got here by accident and I'll be found out.' 'I'm dreading the day when someone is going to get me for that.' 'I'm close to being found out, so I'll hide out where I am.' Expecting acceptance is putting yourself on a par with any other member of the human species. Expecting acceptance is stubbornly and justifiably holding a belief of simple self-acceptance. No one is above you or below you. We are all at the same level."

It's difficult to expect acceptance when you have little or no confidence. On the other hand, it's easy to expect acceptance when you are self-confident. This can become a positive or negative self-fulfilling prophecy. Self-confident people expect to be accepted. Therefore they are and their self-confidence grows. People who are not self-confident expect to not be accepted. Therefore, they aren't and their self-confidence is diminished.

The key is to create your own positive self-fulfilling prophecy. Debra says...

> "Initiate a conscious, deliberate, persistent attitude of expecting acceptance from other humans, regardless of whether they earn more money, carry a loftier title, or appear to have more power, experience, status and so on... Everyone knows people who can intimidate, overwhelm, rankle, derail or overly impress... These people don't have power over you unless you give it to them."

This means that you have to consciously work on building your self-confidence. No one is going to do it for you. Be optimistic. Face your fears and act. Surround yourself with positive people. Find a mentor and absorb his or her wisdom. Mentor others. Do all of these things, and you'll be more self-confident, and able to expect acceptance. You'll be creating your own positive self-fulfilling prophecy.

Here's a personal story. Several years ago, I was working for a large company. I was in the training and development department and was scheduled to do a talk for sales people in one of our divisions. I wanted to make sure I did a good job. I called the Division President and VP of Sales to schedule information-gathering interviews.

I had great conversations with both of them – and their input helped me develop and conduct a dynamite program that was the highlight of the sales meeting. The Division President even sent a nice note to my boss, complimenting me on the job I did.

My boss came to me with the note and asked, "How did you get the guts to call the Division President to do that interview?" My response – "I couldn't do a great talk if I didn't know exactly what he wanted and needed." Reflecting on this many years later, I realize that I expected acceptance. Of course, the Division President would be happy to speak with me. I was someone who could help him run a successful sales meeting. I created my own positive self-fulfilling prophecy.

Sometimes this takes guts. But I have found that the reward is worth the risk. Fear of rejection is one of the biggest human fears. But I have found that if you approach people confidently, openly and honestly, they are very likely to accept, not reject you. To do this, you have to conquer your fear of rejection. You have to do something – like initiate conversation. You have to demonstrate that you expect to be accepted. When you do this, you'll find that your fear of rejection is just that...

F	False
E	Expectations
A	Appearing
R	Real

The common sense career success coach point here is simple. Successful people are self-confident. Self-confident people follow the career advice in Tweet 53 in Success Tweets. "Act as if you expect to be accepted and you will be. This will increase your confidence and help you make a strong personal impact." As Debra Benton says, "Expecting acceptance is putting yourself on a par with any other member of the human species. Expecting acceptance is stubbornly and justifiably holding a belief of simple self-acceptance. No one is above you or below you. We are all at the same level." This is great common sense career advice. Don't put yourself above or below anyone. Accept others as they are. Expect that others will accept you.

Success Tweet 54

Fake it till you make it. Appear to be self-confident and others will treat you as if you are. In turn, this will boost your self-confidence.

This post is a continuation of the advice in the post on Success Tweet 53.

The old saying, "fake it till you make it," is great career advice. If you are nervous about being accepted – in a new job or work group, by a new client, by a community that you want to join – act as if you are confident of being accepted. Think, "Of course, I'll be accepted." This will give you the self-confidence to act in a manner that assumes acceptance – even if you're faking it at first – and people will be likely to accept you.

Here's what one of my favorite philosophers and essayists, Ralph Waldo Emerson, has to say on this subject…

> "The virtue you would like to have, assume it is already yours, appropriate it, enter into the part and live the character just as the great actor is absorbed in the part he plays."

He's right. If you play a part long enough, you become that part.

Dottie Walters, who passed away on Valentine's Day, 2007, is a great example of this. You probably don't know who she was, but in certain circles – professional speakers – she was a legend. Dottie Walters was one of the pioneers of the speaking business. There is no aspect of it that she didn't touch or influence. Her book, *Speak and Grow Rich*, is one of the all-time best sellers in our industry. She also produced several audio recordings, books, booklets, and her news magazine for speakers, *Sharing Ideas*. You could even hear her being interviewed at 30,000 feet, as she often was highlighted in the airlines audio programs. Dottie Walters was a true icon.

However, I'm not writing about her here because she influenced the lives and careers of many professional speakers, mine included. I'm writing about Dottie Walters here because she was one of the most optimistic people I know. She truly believed that she would be accepted in whatever she did. And she began by faking it till she made it.

In 1948, she was a stay-at-home mother of two. Her husband's dry cleaning business was on the verge of collapse due to a recession, leaving them with little income and $5,000 in debt – a sizeable sum in those days. Dottie became a saleswoman for a newspaper; first ads, then circulation. She founded a business, Hospitality Hostess Service, kind of like Welcome Wagon. She built it into a four-office, 285-employee business with 4,000 continuous contract advertising accounts.

She began reading everything she could about sales. She found that all of the books she was reading were written for men. She went to the library to find some books on sales that were written for women. When she asked the librarian where the books were for women in sales, she was told, "There are no women in sales, so there are no books for them!"

That night, in her mind, Dottie saw a copy of a book that had not yet been written on the library shelf. The title was *Never Underestimate the Selling Power of a Woman!* She decided to write that book. It was the first book ever written for women in sales by a saleswoman. Dottie Walters expected that her book and her ideas would be accepted – and they were.

Tupperware bought out the entire first printing, including a front section with a letter and picture of their President. They booked Dottie to speak at their big rallies around the country. Many other direct sales companies followed suit.

She went on from there to produce audio programs, and become one of the founding members of the National Speakers Association. Dottie Walters became a legend because she believed in herself. She acted as if she expected to be accepted – and she was. As Emerson suggests, she "played the role" of a super saleswoman for so long that she eventually became a super saleswoman. She assumed that her book on women in sales was necessary and would sell. She was right. Dottie Walters always looked at the bright side. She assumed she would be accepted even when she was selling newspaper subscriptions while pushing two children in a stroller.

In *The Power of Positive Thinking*, Norman Vincent Peale makes an interesting point about being accepted and liked...

> "The fact is that popularity can be attained by a few simple, natural, normal and easily mastered techniques. Practice them diligently and you will become a well-

liked person. First, become a comfortable person, one with whom people can associate without a sense of strain. A comfortable person is easy-going and natural. He has a pleasant, kindly, genial way about him."

This is great career advice and where acting as if you expect to be accepted comes in. When you expect to be accepted you don't work too hard at getting people to like and accept you – you become a comfortable person; someone who is easy-going and natural with a pleasant, kindly, genial way.

The common sense career success coach point here is simple. Successful people build relationships easily because they are self-confident. They follow the career advice in Tweet 54 in Success Tweets. "Fake it till you make it. Appear to be self-confident and others will treat you as if you are. In turn, this will boost your self-confidence." Norman Vincent Peale suggests that the best way to act as if you expect to be accepted is to become a comfortable person – someone others want to be around. He says that comfortable people are easy-going and natural. I agree with this career advice; when you are easy-going and natural, people sense that you expect them to accept you. While other people's opinion shouldn't be the entire basis of your self-confidence, feeling accepted by others is always a confidence booster.

Success Tweet 55

Stand or sit up straight. Don't slouch. Your mother was right. Good posture is important. It makes you look self-confident.

Several years ago when she was Secretary of State, Madeline Albright delivered the commencement address at Wellesley College. She concluded her remarks by saying, "Congratulations, good luck, and remember to always sit up straight." Great career advice if you ask me.

Good posture not only makes you appear to be self-confident, it helps your self-confidence. When you stand or sit up straight, other people see you as confident, ethical, straightforward, awake, alert and alive – a winner.

I turned on one of the games in the recent NBA Finals a couple of weeks ago. It was late in the game, and they were showing the benches. I knew who was winning just by looking at the players and coaches. The Lakers were winning that game. They were sitting straight and had big smiles on their faces. The Celtics, on the other hand, were slumped down on their bench. The contrast was striking. Winners sit and stand up straight.

In the post on Success Tweet 53, I mentioned Debra Benton's book, *Executive Charisma*. Debra has some things to say about good posture too…

> "Good posture shows confidence, vitality, discipline and youthfulness. Slumped posture implies fright, insecurity, lack of self-acceptance or self control, lack of self discipline, a loser, sheepishness, shame and guilt. To stand tall and straight is to have a demeanor that says, 'I expect acceptance.'"

I don't know about you, but I prefer others to think of me as confident, vital and disciplined; not a frightened, insecure, shameful loser.

Debra offers the following advice on how to stand and sit tall and straight…

> "Lift up, suck in and breathe. Whether you're sitting or standing, for good posture: 1) pull yourself up by lifting your rib cage away from your pelvis; 2) roll your shoulders back and down; 3) pull your stomach in at the belly button

toward your spine; 4) breathe; and 5) maintain the posture and keep breathing... Don't just read these recommendations and think 'It's not that important,' or 'I do it fine already,' or 'I'll try it later.' Stop right now and take yourself through these movements."

The common sense career success coach point here is simple. Successful people have good posture. They follow the advice in Tweet 55 in Success Tweets. "Stand or sit up straight. Don't slouch. Your mother was right. Good posture is important. It makes you look self-confident." This is important career advice. Your vibe tells people a lot about you. When you slouch, you give off a defeated, unconfident vibe. When you sit up and stand up straight, you give off a winner's vibe – that of a confident, poised successful person.

Success Tweet 56

Self-confidence must come from within. Outside reinforcement and strokes can help, but you have to build your own confidence.

"I am not confident, what do I need to do to become more confident?" I get asked this question a lot. Here is how I respond...

Self-confidence is an inside job. Self-confident people are optimistic. Self-confident people face their fears and act. Self-confident people surround themselves with positive people. If you want to build your self-confidence, focus on becoming an optimist, facing your fears and surrounding yourself with positive people. Let's look at each of these in a little more detail.

Optimism

Max More says optimism is "the fuel of heroes, the enemy of despair, the creator of the future". Optimism is the opposite of pessimism, which Denis Boyle says is "as magnetic as any black hole, swallowing one good day after another until there are no good days left". Read that sentence again. It's great career advice for becoming more self-confident – avoid the black hole of pessimism.

In a very interesting article in the March/April 2007 edition of AARP, The Magazine (yes, I'm old enough to be a member), Mr. Boyle makes some great points about optimism and pessimism:

"The essential truth about optimism: the opportunities for it are everywhere. They just get ignored... Pessimism though, is the default state of our psyche, and the easy way out. We tell ourselves there is nothing we can do because life sucks, black holes abound, Murphy's Law rules. Meanwhile, optimism takes effort. Despites tons of information provided by zealous pessimists, optimists believe everything will turn out fine. They are able to do something no pessimist can: they do their part to make sure tomorrow will be better than today. To subscribe to optimism means that you have a role in shaping your own future. Why is this important? Because it's how stuff gets done. No successful individual could conduct business with a set of pessimistic assumptions... Work, progress, great ideas, all are fueled by optimism."

I agree. I am an optimist. I admit that in these days of high unemployment and oil spills it can be difficult being optimistic, but I choose to be relentlessly optimistic. I believe every day is going to be a good day – and set about making it so. I believe I will succeed in every project I undertake. This optimism fuels my self-confidence, and my self-confidence drives my performance.

Tal Ben-Shahar teaches a course in Positive Psychology at Harvard. He had 800 students in his course last year. He offers the following three tips for becoming more optimistic:

1. Give yourself permission to be human – don't beat up yourself about mistakes.
2. Express gratitude often.
3. Engage in activities that give your life pleasure as well as meaning.

Fear

Fear is the enemy of self-confidence. It's also very normal. We're all afraid sometimes. Usually it's a fear of failure. Fear can be debilitating, paralyzing us into inaction. Over the years, I've found how to face up to my fears and to conquer them. Indecision, procrastination and inaction feed fear. Action cures it.

Here are my four easy steps for dealing with fear.

1. Identify it
2. Admit it
3. Accept it
4. Take action to deal with it

In the post on Success Tweet 46, I discussed these four steps for dealing with fear in detail. Check it out if you missed it.

Positive People

Surround yourself with positive people – people who are both positive by nature, and positive about their success in their life and career. Positive people are optimistic – and as I've discussed above, optimism is the first step in building self-confidence.

Positive people help you feel good about yourself, because they feel good about themselves and life in general. Positive people are there when you begin to doubt yourself. They help you build your self-esteem because they have a strong sense of self-esteem. People with a strong sense of self-esteem are not threatened by others. They realize that self-esteem is not a fixed pie. There is an unlimited amount of it to go around. Therefore, you can build your self-confidence just by being around upbeat, positive people.

Self-confident people take the time to identify and build relationships with mentors. Wikipedia defines a mentor as "a trusted friend, advisor, counselor or teacher; usually a more experienced person… Today mentors provide their expertise to less experienced individuals in order to help them advance their careers, enhance their education, and build their networks." Mentors are positive people by definition. You cannot be willing to lend your wisdom and expertise to another person without being hopeful about that person and his or her future.

I have had several mentors over my career: Bert Phillips, Maggie Watson, Dick Pelton, Bill Rankin, Howard Sohn, were all trusted friends and advisors at one time or another in my career. I believe that mentoring is so powerful that, as I turn 60, I am working with three mentors. Russell Brunson, Stephanie Frank, and Nancy Marmolejo are helping me turn the intellectual property that I have developed over the past 35 years into products that can be sold on line.

Mentors challenge you to do better. That's why they are so important in building self-confidence. As they challenge you, they are also telling you that "you can do it". Having someone who believes in you – like a mentor – is one of the best ways I know to build self-confidence.

The common sense career success coach point here is simple. Successful people are self-confident. They understand the career advice in Tweet 56 in Success Tweets. "Self-confidence must come from within. Outside reinforcement and strokes can help, but you have to build your own confidence." You can build your self-confidence by becoming an optimist, facing your fears and acting and surrounding yourself with positive people. Self-confidence is an inside job. You have to create it yourself. But once you do, you'll find that it's an upward spiral. Your confidence will inspire you to take on challenges. Your success in dealing with these challenges will help you become more confident – which in turn, will allow you to take on and meet even greater challenges.

Success Tweet 57

Think only of the best, work only for the best and expect only the best. Forget the mistakes of the past. Press on to better things.

This tweet is a combination of two points of The Optimist Creed. The first part comes from point 5 of the Creed: Think only of the best, work only for the best and expect only the best.

This is an important point. Too many people settle for mediocrity. They take an "it's good enough" attitude. Good enough is certainly not the best. In my opinion, it is not even good enough.

In 2001, Jim Collins published a great book, *Good to Great*. The very first words in Chapter 1 are, "Good is the enemy of great." Later on the first page, he says, "Few people attain great lives, in great part because it is just too easy to settle for a good life."

And that's what the fifth point of The Optimist Creed is all about. Don't just be good, be great. Why not? All it takes is a little more effort.

Here's a personal example. I have found that blogging is a great way to write a book. I blog every day, so I have a lot of material. Last summer, I took many of the posts from this blog and tied them together into a book. I was all set to publish it, when one of the people I had asked to read it said, "This is good, but it could be great. It reads too much like a series of blog posts. Your voice doesn't come through well enough."

I didn't want to hear that. I wanted to get the book published. My first thought was, "This is good enough, I don't want to do a lot of rewriting." My second thought was, "I can write a great book; why settle for a good one?" So I rewrote the book. The first one wasn't a total loss. I published it is an ebook called, *Star Power: Common Sense Ideas for Career and Life Success*. You can get a copy by sending me an email (Bud@BudBilanich.com) with the words "Star Power" in the subject line.

I rewrote *Star Power,* and changed the title to *Straight Talk for Success*. This book came out in both hard cover and paperback editions in February 2008. It became an Amazon.com bestseller. *Straight Talk for Success* is better than *Star Power*. It's better than *Star Power* because I took the time to rewrite, to make my voice come through. I thought only of the best, worked for the best, and expected only the best of myself."

When *Straight Talk for Success* went to the printer, I was proud of what I had written. I think it is great. It is the best I could do. In my heart of hearts, I knew that *Star Power* was good, but that I could do better. Someone challenged me to go from good to great, and I have – in my opinion at least. It will be interesting to see what other people think.

However, for now, I am proud of what I have accomplished. I feel as if I have been true to myself by not settling for something that is merely good when I had the chance to be great by putting in a little more time and effort.

The second part of the tweet comes from Point 7 of the Creed: "To forget the mistakes of the past and press on to the greater achievements of the future."

What happens to you, or the mistakes you've made, aren't important. How you react to it is. Don't dwell on negative stuff or your mistakes; use them as a springboard to action and creativity.

Successful people develop the habit of focusing on the positive and putting the negative out of their minds. Positive habits like this are an important key to career success. Habits are like muscles. The more you use them, the stronger they get. Dan Robey is the King of Positive Habits. His eBook, *The Power of Positive Habits*, is one of my go-to books when I need to give myself a little boost. You can get a copy at www.ThePowerOfPositiveHabits.com. I discussed Dan's ideas in detail in the post on Success Tweet 37. Check it out if you missed it.

In her book, ***Forget Your Troubles: Enjoy Your Life Today***, Evelyn Brooks suggests that you get S.M.A.R.T. about putting past mistakes behind you.

- S   Smash the negative.
- M   Maximize the positive.
- A   Act.
- R   Relax.
- T   Target your next action.

One of my favorite piece of career success coach advice is, "Stuff happens as you go through life; positive stuff, negative stuff, happy stuff, sad stuff, frustrating stuff. The important thing is not what happens, but how you react to it. In other words, smash your negative thoughts; replace them with positive ones. Don't dwell on the negative, use it as a springboard to action and creativity. This will help you maximize the positive in your life."

The common sense career success coach point here is simple. Successful people follow the advice in Tweet 57 in Success Tweets. "Think only of the best, work only for the best, and expect only the best. Forget the mistakes of the past. Press on to better things." This advice comes from The Optimist Creed. The first part is point 5: "Think only of the best, work only for the best and expect only the best." I think the first few words in Jim Collins' book, *From Good to Great*, sum it up well – "Good is the enemy of great." If you never allow yourself to settle for "good enough" you will be expecting only the best from yourself. The second part of the career advice in this tweet comes from point 7 in The Optimist Creed: "Forget the mistakes of the past and press on to the greater achievements of the future. If you want a free .pdf of The Optimist Creed that you can frame and hang in your workplace, go to http://BudBilanich.com/optimist. Remember, it's not what happens to you, but how you react to it. Don't dwell on the negative or past mistakes; use them as a springboard to action and creativity. Smash the negatives in your life and create positive thoughts, habits and routines. Use the negatives that come your way as learning experiences that will help you create the life and career success you want and deserve. The idea of creating positive habits – like not settling for good enough – is a powerful piece of career advice that will help you become the life and career success you deserve to be.

Success Tweet 58

Be as enthusiastic about the success of others as you are about your own. Help all people recognize that they are special.

This tweet contains advice from two more points in The Optimist Creed. Point 6 says, "Be just as enthusiastic about the success of others as you are about your own." Point 3 says, "Make all your friends feel that there is something in them."

Let's talk about Point 6 first...

All teachers know that the best way to really master a subject is to learn to teach it. I learned this firsthand when I was teaching in the Business School at Northeastern University while I was completing my dissertation at Harvard. To be an effective teacher, you have to have complete mastery of your subject. You need to be able to present it in a number of different ways so that people with different ways of thinking will be able to grasp the ideas you are presenting.

I have found that this is true for self-confidence as well. The more you help others develop their self-confidence, the more yours will grow. This is true for me. As I've worked with my career success coach clients, I have seen them grow, develop and flourish. I am really happy when my clients put my career advice to use and succeed. As they grow and flourish, my self-confidence also grows.

In yesterday's post I mentioned my bestselling book, *Straight Talk for Success*. I got the confidence to write this book from watching my coaching clients succeed. As I watched them put to work my career advice, I came to believe that I was really on to something and that I should share my thoughts with a broader audience.

In other words, by being "enthusiastic about the success of others", I became more self-confident and enthusiastic about the chances of success of my books – that's why I wrote *Success Tweets* as a follow on to *Straight Talk*.

It's karmic. I've put out some positive energy – both my career advice and my enthusiasm for other people's success. And I've seen my career success coach clients benefit from this energy. As a result, I have benefited by being able to gather my thoughts, publish them and help more people create the life and career success they want and deserve.

Now let's talk about Point 3 of The Optimist Creed...

Everybody likes to feel special. Mary Kay Ash, the founder of Mary Kay Cosmetics, said it really well. "Everyone has an invisible sign hanging from their neck saying, 'Make me feel important.' Never forget this message when working with people." She's right. That's the main message here.

I'd like to take it one step further. I suggest that you promise yourself to make all the people you meet – not just your friends – feel that there is something special in them. When you do this, two things will happen: 1) You'll make their day; 2) You'll feel better about yourself. And, feeling good about yourself is an important part of self-confidence.

Let me tell you a story. A couple of years ago, I was in New York to facilitate a meeting at a client's office. The meeting was scheduled to begin at 7:30. I always like to turn up early for meetings I am facilitating.

I arrived at the client's office about 6:50. Since 9/11, they have a security card system. Because I do a lot of work for them, I have a contractor security card. When I swiped the card on Tuesday, I was denied access. The Security Guard on duty looked at my card and told me that I have limited access – 7:00 a.m. to 7:00 p.m. – to the building and that I would have to wait 10 minutes.

I didn't know this. I'm usually not there that early. It was winter. I was cold. I was tired. I had arrived at my hotel at 12:30 a.m. the previous night. I tried to convince the guard to let me in to the building. He was unyielding (as he should have been). I expressed my frustration at this "silly rule," and went to the coffee shop next door to wait until 7:00.

When I came back at 7:02, I apologized to the Security Guard. He was genuinely surprised. He said that similar situations happen a couple of times a week, and a lot of people get really angry at being made to wait. He told me that I was actually quite pleasant for someone who was being denied access to the building.

And that's the common sense point here. I apologized to the guard and told him that he was not only "just doing his job", but that he was doing a good job. He was firm in upholding the company's policy, but he did it in a professional, non-confrontational manner. This was some positive feedback for someone who is in a role where positive feedback isn't all that common.

I could tell that he appreciated my comments. He felt a little better about himself because he did the right thing – and that someone who was frustrated by him doing the right thing recognized and appreciated the value of what he did. He began his day with a smile.

On the other hand, I felt better about myself because I chose to apologize for the little bit of grief I gave him, and I did something small to make his day just a little bit brighter.

Self-confident, optimistic people feel good enough about themselves to help others feel good about themselves. This is a powerful way to build relationships with others and to become a life and career success. Try it. Look for ways to help everybody you meet feel as if there is something special in them.

The common sense career success coach point here is simple. Self-confident, successful people aren't threatened by, or envious of, the success of others. They follow the career advice in Tweet 58 in Success Tweets. "Be as enthusiastic about the success of others as you are about your own. Help all people recognize that they are special." I am reminded of a quote from Jackie Robinson, the man who broke the color barrier in major league baseball, here. "I'm not concerned with your liking or disliking me… all I ask is that you respect me as a human being." Being enthusiastic about others' successes and helping others recognize that they are special are two great ways to respect them as human beings. No one of us can succeed on our own. We need the help and support of others. The best way to gain the help and support of others is to help and support others. Being enthusiastic – not envious – of others' success is a good way to start.

Success Tweet 59

Give so much time to building your self-confidence and improving yourself that you have not time to criticize others.

This tweet has its roots in Point 9 of The Optimist Creed. "Give so much time to the improvement of yourself that you have no time to criticize others."

Like everything else in The Optimist Creed, this is great common sense. I know that I have a lot to learn. There are many things about me on which I can improve. I'm just guessing here, but I bet that's true for you too. That's why I choose to focus on improving me rather than criticizing others.

I'm not a real religious guy, but I do remember a few Bible stories. Remember the one where people are gathered to stone a woman who is accused of adultery and Jesus disperses the angry crowd by telling them, "Let he who has not sinned cast the first stone?" I know I am in no position to be casting stones. I doubt if you are either. None of us is perfect. If we both choose to put our energy into building our self-confidence and improving ourselves – not criticizing others for their failings – we will be happier, more confident and successful, and the world will be a less contentious place.

I first learned about Abraham Maslow's hierarchy of human needs when I was in college at Penn State. The model was structured as a pyramid with "self actualization" at the top. Dr. Maslow defined self actualization as "being all that you can be" – something the US Army borrowed for its TV recruiting commercials several years ago.

According to Dr. Maslow, self actualization is an unattainable state, because no matter what you achieve, you soon realize that you can achieve even more. You can take this one of two ways. You can see it as negative and frustrating because you'll never reach the goal of being self actualized. Or you can see it as positive and inspiring because you'll always have another dream to chase, another goal to reach.

I choose the latter. I was telling someone the other day that the whole web 2.0 phenomenon has been great for me, because I have begun really learning lately. I've always kept up in my field, but I've felt for the past few years that most of my learning was incremental. I wasn't making any quantum leaps forward.

However, since I've begun blogging and tweeting, I've learned a lot – really a lot. And, as the ninth point of the Optimist Creed points out, I haven't had the time, or the inclination, to think about what others are doing, much less criticize them. I'm busy learning and growing – and that's cool and fun and exciting.

The common sense career success coach point here is simple. If you want to build your self-confidence, work on improving yourself and achieving your goals. Don't worry about what others are doing, or comparing yourself to them. Be too busy with your own growth to worry about anyone else. Follow the advice in Tweet 59 in Success Tweets. "Give so much time building our self-confidence and improving yourself that you have not time to criticize others." This is great career advice. Criticizing others is a waste of your precious time. It robs you of the ability to set and achieve your goals and create the life and career success you want and deserve. Besides that, you're probably not in the position to be casting stones anyway – I know I'm not.

Success Tweet 60

**Take stock of yourself. What are your strengths? What are your weaknesses?
Confident people emphasize their strengths.**

I saw a great quote on line a while back...

"What we are is God's gift to us. What we become is our gift to God."

It was from Eleanor Powell. If you don't know Ms. Powell, she was a well-known dancer
and actress who appeared in many musicals in the 1930s and 1940s. She was a good
dancer, but an amazing tap dancer. In her day, she was known as "the world's greatest
tap dancer."

I love the quote – it gets at the heart of self-confidence and commitment to taking
personal responsibility for your life, career and success. God (or the universe, if you are
so inclined) gives each of us certain talents and abilities. It is up to us to take those
talents and abilities that we have been given and develop them, make full use of them.
This is our gift back to God (or the universe).

Eleanor Powell was given the gift of dance. She began dancing in Vaudeville when she
was 11 and was on Broadway when she was 17. She developed her dancing talent to a
very high level.

I have been given several gifts – the ability to write clearly, the ability to simplify the
complex, empathy and common sense. I've worked hard to develop these gifts. I use
them to help others grow and develop and to create the life and career success they
want and deserve. I believe that I owe it to myself, God, and the people who read the
career advice I write, and those who avail themselves of my career success coach
services, to keep learning, growing and developing my skills.

That's why I started blogging. That's why I write books. Both give me the chance to use
and develop my writing skills, and my ability to simplify complex things, like creating a
successful life and career. I created my *Career Success GPS System* for the same
reasons – to continue to develop my skills and to help others.

When you focus on your strengths, you are emphasizing what you do well naturally.
And this is important. When I was young, I realized that my strengths lie in my ability to

think and communicate. I could always write clearly and persuasively. I wasn't so good at math and science. For a long time, I focused on my weaknesses – taking advanced placement chemistry, physics and calculus courses in high school. I didn't enjoy these courses, but I suffered through them – and did OK grade-wise too. I did this because in those days, I was the Protestant Work Ethic in overdrive. The less I liked something, or showed a natural talent for it, the more I chose to master it.

What a waste! I should have been spending my time on the things I liked – and for which I have a natural talent. My four years at Penn State cured me of my tendency to focus on my weaknesses. That was the best thing I got out of my time there – the idea that I should focus on and develop my strengths, the things that came naturally to me, the things at which I could excel because I enjoyed them and they were easy for me.

That's what you need to do, too. Focus on your strengths. Build on them. This will help you build your self-confidence and create the life and career success that you want and deserve. Don't ignore your weaknesses – do what you can to improve on them, but don't make them the focus of your self-improvement work. My best career advice on self-confidence can be summed up in four words: "Focus on your strengths."

The common sense career success point here is simple. Successful people commit to taking personal responsibility for developing their self-confidence. They apply the advice in Tweet 60 in Success Tweets. "Take stock of yourself. What are your strengths? What are your weaknesses? Confident people emphasize their strengths." As Eleanor Powell said, "What we are is God's gift to us. What we become is our gift to God." She took personal responsibility for using her God-given dance talent to become the world's greatest tap dancer, and become a vaudeville, Broadway and Hollywood star. What are your God-given talents? What have you done to develop them? Commit to taking personal responsibility for developing your talents. It's the best way to give thanks for them, to help others, and to create the life and career success you want and deserve.

Success Tweet 61

Create and nurture your unique personal brand. Stand and be known for something. Make sure that everything you do is on brand.

What products come to mind when you think of great brands? Coca Cola? Levis? The New York Times? Apple? Scotch Tape? All of these come to my mind when I hear the word "brand." People can be brands too: LeBron James, Oprah Winfrey, Martha Stewart, Tiger Woods, are all strong brands – although Tiger's brand has taken a hit in recent months. In fact, they are all readily recognizable by their first names.

If you want to create the life and career success you want and deserve, you need to brand yourself too. Your personal brand differentiates you from everyone else in the world. My brand is "The Common Sense Guy." Because of my brand, people know that they can rely on me to provide them with common sense advice that will help them reach their life and career success goals. They also know that they will get this advice in a straightforward, easy to understand and apply manner, because after all, I'm just a guy.

You need to spend time crafting your brand. Your brand is the two or three words you want people to associate with you. Decide what you want these words to be, and then go about making sure that all of the people with whom you come into contact think of you that way.

When my name comes up, I want people to think of two things – "common sense," and "guy." I do everything I can to get people to think of me this way. My writing is simple, straightforward and to the point. The career advice I give my career success coach clients is always based on ideas they can put to use immediately – never filled with a lot of theory, even though it is based on the latest life and career success literature.

This is important, because nature abhors a vacuum. If you don't brand yourself, others will. It's better to be in control of your personal brand by creating it yourself, than it is to let others create it for you.

Here's a real life example. I have a very successful friend. He owns a high-profile and growing advertising agency. We met when we were both working for a very large

Fortune 500 company. My friend is a fun guy, a big sports fan and very witty. Somehow his fun personality got him tagged as "immature." This is ironic because he is one of the most mature and hard-working people I know.

No matter, his immature brand cost him several promotions at the company where we worked. Whenever his name came up in promotion discussions, the dreaded "immature" tag came up too. He finally had to leave that company and begin someplace anew where he could establish a more positive brand. It worked out well for him, as he is entrepreneurial by nature and is much happier running his own company than he would be working in a very large corporation.

Let this story be a lesson to you. If you don't brand yourself, others will – and sometimes the brand with which you're stuck may not be the brand you want. Pay attention here. This is important career advice.

Creating a strong personal brand is simple, conceptually. Ask and answer these simple questions: "How do I want people to think of me?" "What words do I want to people to use to describe me?"

Think about these questions. Take your time. Don't settle for the first answer. Work to come up with the one that truly describes how you want to brand yourself. Then – and this is very important career advice – do whatever it takes to make sure that other people think of you that way. In other words, act in a manner that consistently and constantly promotes the brand you've chosen for yourself.

For example, if you decide that "hard-working" is a term which you would like others to associate with you, then work hard. Do your assignments well and on time. When you finish one task, ask for another. Come early, stay late. Ask questions to help you understand the business. Pretty soon, people will begin thinking of you as a hard worker – "someone who does everything we ask, and then asks for more." Once this happens, you'll know that you're on your way to creating your own special and unique personal brand as a hard worker.

The important thing is to choose your brand, then consistently and constantly do the things that will build the brand that is uniquely you. That's why I blog. That's why I write books. My books are short. They are not filled with a lot of fluff – in my opinion, fluff and common sense don't work together. That's why Success Tweets is written as a series of tweets – common sense information, presented in a down-to-earth, easily readable manner. That's also why I am writing this series of blog posts. Common sense says that some people will want more than 140 characters on some of the advice in Success Tweets.

The common sense career success coach point here is simple. Successful people are clear on their purpose and direction in life; commit to taking personal responsibility for their success; are confident and are competent. The ability to create positive personal impact is the first of four key competencies that all successful people have mastered. Developing and nurturing your unique personal brand is the first step in creating positive personal impact. Follow the career advice in Tweet 61 in Success Tweets. "Create and nurture your unique personal brand. Stand and be known for something. Make sure that everything you do is on brand." There are two steps to building your personal brand: 1) Figure out how you want others to think of you; 2) Consistently and constantly act in a manner that will get them to think this way.

Success Tweet 62

Your personal brand should be uniquely you, but built on integrity. Integrity is doing the right thing when no one is looking.

There are two common sense steps for developing and nurturing your personal brand.

- Figure out how you want people to think of you.
- Consistently and constantly act in a manner that will lead them to think of you that way.

While your brand should reflect you and your uniqueness, it has to be built on integrity.

According to Wikipedia, "Integrity is consistency of actions, values, methods, measures and principles." Integrity and consistency are intertwined. People who are consistent in their actions are seen as people with a high degree of integrity.

Oprah says, "Real integrity is doing the right thing, knowing that nobody's going to know whether you did it or not." This is true. If you practice situational ethics – doing the right thing only when you're in the public eye — you aren't really a person of high integrity, you're just pretending to be one.

Besides, it's hard to act one way in public, and another in private. So to be safe, resolve to act like Oprah. Do the right thing because it's the right thing to do – not because you'll get credit, or avoid getting into trouble.

John Maxwell is a well-known business author. One of his books sends the same message. It's called, *There's No Such Thing As Business Ethics: There's Only One Rule for Making Decisions*. According to John, that rule is the Golden Rule: "Do unto others as you would have them do unto you." In other words, do the right thing.

There's a practical side to this too. Mark Twain once said, "If you tell the truth, you don't have to remember anything." In other words, if you're always a person of high integrity, it's easy to be a person of high integrity; there are no complicating factors – like remembering what you did or said in a given situation.

Polonius gave similar advice to Hamlet. "To thine own self be true, and it must follow as the day the night, thou canst be false to no man." Roy Blackman, my father in law, passed away a few years ago. This quote was his epitaph. It was on the program handed out at his funeral. Roy embodied it in how he lived his life. It was the only piece of advice he gave his grandson, Matt, as he went off to college.

Oprah, John Maxwell, Mark Twain and Shakespeare are all in agreement on one common sense piece of career advice. If you want to become known as a person of high integrity – and I believe integrity is the cornerstone of any personal brand – act as a person of high integrity all the time – not just when it suits you, or when someone might notice.

Here's a story to illustrate this point. Cathy, my wife, was a flight attendant for 36 years. Seniority is a very important thing in the airline industry. It governs how you bid for trips, positions on the airplane and vacations – almost anything important to a flight attendant's quality of work life.

Cathy was very active in her union. And seniority was one of the union's most sacred principles. A few years before she retired, Cathy's airline made a big push into the international market. International flights were plum assignments; they went to people with high seniority.

However, the airline realized that it would be to their advantage to have some flight attendants who spoke the language of the country to which they were flying on these international flights. Most flight attendants in her airline spoke English only. The airline proposed putting two "language speakers" on each international flight. Many people, including Cathy, were upset with this arrangement as they felt it violated the seniority concept.

Cathy used to fly from the US to London. One day I said to her, "This whole language speaker issue doesn't really affect you. You fly to London; there are no language speakers on those flights. Why do you care so much?" She said, "I believe in the concept of seniority. It doesn't matter if I'm affected by language speakers. It's the principle of the thing." That's consistency – and integrity — in action.

On the other hand, there's Tiger Woods. Tiger had one of the best personal brands in the world. He earned close to $100 million in 2009 on it. If you were following the news in late 2009 and early 2010 (how could you miss it?), you know that the Tiger brand is in serious jeopardy because of some of his indiscretions which have come to light.

Sadly for Tiger, his integrity is now in question – and that's being kind. His wife has left him, taking the kids. Several sponsors have dropped him. And, his golf game is suffering. I'm not writing this post to pass judgment on Tiger – enough people have done that already. I am writing it however, to reinforce my point of building your personal brand on integrity.

The common sense career success coach point here is simple. Creating positive personal impact is one of the competencies all successful people possess. You create positive personal impact by developing and nurturing your unique personal brand, being impeccable in your presentation of self, and knowing and following the basic rules of etiquette. Your personal brand should be uniquely you, but it should be built on integrity. Follow the advice in Tweet 62 in Success Tweets. "Your personal brand should be uniquely you, but built on integrity. Integrity is doing the right thing when no one is looking." As Tiger Woods's case demonstrates, a lack of integrity can lead to serious consequences for a carefully crafted brand. Now, everyone is looking at Tiger and most people don't like what they're seeing. So take a lesson from Tiger – one he's learning the hard way – build your personal brand on integrity.

Success Tweet 63

Be visible. Volunteer for tough jobs. Brand yourself as a person who can and does make significant contributions.

Being visible is a great way to create positive personal impact. Volunteering for tough jobs is the best way to become visible. Tough jobs usually come in two flavors: 1) things no one else wants to do; and 2) tasks in which success is not guaranteed. Volunteering for both types of jobs will get you noticed in a positive way. Trust me here. This is good career advice.

Let me give you an example. Several years ago, I was working for a very large company. This company was committed to supporting the United Way. Every year, they conducted a huge campaign encouraging all employees to contribute. This was a job no one wanted to do. Who wants to ask their coworkers for money?

One year, I volunteered to run the headquarters United Way campaign. Actually, my boss suggested that I volunteer, so I did. I ran a successful campaign, bringing in a higher percentage of donors and a higher absolute dollar amount than the previous year. It was a lot of painstaking, detail work. I also had to manage a group of other volunteers who were canvassing their departments.

What started out as something I felt I had to do, turned into a great experience. I met several senior executives in the company. I met several influential people in New York City. And I demonstrated my ability to manage a large, complex project and bring it to a successful conclusion. And, I felt good about myself when I visited a couple of the agencies who were receiving funds from my company's contributions.

I ended up getting a promotion as a direct result. One of the executives I met during the campaign liked what he saw in me, and offered me a position in his business unit. I created positive personal impact (with her at least) by taking on a job no one wanted and doing a good job with it.

Taking on a job in which success is not guaranteed is also a great way to create positive personal impact. I have a friend who took on a very difficult job when he was a Sales

Manager. His company's CEO had a son who was a slacker. He had a couple of jobs with the company and had failed miserably in all of them. My friend was asked if he would fill one of his open sales positions with the CEO's son. Several of his friends advised him against this – telling him that the son was not a good performer, and never would be.

My friend took on the task. He welcomed the CEO's son to his sales team. He worked with him extensively. By the time he was finished, the CEO's son was a good performer – not a great performer, but a good one. My friend took on a tough job, one in which success was far from guaranteed, and succeeded in it.

He created such powerful positive impact with the CEO that his career success moved rapidly. He went from District Sales Manager, to Regional Sales Manager, to VP of Sales, to the President of his business unit, in the space of six or seven years. Some people said he was in the right place at the right time. While that may be true, he took advantage of an opportunity that many people told him to avoid.

Stephen Covey suggests thinking of jobs in one of four ways.

- Not Important, Not Urgent

- Not Important, Urgent

- Important, Not Urgent

- Important, Urgent

Volunteering for tough jobs that no one else wants to do falls into the Important but Not Urgent bucket. Important but Not Urgent tasks will give you the most payback. We all tend to get trapped by urgency. However, non-urgent tasks that are very important to your success can slip through the cracks if you don't force yourself to spend time with them every day.

You don't have to volunteer for every tough job that comes along. However, by doing so on occasion you will be creating positive personal impact. Creating positive personal impact is an important, but not urgent task. You don't have to be building your reputation every day, but if you never take on a job that will help you build it, you won't achieve the kind of life and career success you want and deserve.

While it's important to volunteer for difficult jobs, it's also important to do the job with enthusiasm.

A while back, I read an article on enthusiasm by Judy Williamson, Director of the Napoleon Hill World Learning Center, at Purdue University Calumet.

> "Enthusiasm is a powerful motivator when it is sincere and heartfelt. It is a spirit that inspires us to move forward positively in a direction of our own choosing… Only the results of enthusiasm can be seen, not enthusiasm itself, because it is an abstract concept. Love, faith, honor, loyalty, and beauty are also abstract concepts. They cannot be perceived directly with the naked eye, but can be seen indirectly in the results that they cause to happen…
>
> "A certain charisma develops within the enthusiastic person. Crowds respond to the 'electricity' that this person generates when they walk into a room, address a crowd, deliver a speech, or just work for their cause. Enthusiasm becomes a catalyst for change when it is sincere. People jump on the bandwagon of an enthusiastic person because they want to feel the energy for themselves. Greatness demands enthusiasm.
>
> "To be enthusiastic, act enthusiastically. Allow yourself to feel the energy and lightness of being that develops when you embrace the higher vibrations of your spirit."

The "charisma" that Judy describes is what I call creating positive personal impact. When you create positive personal impact, you are building your life and career success, because others will notice you, want to associate with you, help you and follow you.

Enthusiasm will help you create positive personal impact. People respond to enthusiastic people. When you're enthusiastic about what you're doing, you and other people feel that you can overcome great obstacles. It will seem as if the entire universe is lining up to help you achieve whatever you have your heart set on achieving.

The common sense career success coach point here is simple. Successful people create positive personal impact. Visibility is a key to creating positive personal impact. Follow the career advice in Tweet 63 in Success Tweets. "Be visible. Volunteer for tough jobs. Brand yourself as a person who can and does make significant contributions." Taking on tough jobs is an important, but not urgent task. You don't need to take on one after the other, but you do need to find places where you can shine and volunteer for the job. If you never volunteer for tough jobs you will be losing the opportunity to create positive personal impact. When you volunteer for tough jobs, do them with enthusiasm. Enthusiasm will help you create positive personal impact and build your career success brand.

Success Tweet 64

Build your personal brand. Do whatever it takes to make sure that people think of you in the way you want them to.

Abraham Lincoln once said something that applies here: "Don't worry when you are not recognized, but strive to be worthy of recognition." The idea of constantly striving "to be worthy of recognition" captures the essence of creating positive personal impact.

As I point out in *Success Tweets*, I have found in my career success coach work that people who create positive personal impact have three things in common:

- People with positive personal impact develop and nurture their unique personal brands.
- People with positive personal impact are impeccable in their presentation of self.
- People with positive personal impact know and follow the basic rules of etiquette.

If you develop and nurture your unique personal brand, present yourself well and use the basic rules of etiquette consistently, you will become recognized as a person with positive personal impact. There are two keys here. First, work constantly and continually at creating positive personal impact and on building your personal brand. Second, realize that this won't come overnight. You have to work at it. That's the idea behind the first part of Mr. Lincoln's quote – "don't worry when you are not recognized."

I'll use myself as an example. I have been working on my personal brand, The Common Sense Guy, for over ten years. Yet, I never miss an opportunity to reinforce it. My business card says, "Bud Bilanich, The Common Sense Guy." As I'm sure you've noticed, I tend to end most of my blog posts by saying something like, "The common sense point here is simple…" When I speak, I always make sure that my audiences know the career advice I am dispensing is based in common sense. When I complete on line forms, I always enter "The Common Sense Guy" for both my company and my title.

It's the same when it comes to attire. When I pack for business trips, I pull out two or three pairs of dark charcoal gray slacks, a black or blue blazer, several white shirts and striped ties. I always wear white shirts and striped ties when I visit my clients. Often, they tell me that I don't need to dress up as they are a business casual office. I always reply by saying, "I put on my tie today because I knew I would be seeing an important person – you." This comment always gets a smile – and from what I can tell, people are flattered by it. It helps me create positive personal impact.

My white shirt and striped tie look has become so well-known among people whom I see regularly, that they are surprised when I deviate from it. A couple of months ago, I was getting dressed and noticed a favorite foulard patterned tie on my tie rack. I decided to be a little wild and crazy and wear it. Sure enough, one of my clients asked if I were changing my look – from striped to patterned ties. This little story illustrates the power of consistency. I had never discussed my preference for striped ties with this woman. However, at some level, she noticed my white shirt and striped tie presentation. It must have registered, or she would not have mentioned it when I deviated from my normal tie selection.

What is your personal brand? What do you do every day to reinforce it? What else can you do? If you want to learn more about personal branding, Dan Schawbel and William Arruda are the two best sources I know. Check out Dan's personal branding blog, and William's site. William was featured in the August 2010 issue of Money Magazine.

When it comes to etiquette, I have one simple piece of advice – do whatever it takes to make the people around you feel comfortable. I have an acquaintance who is an etiquette nut. She can quote you chapter and verse from Emily Post. Unfortunately, she is so correct in her behavior, and her expectations of others, that dining with her is an unpleasant experience. I am pretty well versed in dining etiquette; yet when I dine with this woman I spend way too much time worrying about the more esoteric dining etiquette rules. I spend so much time worrying about the rules that I never enjoy my meal. This is probably more my fault than hers, but she contributes to a general feeling of discomfort in these situations.

Polite people never call attention to social faux pas. In fact, they do just the opposite; they do whatever they can to avoid making other people feel uncomfortable. A few years ago, my niece graduated from college. Cathy and I were at a dinner in her honor. The man sitting to my left used my bread plate. Like a lot of guys, he didn't know that his water glass was on the right, and his bread plate on the left. I said nothing and placed my roll on the edge of my plate. Cathy noticed, and whispered that I should be using my bread plate. I whispered back, "I would but Joe is using it and I didn't want to embarrass him."

The common sense point here is simple. Follow the common sense career advice in Tweet 64 in Success Tweets. "Build your personal brand. Do whatever it takes to make sure that people think of you in the way you want them to." Heed Abraham Lincoln's advice – strive to be worthy of recognition. I love this career advice. If you strive to be worthy of recognition, you'll be doing the right things. If you strive merely to be recognized, you may take some short cuts and do damage to your personal brand. Be worthy of being recognized by developing and nurturing your personal brand; being impeccable in your appearance; and helping the people around you to feel comfortable in social situations. If you do just three things, you'll create powerful positive personal impact and build a solid personal brand.

Success Tweet 65

A good personal brand highlights your uniqueness. Be unconventional. Break rules.

I love the movies. I was really pleased when I was asked to review a book called *The Big Picture: Essential Lessons for the Movies.* Authors Kevin Coupe and Michael Sansolo do a great job of discussing the life and career success ideas in over 200 movies. This is a very thoughtful book.

Kevin and Michael make some great points about success that pops up in some unlikely movies. For example, they use the movie *Babe* to make the point that it's important to be different – and break some rules — if you want to get recognized and succeed. That's great personal branding and career advice. Creating and nourishing your unique personal brand is the first step in creating positive personal impact.

Here's some of what Kevin and Michael have to say about *Babe…*

> "Babe is a simple story, but it contains an important lesson. Think of how many businesses have stuck to the way things always are and completely missed the opportunity to become something entirely new, bigger and better.

> "MTV didn't invent video or records, but pulled them together in an entirely new cable channel. CBS, in contrast, owned a television network and a record company, but missed the chance."

I experienced a rule-breaking moment the other day. I was in a local bookstore looking for a book on fitness. As you can imagine, there was no shortage. As I opened various books to check them out, I found Tamba Mbawa's business card in every one of them. I purchased a book and took it home. When I got there, I went to Tamba's website to see what he is about. Not surprisingly, Tamba is a personal trainer and fitness coach.

I thought this was a great example of breaking the rules and personal brand building. Tamba spent the time to go to a local Barnes and Noble and place his card in every one of the fitness books they have on the shelf. He was getting his name in front of a very targeted audience: people who purchase books on fitness. Pretty cool idea in my book. And one that is a perfect manifestation of what Kevin and Michael have to say about breaking the rules to get recognized for your uniqueness.

When I first started blogging, my dad read a few of my posts and said, "You're giving away some of your best ideas. You shouldn't do that. You need to be selling your advice, not giving it away." At the time, content-rich blogs ran counter to the rule of jealously guarding your proprietary information. I told my dad that I'm happy when people read my blog and find ideas they can put to use. More power to them. I also told him that people who find my ideas helpful are more likely to look to me for career advice when they run up against a problem they can't solve on their own. I was breaking a rule to build my brand.

Interestingly, giving away solid, useful information is the new rule. Ask any Internet marketer or marketing guru. They will all tell you to build a relationship and establish credibility with your target audience by providing them with useful information at no cost. Funny how things change.

George Bernard Shaw is my favorite playwright. There is nothing so good as a well-performed Bernard Shaw play. He also had something to say about breaking rules...

> "All great truths start out as blasphemies."

> "The reasonable man adapts himself to the world; the unreasonable one persists in trying to adapt the world to himself. Therefore all progress depends on the unreasonable man."

So go ahead, break a few rules. Be a little unreasonable. Be unconventional, make your brand uniquely you.

One last story. Tim McKernan had one of the most unique personal brands I have come across. He was The Barrel Man. You might say that Tim was a superfan of the Denver Broncos. For 30 years and in all kinds of weather, he attended every Bronco home game wearing nothing but an orange barrel with a Broncos logo and a cowboy hat and boots.

He wore his costume for the first time in 1977. He had a $10 bet with his brother. He bet that the costume would get him on TV. He won that one, and was on TV every time the Broncos were for the next 30 years. John Madden always mentioned him when he was doing a game in Denver.

Tim's unique brand got him inducted into the Visa Hall of Fans at the Pro Football Hall of Fame. He passed away in 2009. He was in the stands for both of the Broncos' Super Bowl victories.

You don't have to go to the lengths Tim McKernan did when building your brand. But I encourage you to think like Tim. Being a little outrageous, like wearing only a barrel to football games in December in Denver, can help you stand out from the crowd and get recognized.

The common sense career success coach point here is simple. Successful people build personal brands that are unique. Breaking a few rules is one way of building a unique brand. By breaking the rules, I don't mean doing something illegal or unethical. I mean thinking outside of the box and not being constrained by conventional wisdom. In the movie "*Babe*," Babe the pig succeeds because he doesn't act like a pig. He is friendly and mannerly – characteristics not usually associated with pigs. What rules are holding you back from building a great personal brand? How can you break them to demonstrate your uniqueness? Follow the career advice in Tweet 65 in Success Tweets. "A good personal brand highlights your uniqueness. Be unconventional. Break rules." Don't do anything that will land you in jail, or get you fired. But think outside the box, find ways to create a Cherry Garcia brand, not one which is plain vanilla. Think of new ways to combine ideas. An iPod after all, is nothing more than a hard drive with a set of headphones. Figure out how you can become the iPod in your work team. Create a brand that shows how unique and fascinating you really are.

Success Tweet 66

Nurture your network. What your friends, colleagues and customers say about you is how others will think of your brand.

Successful people build strong networks. Strong networks are a great way to develop your personal brand – or to wreck it. Here's a true story about one of my career success coach clients.

James was with his company for close to 30 years and was a very senior executive. He had risen through the ranks and was well-regarded by almost everyone who knew him. But, a couple of years ago, he was asked to resign.

James became the protégé of a senior manager early in his career. As the manager moved up, James moved up with him. The manager had great faith in James' business acumen and his problem-solving ability. Whenever a problem arose, James' manager would ask him to "look into it and fix it."

James enjoyed these challenges. He was smart, and had an uncanny ability to zero in on what was going wrong. He was equally adept at coming up with solutions to problems.

James created issues for himself though. Most of the time, the problems he was asked to fix were not in his area of responsibility. They were problems that his peers, other people at his level who reported to his boss, were experiencing. In pleasing his boss and solving problems, James stepped all over the toes of his peers – sometimes not so gently. They came to resent him for it. And this hurt his personal brand.

One day, his boss left the company. One of James' peers was appointed to take his place. Three months later, James was asked to resign. He was asked to resign not because of his performance. In some ways, it was because he was too competent. He was asked to resign because he hadn't built strong relationships with his peers. Often, by doing what his boss wanted, he alienated the people closest to him.

James and I began working together. My career advice was to build his brand by working on his interpersonal skills. I helped James understand that it was important not only to do a great job, but to do so in a way that did not alienate those around him.

I'm happy to say that James landed a job as President of a small company in his industry. We still speak. He tells me that the secret to his new-found success comes from both his willingness to work hard and to build and maintain relationships with people at all levels of his company.

James' story illustrates an important point about career success. Successful people realize that relationships are the key to building a winning personal brand. No one can go it alone and succeed. You have to build and nurture a strong network of colleagues and peers.

The common sense career success coach point here is simple. Successful people's personal brands identify them as being interpersonally competent. Interpersonally competent people build and maintain strong relationships with the people close to them. They also resolve conflict in a manner that enhances, not detracts, from these relationships. If you want to build a brand that identifies you as being interpersonally competent, follow the career advice in Tweet 66 in Success Tweets. "Nurture your network. What your friends, colleagues and customers say about you is how others will think of your brand." Put as much effort into building strong relationships with your colleagues as you do into producing good results. Remember, success depends not only on what you do, but how you do it.

Success Tweet 67

Demonstrate self respect. Be impeccable in your presentation of self – in person and on line.

Successful people, those who create positive personal impact, dress well, and don't post stupid things on line. You don't have to spend a fortune to dress well. Here are my best tips for looking good at work.

Business Casual…

Men should wear khaki or light gray slacks, an oxford cloth button-down shirt and a blue blazer, and carry a "just in case" tie in their briefcase. Women should wear slacks or a skirt, blouse and jacket.

If you don't know, err on the safe side. Men and women should wear suits, and men should wear a tie. It's always OK to ask about a company's dress code when you are arranging a first meeting.

Quality matters…

All of your clothing should be of quality fabric, clean and neatly pressed. Shoes should be shined. Heels should not be worn down.

Grooming…

Wear your hair neatly styled. Make sure your breath is fresh. Keep your fingernails trimmed and clean.

Hosiery…

If women don't wear hosiery, they should make sure their legs are well maintained. They should wear professional shoes in the office. Save the strappy sandals for weekends and get-togethers with friends.

Have an "Outfit B"…

It's a good idea to keep a backup business outfit in your office. This can help when you have an unexpected meeting come up – or worse yet – if a waiter spills something on you at a business lunch.

Here's an example of the importance of "Outfit B." The idea really hit home with me. Several years ago, I was conducting an off-site team-building retreat. We were in a meeting room at a hotel. We adjourned to the dining room for lunch. The person next to me order fried mozzarella sticks as an appetizer. They came with a side of marinara sauce. We were squeezed in pretty tight. When the waiter came with the fried mozzarella, he was balancing the cheese and marinara sauce on a small tray. My friend said, "Let me help you," and picked up the mozzarella sticks. That upset the balance of the tray, and the marinara sauce spilled all over me. I was wearing a pair of light-colored khaki slacks and a light pink button-down shirt. Both were ruined.

Fortunately, I was staying at the hotel where the meeting was taking place and was able to go to my room and change. However, from that day forward, I always kept a change of clothing in the closet in my office at work. I never needed them, but I felt better being prepared.

A while back I came across a great article on HRGuru.com called, "What Professionals Should Never (Ever) Wear." Here are the items that the authors suggested you should not wear to work. Some are funny. Some are downright stupid. They all are just not good common sense...

- Crocs
- Uggs
- Fanny Packs
- Scrunchies
- Sweatshirts and Sweatpants
- Footless Leggings and Spandex/Yoga Pants
- Leather Pants
- Face Tattoos
- Velour/Juicy Tracksuits

- Message T-Shirts

- Too Much Exposed Skin

- Heavy – or no – Makeup

- What You Wore Yesterday

- Sequins

- Flip-Flop Sandals

- Excessive Jewelry

- Sports Teams Jerseys

- Hats and Caps

- Long Fingernails

- Messy, Wrinkled or Torn Clothing

- Wallet Chain

- Glitter

- Sunglasses Indoors

- All-Over Animal Print

- Short Shorts

You'd think that people would have the common sense to avoid wearing these items at work. However, I can recall seeing each of these fashion faux pas – with the exception of Mike Tyson face tattoos – in places where I have worked. One of my professors at the Harvard Business School used to wear a wallet chain. He looked like a biker in a suit.

Finally, your on line presentation of self is important too. My best career advice is to Google yourself. See what comes up. If it's something embarrassing, or something you wouldn't want your employer to see, make sure you remove it. This holds true for your Facebook and LinkedIn profiles. Be just as impeccable in your on line presentation of self as you are in person.

The common sense career success coach point here is simple. Successful people create positive personal impact. You can create positive personal impact by being impeccable in your presentation of self – in person and on line. Follow the career advice in Tweet 67 in Success Tweets. "Demonstrate self respect. Be impeccable in your presentation of self – in person and on line." Professionals should dress in a professional manner. Your attire and grooming are important keys to creating positive personal impact. It's important to look good. Wear quality clothes and shoes that are in good repair. Keep your hair neat. Dress a little better than you have to. And, look in the mirror on your way out the door. Ask yourself, "Does what I'm wearing today demonstrate that I respect myself and the people I will meet today?" If yes, get going and have a great day. If no, take a few minutes and change into something more appropriate. You'll build a professional brand.

Success Tweet 68

Be well groomed and appropriate for every situation. Always dress one level up from what is expected. You'll stand out from the crowd.

Your appearance says a lot about you. My best career advice on how your attire can help you create positive personal impact is simple common sense. Dress one level up. In other words, dress a little nicer than you have to. For example, if your office is casual, wear a dress or a suit every once in a while.

I always get dressed up when I am meeting clients. Many of my clients dress casually. When they tell me, "You didn't need to wear a suit today," I say, "Yes I did. I'm meeting with an important person – you." Show respect for yourself and the people around you by dressing well and looking good.

Accessories are an important part of your appearance. In general, you want your accessories to complement, not overpower your clothing. Keep them understated and elegant. Large rings and earrings, bracelets that jangle every time you move, can distract from your look and your professionalism. Save the bling for evenings out; tone it down at work.

Pay attention to your electronic accessories. A couple of years ago, I saw a Wall Street Journal article about electronic accessories. It made some interesting points about cell phones, PDAs and other electronic helpers – all small enough to tote around with us all the time – and how they can hurt your image as a professional. Look around, you'll see that most senior executives aren't overburdened by electronic accessories. They don't wear cell phone ear-pieces and don't clip their phones on their belts. Keep your electronic accessories in your briefcase or purse, not on display. You will be projecting a more professional image.

In *Wildly Sophisticated*, my friend Nicole Williams lays out ten fashion commandments. I think they are invaluable advice for creating a professional look and helping you dress one level up.

1. **Sweat the small stuff.** People don't necessarily notice if you're groomed, but they definitely notice when you're not.

2. **Restrain yourself.** Never let your accessories wear you.

3. **Know your body.** Recognize that every style trend is not designed for you. This isn't a limitation – it's just reality.

4. **Black is your friend.** Black staples – pants, skirts and jackets – are clean, classic and they always look good. They're flattering, will work with everything else in your closet and will stretch your clothing budget.

5. **Focus on your feet.** A great pair of shoes can make all the difference in your look. Make sure your footwear is polished and clean. This is another one of those details that people really do notice.

6. **Welcome the three-way mirror.** Make sure your clothes fit well. Clothes that fit well make you look more professional and help your confidence.

7. **Work it.** Style is really a synonym for self-expression. You'll feel and look better when your clothes reflect your personality. I'm a big guy. I look better in conservative clothing, so I wear Brooks Brothers – and often get complimented on my appearance.

8. **Buy quality.** In the long run, quality clothes will actually save you money.

9. **Invest in accessories.** Your bag or briefcase is a constant companion. Clients, employers and colleagues notice what's on your arm. Invest in a quality piece that reflects your style. And in this age of laptops, cell phones and PDAs, a bag that will carry your hardware is a lifesaver.

10. **Relax.** Bottom line? It's just fashion. Give it your best shot; know that style matters and that looking groomed and professional are important for your career.

The common sense career success coach point here is simple. Follow the career advice in Tweet 68 in Success Tweets. "Be well-groomed and appropriate for every situation. Always dress one level up from what is expected. You'll stand out from the crowd." "Act as if" is one of my pieces of career advice I often offer my career success coach clients. One way to "act as if" is to dress as if you're in the position to which you aspire.

That means dressing at least one level up from what is expected of you. For men, a blazer and slacks with a nice shirt and tie, or for women, a suit with a silk blouse and tasteful accessories will help you create the look of a successful professional – someone who is going places.

Success Tweet 69

Demonstrate respect for yourself and others in your dress. People will notice and respond positively to you.

How you dress says a lot about how much you respect yourself, and how much you respect other people. You read that right. Your attire is about respect. If you respect yourself, you will dress well and look good. If you respect other people, you will dress well and look good. It's as simple as that.

Just this morning, I saw something on line from the Napoleon Hill Foundation that applies here.

> "If you haven't the willpower to keep your physical body in repair, you also lack the power of will to maintain a positive mental attitude in other important circumstances that control your life."

While this quote is directed at your physical condition, it applies to the condition of your wardrobe as well. You have to take the time to keep your clothes in good repair. Clothes that are clean and pressed, fit well, and are in good repair show that you care.

Clothes that are wrinkled, have spots from previous wearings, are too tight – or too big – and have missing buttons or undone hems characterize you as someone who doesn't care. Someone with little self respect. Someone with little respect for other people.

People notice how you look. It's as simple as that. So put a little thought into getting dressed each day. Make sure that what you wear reflects the professional you are. You don't have to spend tons of money on your wardrobe. But you do need to maintain it. Pay attention here, this is solid career advice.

When I was in high school, I saw a movie called "To Sir, With Love." Sidney Poitier played a teacher in a tough neighborhood in London. He was determined to teach his students life lessons in addition to the regular curriculum.

He had only a couple of shirts and ties. But he washed and ironed his shirts after every wearing. He looked good in the classroom. He did this because he respected himself and his students. He wanted to be a positive role model.

That movie is over 40 years old, but Sidney Poitier's dedication to pride in personal appearance has stuck with me all these years – and it's the main lesson that comes from today's career success tweet.

The common sense career success coach point here is simple. Successful people respect themselves and the people they meet. Your appearance is one way to demonstrate self-respect. Follow the advice in tweet 69 in Success Tweets. "Demonstrate respect for yourself and others in your dress. People will notice and respond positively to you." Taking a few minutes each day to make sure that your clothes are clean and in good repair shows that you care. And when you care, other people notice and respond positively to you. Showing that you care is a great way to create positive personal impact.

Success Tweet 70

Business is the first and most important word in "business casual." Dress like you're going to work, not a sporting event or a club.

I saw a tweet on line yesterday that said…

> "The impression you make when first meeting someone is 7% verbal, 28% body language, and 65% visual."

I retweeted this bit of information. I'm not sure if the numbers are 100% accurate, but they are pretty much aligned with my personal experience. That's why the career advice in this tweet is so important. When you're going to work, look like you're going to work.

Recently, I came across the website of a company called Personal Impact International www.personalimpact.ca. The "quick tips" button on their website yielded some great information on how to dress appropriately at work. Take a look…

Personal Impact Quick Tips from Personal Impact International

When in doubt dress up
In business, it's better to be over-dressed than under-dressed.

Dress to Impress
Impress your boss – Dress at the same level or one level down. Impress your client – Dress at the same level or one level up.

Impress with Less for Less
Buy quality, timeless styles. The best you can afford. Colors and styles that mix and match create Wardrobe Capsules that save you money.

Play it Safe all Year Round
Choose seasonless fabrics, such as lightweight wools, fine cottons, and silks. Natural fibers look and feel more expensive.

Love What You Buy
Don't buy anything on sale you wouldn't have paid full price for.

Think in Three's
Less is better when in comes to color. Wear no more than three colors at once including accessories. Patterns count as one color.

Plan Ahead for Professional Polish
It's the little things that count. Grooming really does make a difference. You – and your clothing – should be in tip-top condition.

Add a Little Pizzazz
Take it easy on the accessories. Accessories can create the look that says 'me'. Accessories are the extras that can give you individual style. But remember, in business less is more.

Make a Statement in Shades
A dark or muted jacket worn with a light or contrasting top highlights the face, adding authority and presence.

Dress Down with Style
Even on casual days, be prepared. Keep a coordinating jacket handy for the unexpected meeting with the boss or clients.

Avoid Image Blunders
Everything has its time and place. Sexy, frumpy and sweaty have no place in the work place – even on casual day. Clothing worn for special activities should be saved for those activities.

Make a Little Adjustment
Making small alterations to the sleeves, hemline and waistline or simply changing the buttons can make your clothing look custom tailored, and you look like a million.

Common Sense Prevails
If it doesn't seem quite right, it probably isn't. Common sense and tasteful good judgment can create impressions that help you soar to the top.

I like this advice – if for no other reason than the last point – "common sense prevails." The Personal Impact people are right – "if it doesn't seem quite right, it probably isn't."

Things have changed and are more casual. Way back in 1983 I showed up for work in a blue blazer and dark charcoal slacks, white shirt and tie. My boss called me into his office and told me that a blazer is a "sport coat" and that I was at work, not a sporting event. He suggested that in the future I should stick to suits for work.

That was then. This is now. Times change, and the workplace is more casual. Today, a nice blazer and slacks with a tie is considered quite dressy. However, the point remains. When you go to work, dress to make a positive impression on those around you.

The common sense career success coach point here is simple. Successful people create positive personal impact. To create positive personal impact, follow the career advice in Tweet 70 in Success Tweets. "Business is the first and most important word in "business casual." Dress like you're going to work, not a sporting event or a club." As I've mentioned, when you're going to work, dress like you're going to work. It's always better to be over-dressed than under-dressed at work. When I'm working at home, I may be dressed in my exercise clothing. However, when I go out – even for a meeting with a client I know well – I shower, shave, comb my hair and put on clothes appropriate for the meeting. A lunch or coffee appointment usually means a pair of nice slacks, a blazer and an open collar, button-down shirt. A visit to a client's office always means a jacket and tie. Work is work, fun is fun. Dress appropriately for each.

Success Tweet 71

Observe successful people in your organization. What do they wear? Dress like them and you won't go wrong.

This tweet is pretty self explanatory, so this will be a brief post. That doesn't mean that the career advice isn't important though.

If you're like most people and work for a large company, you'll notice that your senior executives dress well. Most days, they'll be wearing a suit. You don't have to wear suits all the time, but you should follow their example.

In general, you'll find that executives wear clothing that fits well, is clean and in good repair – you should too. Here are a few of my best tips for dressing like an executive. They are good career advice for anyone who aspires to becoming an executive.

If you're a man…

> Wear nicely tailored wool slacks – not khakis.

> Wear long-sleeved collared shirts – not golf shirts.

> Tuck in your shirt.

> Wear a tie every couple of days.

> Keep your shoes shined. Wear tasseled loafers or brogues.

If you're a woman…

> Wear a conservative hem – no more than two inches above the knee.

> Make sure your blouses fit, that they don't gap.

> Wear heels that are no more than two inches high.

> Wear hose that are flesh color or darker.

> Make up should be understated. Wear a mild fragrance.

There are exceptions to any rule. Steve Jobs, Apple CEO, comes to mind. His business attire seems to consist of black mock turtle necks, jeans and sneakers. If you work for Apple you might be able to get away with this type of attire.

However, you probably don't work for Apple. You probably work for a large company where the executives dress more conservatively. That means you should follow their lead.

The common sense career success coach point here is simple. Successful people create positive personal impact. Your attire has a lot to do with the personal impact you create. Follow the advice in Tweet 71 in Success Tweets. "Observe successful people in your organization. What do they wear? Dress like them and you won't go wrong." This is important career advice. If you follow the lead of senior executives and other successful people when it comes to your attire, you'll be a step ahead of the game. Sometimes this means dressing up more than you would like. But, it will put you on the road to the life and career success you want and deserve.

Success Tweet 72

21st-century technology has created new etiquette rules. Learn and use them to appear polished on line and off.

People with positive personal impact are always polite. They know and understand the basic rules of etiquette. But 21st-century technology has created new etiquette challenges. Here are a few thoughts on how to be courteous while using your latest gadget.

- Never text and drive – never. If you want to make a call, use your hands-free device. Better yet, wait till you get where you're going to make cell phone calls.
- When you are in a public place, like an airport concourse, don't stretch your laptop power cord across the floor. You can cause a serious accident. Find a place to sit where you can be close to the power source – even if it means sitting on the floor while you charge your battery.
- Listen to local people in your car, instead of relying on your GPS device. It's the polite thing to do – and you will probably get where you're going sooner.
- If a stranger offers to take your picture, return the favor. Ask if he or she has a camera and would like for you to take a photo of him or her and friends. If not, ask if they have an email address where you can send a picture of him or her that you will take with your camera.
- Use the "reply all" button only when everybody on the original email list will really want to hear your thoughts. In most cases, it's better to reply to the sender only.
- Don't wear your Bluetooth earpiece if you are not on a call. At best, you look like a limo driver. At worst, you look foolish.
- Finally, DO NOT TYPE EMAILS IN ALL CAPS. All caps indicate that you are yelling. It is bad form and does not help you make a positive personal impact.

Computers and airplanes present other potential etiquette gaffes. Here are my thoughts on airplane computer etiquette.

- When you're on a plane and your neighbor is working on his or her laptop, don't snoop. That spreadsheet is none of your business.
- Don't stare at your neighbor's movie. If you'd like to watch it without sound, ask first.

- On the other hand, be neighborly. If you see someone straining to peek at your movie or music video, invite him or her to watch. You might make a new friend.
- Bring headphones. If you plan to watch a movie or play a game with sound, spare your neighbors the noise. If you forget, ask a flight attendant for airline headphones.
- Defend yourself. Bring earplugs or noise-canceling headphones to shut out others' laptop sounds.
- Speak up. If you have a problem with the sound or the content coming from your neighbor's laptop, tell the person. If that doesn't work, contact a flight attendant.
- Be considerate. Leave the porn and gore flicks at home.

But cell phones are the most abused electronic devices. Here are my thoughts on what to do and what not to do when it comes to creating positive personal impact with your cell phone. You probably don't know it, but July is National Cell Phone Courtesy Month.

- Avoid speaking loudly on your cell phone when you are in a public place – a restaurant, airport concourse, airplane (before the door closes). No one wants or needs to hear your conversation. This is good advice for two reasons. First, you won't be disturbing the people around you. Second, your business will remain private.
- Ask permission first. When you think that you may be receiving an important call, let others know and ask their permission to leave your phone on and to take the call.
- Excuse yourself. When the all-important call comes, excuse yourself and find that secluded spot.
- Turn your cell phone off. Whether you are attending personal or professional functions, just turn off the phone. You can check your messages later. Few of us are so indispensable that we cannot be out of contact for a few minutes or hours.
- Use the silent ringer or vibrate function appropriately. When you are in the presence of others, it is just as inconsiderate to check the incoming call as it is to answer it. If your phone vibrates, excuse yourself to check the call, or better yet, check it later. You are really discounting a person to whom you are speaking if you suddenly say, "Do you mind if I check my phone and see who this is?" You almost hold your breath waiting to see who will win the attention of your companion, you or the caller?

- Keep your voice down. The phone may look tiny, but it picks up sound perfectly well.
- Behavior is the problem, not the phones.

The common sense career success coach point here is simple. Successful people create positive personal impact. They follow the career advice in Tweet 72 in Success Tweets. "21st-century technology has created new etiquette rules. Learn and use them to appear polished on line and off." New electronic devices can help you stay in touch 24/7. They can also lead you to break simple rules of etiquette and civility. Use your common sense when using your electronic gadgets – especially the text function on your cell phone. Never text and drive. Texting and driving is dangerous, illegal in most states, and an accident waiting to happen.

Success Tweet 73

Be gracious. Know and follow the basic rules of etiquette. Everybody likes to be around polite and mannerly people.

A couple of years ago, I published a book called *Straight Talk for Success*. A few months after it came out, I received an email from a young guy named Jim whose boss had given him a copy of *Straight Talk*. In part, here's what it said...

> Bud:
>
> I read your book *Straight Talk for Success*, excellent. You are indeed the common sense guy! I have learned a ton from reading that book from how to brand myself, to dinner etiquette (glass on the right, bread dish on the left, outside-in with utensils). Truly found your book easy to read and loved it...
>
> I am 27 and feel like a sponge for all this information.
>
> Just wanted to thank you for your words of wisdom and for writing about some of the unwritten rules in business.

That was great. I always like to receive positive feedback on what I write. However, I was gratified that by sending me an email, Jim was putting to work some of my advice on creating positive personal impact. He showed me that he is a guy who understands the basics of etiquette.

Have you ever sent an email to an author thanking him for what he's written? Did you get a response? Please leave a comment sharing your experience – positive or negative – with us.

Here's a personal story about this. A while back, I was in the New York City area. When I'm there I listen to Q 104.3, the classic rock station. Maria Milito was on as I was driving to the airport. She played a great set. When I got to the airport, I logged on to the Q104.3 site and sent her an email telling her I enjoyed her show. I got a response from her in less than a half hour. Everybody likes positive feedback – trust me on this career advice.

Back to Jim's email to me — sending a thank you note to someone who has done something for you is common sense and proper etiquette. Sending a note to a stranger whose book you read and enjoyed is even better. By doing so, Jim branded himself (in my mind at least) as an interpersonally competent guy, and someone who is business savvy.

In reality, there is no difference between business etiquette and social etiquette. Well mannered people always focus on making other people feel comfortable and appreciated – whether in a business or social setting.

As Jim points out when he mentioned business dining etiquette, there are some rules to follow. But the rules only make it easier to concentrate on the conversation instead of worrying about making a social gaffe. Most people will overlook minor faux pas if you are truly gracious. It is a good idea to brush up on dining etiquette before important business lunches or dinners and interviews.

Sharon Hill is a friend and etiquette consultant. She once told me a story of a young man who lost a sales job because he didn't know how to properly eat a foil-wrapped baked potato. Do you know how to eat a foil-wrapped baked potato properly? I'll send a signed copy of *Straight Talk for Success* and *Success Tweets* to the first person who responds to this question.

Personally, I think that this is a sad story – for the young man and his potential boss. Not knowing a minor point of dining etiquette shouldn't disqualify an otherwise qualified candidate from a job offer. If that's the candidate's only flaw, he can learn that lesson once and be on his way to a successful career. However, in this case the hiring manager saw it as a deal breaker – and he had the ultimate say-so.

When it comes to etiquette there is an old saying…

> Those who know, know. Those who don't know, don't know. Those who know, always know those who don't know.

Think about it. Take the advice of this career success coach. Learn and follow the basic rules of etiquette – especially dining etiquette. You'll look polished. You'll present well. More important, you won't have to worry about the rules when you're in a social situation. You'll be able to concentrate on the conversation – which is the important reason for any business meal

The common sense career success coach point here is simple. Successful people create positive personal impact. You can create positive personal impact by becoming known as a gracious person. Follow the career advice in Tweet 73 in Success Tweets. "Be gracious. Know and follow the basic rules of etiquette. Everybody likes to be around polite and mannerly people." Small things – like saying "please" and "thank you," smiling at others, taking a second to hold a door for someone who has an arm-full of packages, allowing someone to cut in front of you in traffic – are the marks of gracious people. A strong personal brand also helps create positive impact. If you build your personal brand on gracious and ethical behavior, you will be well on your way to success in your life and career.

Success Tweet 74

When someone compliments you, just say "Thank you." When someone criticizes you, say "Thank you. I'll work on that."

Giving feedback is a difficult interpersonal skill to master. Receiving feedback graciously may be an even more difficult to master. I think it all comes down to self-confidence.

Confident people accept positive feedback in the spirit in which it was given. They don't discount it. On the other hand, confident people accept negative feedback for what it is – the opinion of one other person. They listen to what is being said, and then decide what – if anything – they're going to do about the feedback.

Whether it's positive or negative, confident people respond to feedback in a gracious manner.

If your confidence or self-esteem is a little low, you might have a tendency to respond to positive feedback inappropriately. When someone compliments you, do you say something like, "It was nothing," or "Anybody could have done it," or "It really wasn't that big of a deal?" This is unassertive behavior and it marks you as someone lacking in confidence.

Besides that, it discounts the feedback and the person who is giving it to you. When someone compliments you on a job well done and you say, "It was nothing," you're questioning the other person's judgment. You may not realize it but you are. He or she took the time to compliment you. The appropriate response is, "Thank you." You might want to add something like, "Your feedback means a lot to me. I value your opinion."

Don't discount yourself, your accomplishment, or the other person by minimizing what you accomplished. On the other hand, don't overinflate the feedback. Take it for what it is: a comment on something you did well.

Negative feedback can be a little more difficult to take. You can feel attacked personally. My best career advice is to not take negative feedback personally. Don Miguel Ruiz's little book, *The Four Agreements: A Practical Guide to Personal Freedom,* is a favorite of mine. "Don't take anything personally" is the second of the four agreements.

Don Miguel Ruiz explains it this way...

> "Nothing others do is because of you. What others say and do is a projection of their own reality, their own dream. When you are immune to the opinions and actions of others, you won't be the victim of needless suffering."

This is great advice for accepting negative feedback. Remember that feedback is a projection of the other person's reality. It may be correct. It may be incorrect. That's why I always advise my career success coach clients to respond to negative feedback by saying, "Thank you. I'll work on that." By saying this, you are acknowledging the feedback and the person who provided it. You are not committing to doing anything specific about it.

You should think about the feedback and then decide what to do. It may be nothing, or you may choose to make some significant changes in your behavior. The important career success coach point here is that you get to decide how you will deal with feedback.

Here are some common sense coach points on what to do when you're presented with negative feedback...

- Avoid being defensive – don't try to justify what you did or didn't do. Listen to understand. Ask questions to make sure you completely understand what the other person is saying.

- Don't fight – accept the feedback, even if it makes you angry. Take time to reflect. You can always have another conversation if you think the feedback was inaccurate or unfair. You'll be calm, and in a better position to make your points.

- Listen attentively – make sure the other person knows you're paying attention by your body language, facial expression and questions.

The common sense career success coach point here is simple. You can create positive personal impact by responding to feedback – both positive and negative – appropriately. As Don Miguel Ruiz says in *The Four Agreements*, never take anything personally. Follow the career advice in Tweet 74 in Success Tweets. "When someone compliments you, just say 'Thank you.' When someone criticizes you, say 'Thank you. I'll work on that.'" If you follow this advice, you will become known as someone who responds to feedback graciously. And, those kinds of people always create positive personal impact. This is great common sense career advice. I urge you to put it to work.

PS: I think the Four Agreements are powerful. Here is a quick synopsis of all four from Wikiquotes...

- **Be Impeccable With Your Word.** Speak with integrity. Say only what you mean. Avoid using the word to speak against yourself or to gossip about others. **Use the power of your word in the direction of truth and love.**

- **Don't Take Anything Personally.** Nothing others do is because of you. What others say and do is a projection of their own reality, their own dream. When you are immune to the opinions and actions of others, you won't be the victim of needless suffering.

- **Don't Make Assumptions.** Find the courage to ask questions and to express what you really want. Communicate with others as clearly as you can to avoid misunderstandings, sadness and drama. With just this one agreement, you can completely transform your life.

- **Always Do Your Best.** Your best is going to change from moment to moment; it will be different when you are healthy as opposed to sick. Under any circumstance, simply do your best and you will avoid self-judgment, self-abuse and regret.

Success Tweet 75

Learn and use simple table manners. Good manners make you look polished and poised.

In a recent post, I told the story of a young man who lost a sales position with a very prestigious company because he did not know the proper way to eat a foil-wrapped baked potato. The proper way, by the way, is to cut into the potato with the foil on, open the potato, add condiments (butter, sour cream, etc.) and eat the potato while it is still in the foil, leaving the foil and potato skin on your plate when you are finished. The young man I described removed the potato from the foil, balled up the foil and placed it on the table.

As I mentioned in that post, I think that the sales manager who decided not to hire him was a bit impulsive. If this young man was an otherwise outstanding candidate, I'm sure that once he was told how to properly eat a foil-wrapped baked potato, he would not have repeated the mistake. Unfortunately, he lost the job because of this gaffe.

If you know basic table manners, you won't have to worry about faux pas like this. And, you'll be comfortable at the dinner table because you'll be able to focus on the conversation, not on worrying about the rules of dining etiquette.

Business meals provide you with a great opportunity to make a positive personal impact. They also can be disasters waiting to happen. If you know and follow the simple rules of dining etiquette, you'll be fine.

Here is some advice on making the best of the opportunity that business meals afford you. First, use your common sense. These rules aren't all that complicated, and your common sense will tell you what to do.

Learn basic table manners and etiquette. Place settings can be a bit of a challenge, especially when there are a lot of people crammed around a small, round table. If you remember that your water glass is to your right, and your bread and butter plate is to your left, you'll be off to a good start. If one of your fellow diners uses your bread plate, don't comment. Use your main plate for your bread. In this way, you won't inconvenience the person to your right, nor embarrass the person to your left.

Your salad fork is the little one on the far left, and your soup spoon is the big one on the far right. If you remember this, and work from the outside in, you'll be unlikely to make any cutlery mistakes. Sharon Hill has come up with a clever way of remembering where things are on a table: BMW. Moving from left to right, you will find your bread plate (B), then your meal plate (M) and finally your water (or anything wet) (W).

There are a few simple courtesies that can help you get through any business meal. Place your napkin in your lap as soon as you sit down. Sit up straight. Keep your elbows off the table. You can rest your wrists on the table.

Cocktails and beer are before dinner. Wine accompanies dinner. Drink alcohol in moderation.

If you choose not to drink wine with your meal, do not turn over your wine glass. Simply say "no thanks" when the waiter is pouring for the table.

Wait until everyone at the table has been served before you begin to eat. If one person's food is delayed and he or she suggests that you should begin eating, feel free to do so. Order things that are easy to eat.

Order with care. It's almost impossible to eat pasta that needs to be twirled and look sophisticated doing it. Order foods that are easy to eat. Lobster, snails, shrimp with the tails on, are good things to avoid when you are business dining.

Break – don't cut – your bread or roll. That's why dining is sometimes called "breaking bread." Pass the salt and pepper shaker as a pair – even if someone asks for only one. Spoon soup away from you. This will help you avoid spilling it on you. Sip, don't slurp soup.

When you are finished eating, place your knife and fork on your plate at 4 o'clock. Fold your napkin and place it to the left of your plate. This will indicate to the server that you are finished with your meal.

These are simple rules that should help you get through business meals with grace and aplomb. One final thing to remember: business meals are not about the food. This is so important that I have devoted an entire rule to it. Read on.

Today, I'd like to tell you an embarrassing business dining story from my youth...

As I mentioned above, order with care. About 30 years ago, I had just accepted a job as the Training Manager for a division of a large company. Our division was located in New Haven, CT, a city with a large Italian population and a lot of great Italian restaurants.

About a month after I began my job, the VP of Human Resources for the corporation was hosting a two-day meeting of all of the senior HR people in the company at our location. Since the meeting was at our location, junior people like me were invited to a dinner held the evening of the first day of the meeting. I was looking forward to this dinner. It was an opportunity for me to impress some senior people in other divisions.

One of my junior colleagues was a local woman. She was excited about the choice of the restaurant. Of course, it was an Italian restaurant. She had been there on special occasions with her husband. She was very fond of a dish called *zuppa de pesce,* a medley of seafood served over spaghetti. A couple of days before the meeting she told me about this dish and that it was available for two only and asked if I would be willing to share it with her. I said, "Sure."

We arrived at the restaurant, and sure enough, *zuppa de pesce* was on the menu. My friend and I ordered it. What a disaster!

First, the waiters brought lobster bibs for both of us. No one else had ordered this dish, so we were the only ones wearing our bibs. When the food arrived, everyone had a dish of pasta, or some grilled fish, or a steak. The *zuppa de pesce* was served on a silver tray so big that the waiters had to bring a side table for it. There was enough fish and pasta to feed the entire table. My friend dug in and really enjoyed her dinner. I felt like I was a character in *The Godfather*.

I spent my time trying to carry on an intelligent conversation with people I wanted to impress while I was wearing a lobster bib and working hard to make sure that I didn't spill any red sauce, or "gravy" as the waiter called it, on my suit.

I didn't lose any points that night – but I didn't make any either. It was pretty apparent to most people that I was there for the food, not for the conversation.

I learned a lesson that day. Always order something that is easy to eat and won't call attention to you as you eat it. I try to be a good friend, and in social situations, I will often share an entrée that is available for two only – but I never do that in a business situation. Because business dinners are not about the food: they're about the conversation.

The common sense career success coach point here is simple. Business meals are not about the food. They're about the conversation. That means you need to follow the career advice in Tweet 75 in Success Tweets. "Learn and use simple table manners. Good manners make you look polished and poised." You want to look polished and poised during business meals. If you know the rules, you'll be able to spend time focusing on the conversation – not worrying about which fork to use.

Success Tweet 76

Always act like a lady or gentleman. It's not old-fashioned; it's smart business and leads to a successful life and career.

Last year, I did a series of podcasts on career and life success. Lydia Ramsey was one of my guests. Lydia is the author of a great book, *Manners That Sell*. She is a leading authority on business etiquette and protocol. She works with corporations, non-profit and educational institutions, helping people avoid the faux pas that can derail a career. She also writes a weekly business etiquette column in the ***Savannah Morning News***.

Here is an excerpt of my interview with Lydia.

Bud: One of the things I'd like to discuss is a word I use a lot. And that word is "gentleman". I tell people that I try to conduct myself as a gentleman at all times. When I say this, I sometimes get some pretty weird looks. I'm wondering what your take is on this. Is being a gentleman or being a lady a dated concept?

Lydia: Well, in some ways I think that it has become that way. We've gotten so politically correct with the terms that we use that we've lost some important words in our language, like gentleman and lady. We're just overly cautious. Many people in business don't necessarily want to be referred to as gentlemen and ladies. They want to be men and ladies. On the other hand, there are organizations like the Ritz Carlton who want everybody to be referred to, including their own employees, as ladies and gentlemen. Their motto is "ladies and gentlemen serving ladies and gentlemen".

Bud: That's really interesting. I take it just from what you write and your whole focus on etiquette that being a gentleman or a lady can never be harmful to your career.

Lydia: Right, you can never be too nice. And you can never be too courteous and respectful of other people. That's really what etiquette is about and what manners are about.

Bud: I agree. So why are manners and etiquette so important for success?

Lydia: Well, I like to think about etiquette and manners as not necessarily about the rules, but about the relationships that we have with people and the way that we treat people. And all of this, as you know, is really built on relationships... relationships with your clients, with your customers, with your coworkers. Treating people well and with courtesy and respect is a way to build those relationships and to maintain them.

Bud: That's interesting. Tell me a little bit more about this – not rules, but relationships. I'm interested because I think a lot of people feel they need to pull out their Amy Vanderbilt or Emily Post book and make sure that they do things exactly correct. What I'm hearing you say is that's not as important as the way you treat other people.

Lydia: That's right. If your mindset is really about being courteous to other people and just basically being nice to other people then you're going to be exhibiting good manners. That's really what it's about. It's not about a whole set of rules that somebody came up with that were designed to make us all a little crazy or paranoid or whatever. But it's really about knowing what to do in certain cases. Obviously you want to do the right thing. But you will be doing the right thing if you're thinking about the other person's comfort and the other person's ease.

Bud: So the real key thing is to think about the other person, put yourself in their place, try to make them feel comfortable and you're likely to not go too far wrong from an etiquette or a manners point.

Lydia: That's right.

I like Lydia Ramsey's common sense approach to etiquette:

- Think about other people,
- Put yourself in their place,
- Try to make them feel comfortable.

If you do this, you won't go wrong from an etiquette or manners standpoint. What could be easier or more common sense? In other words, most etiquette comes down to behaving like a lady or gentleman – the point I make in Success Tweet 76.

The common sense career success coach point here is simple. Etiquette is a matter of common sense. Lydia Ramsey, a leading etiquette consultant, says it's as simple as one, two, three: 1) Think about other people; 2) Put yourself in their place; 3) Do whatever you can to make them feel comfortable. Follow the career advice in Tweet 76 in Success Tweets. "Always act like a lady or gentleman. It's not old-fashioned; it's smart business and leads to a successful life and career." Ladies and gentlemen are gracious. They don't worry about the rules. They worry about making other people feel comfortable and accepted.

Success Tweet 77

Keep your breath fresh. Brush after meals and coffee. Use the strips. Don't chew gum. Ever. It makes you look like a cow.

I am always surprised when I meet an otherwise well-groomed person who has bad breath. Usually, these people are unaware of the problem. I was in the mall the other day getting fitted for a pair of new glasses. The woman helping me had breath that smelled like stale coffee. It wasn't very pleasant. I'm sure she was unaware of it. I didn't know her, so I said nothing.

A couple of months ago I was getting a haircut. My stylist had been eating some kind of snack food that had a lot of garlic. His breath was overpowering. I know him reasonably well, so I was comfortable telling him that the snack food he had eaten really caused bad breath. He thanked me, and popped a piece of gum into his mouth to mask the smell.

That helped, but then he began smacking his gum – not very attractive to watch in the mirror, nor to listen to. I like gum. But thanks to Cathy, I've broken the habit of chewing it. It's difficult to chew gum and not smack it or look vapid. I have limited my gum-chewing to when I'm riding my bike or exercising. Even then, I keep my mouth closed and avoid smacking it.

People often chew gum on airplanes to help their ears adjust to the changes in cabin pressure. While chewing gum can help your ears, it does little for your image as a professional. My best career advice is to not chew gum ever. There are better ways to control bad breath.

Many otherwise well-groomed people forget about their breath. Fresh breath is the mark of a well-groomed person. Brushing after lunch is the best way to keep your breath fresh. However, if you don't want to bring a toothbrush to work, the breath strips do a pretty good job of keeping your breath fresh. Use them after coffee, and after eating – especially when you eat food seasoned with garlic, or after sushi. Cathy always reminds me when I have wasabi breath.

The common sense career success coach point here is simple. It's the little things that mark you as a well-groomed person. Too many people don't pay enough attention to their breath. Bad breath is not pleasant. Follow the advice in Tweet 77 in Success Tweets. "Keep your breath fresh. Brush after meals and coffee. Use the strips. Don't chew gum. Ever. It makes you look like a cow." Brushing can be inconvenient, so I recommend the breath strips. I always encourage my career success coach clients to avoid gum. It can sweeten your breath, but it also makes you look unsophisticated.

Success Tweet 78

Say "thank you" often. You'll succeed, build a strong personal brand and build a legacy of being a nice person.

Zach Bussey is a Twitter friend of mine. He lives in Toronto and I live in Denver. Isn't the Internet a great thing? Zach really understands social media. You should check out his site. The other day, Zach and I exchanged a few tweets on the importance of saying thank you. Here's one of the tweets Zach sent me…

> "The word 'thanks' is used less and less. It's unfortunate, because it's the kind of word that can change someone's day."

I agree. A sincere "thank you" always makes my day. I really appreciate the people who take the time to thank me for these blog posts and my daily success quotes. My day gets a little brighter every time someone thanks me.

That's why I end every one of my blog posts with something like, "thanks for reading." I really appreciate the time you take to read my blog. Thanking you is the least I can do to show this appreciation. From time to time I offer things for free here to show my thanks. Today, I'd like to thank you by sending two inspirational movies your way.

Check out "Acres of Diamonds" at http://www.lifesecretsonline.com/movie/?t=TCSG&m=AcresofDiamonds.

And you might like "Carrots, Eggs and Coffee." http://www.lifesecretsonline.com/movie/?t=TCSG&m=CarrotsEggsCoffee.

A while back, I did a blog post where I featured Jeff Hajek's book, *Whaddya Mean I Gotta Be Lean?* I like this book. And, as I pointed out in the post, Jeff provides some great career advice in a book that at first glance doesn't seem to have much to do with career success.

Jeff sent me an email the day after the post ran, thanking me for my favorable comments about his book. I thought that was great – and for me it was enough. However, a couple of days later, I received a handwritten note in my snail mail from Jeff. It read…

Bud,

I appreciate you taking time out of your busy schedule to review *Whaddya Mean* on your blog. I am cognizant of the fact that you have gone out of your way to help me, so if there is anything I can ever do to return the favor, please don't hesitate to ask.

Best wishes,

Jeff

Handwritten notes are not very common these days. I was touched that Jeff took the time to write one and send it to me. By sending it, he really strengthened his relationship with me. The next time he asks for my help, I am very likely to give it to him. Also, he offered his help to me. I feel that I can go to him if I need assistance in his area of expertise. Jeff used a simple technique – a handwritten note – to build his relationship with me.

My post helped Jeff – any exposure helps. But I reviewed his book because I thought it would be useful to readers of this blog. My intent was to provide readers of this blog with useful information. So my review was a win/win/win Good for you, good for Jeff, and good for me because I am meeting one of my goals – helping others create the life and career success that they want and deserve. All of us benefited.

Jeff purchased a thank you card for his note to me. That was great, but I have an even better idea. I have invested in a set of note cards with my name printed at the top and my return address on the back flap of the envelope. I suggest that you do the same – you'll find yourself writing more thank you notes when you have a card handy.

One of the companies where I do a lot of consulting and coaching work has picked up on this idea. They have placed blank thank you notes – with one of their core values on the front of the card – at convenient locations in their offices. Their intent is to get employees to thank one another for good work. And it worked. People are sending more of these handwritten notes to their colleagues, strengthening relationships within the company.

The common sense career success coach point here is simple. Successful people are interpersonally competent. Interpersonally competent people are good at building relationships. Thanking people when they help you is a great way to build relationships. Follow the career advice in Success Tweet 78. "Say "thank you" often. You'll succeed, build a strong personal brand and build a legacy of being a nice person." Besides thanking people in person, handwritten notes are a great way of saying thank you. Handwritten thank you notes establish you as someone who cares about other people and is willing to go a little out of your way to build relationships – the hallmark of interpersonally competent people.

Success Tweet 79

Be courteous. It costs you nothing and it can mean everything to someone else. It also helps in getting what you want.

A while back, I was in New York City and had dinner with Gary Steele, a close friend. Gary is an interesting guy. He had plenty of opportunities to play major college football, but he chose service and enrolled at the United States Military Academy. He retired after 23 years in the US Army as a full Colonel.

He also played football when he was at West Point. As it so happens, 40 years ago, he played a game at Penn State when I was student there. I saw him play that day. What a day it was. Penn State was the Number 2 team in the country that year. Gary and his mates almost beat us. It took a fluke play at the end of the game to clinch the win for Penn State. By the way, Gary caught eight passes for 156 yards that day.

Over dinner, Gary and I were talking about the importance of treating all people with the dignity and respect they deserve as fellow human beings. That's what interpersonally competent people do. Later that evening, Gary sent me an excerpt from an 1879 address made by the West Point Commandant, John McAllister Schofield, to the corps of cadets. In part it reads as follows...

> "The discipline which makes the colleagues of a strong organization effective in operations is not to be gained by harsh or tyrannical treatment. On the contrary, such treatment is far more likely to destroy than to make a strong organization. It is possible to impart guidance and to give directions in such a manner and such a tone of voice to inspire in a colleague the feeling of an intense desire to obey, while the opposite manner and tone of voice cannot fail to excite strong resentments and a desire to disobey. The one mode or other of dealing with colleagues springs from the corresponding spirit in the breast of the leader. He who feels the respect which is due to others cannot fail to inspire in them regard for himself, while he who feels, and hence manifests, disrespect towards others, especially his subordinates, cannot fail to inspire hatred against himself."

General Schofield's words work for anyone, not just leaders. I love the line, "He who feels the respect which is due to others cannot fail to inspire in them regard for himself." That says it all. Respect others and they will respect you. Strong relationships are based on respect and trust.

The common sense career success coach point here is simple. Follow the career advice in Success Tweet 79. "Be courteous. It costs you nothing, and it can mean everything to someone else. It also helps in getting what you want." Interpersonal competence is an important key to career and life success. The ability to build strong relationships is a key to becoming interpersonally competent. If you want to build strong relationships with the important people in your life, be courteous and respect them. Your courtesy and respect will pay big dividends. As General Schofield pointed out way back in 1879, when you respect others you cannot fail to inspire high regard for you in them.

Success Tweet 80

Learn and use the basic rules of etiquette. Social faux pas might not ruin your career, but they certainly won't help it.

All that stuff your Mom told you about being polite is true and great career advice. You can never go wrong by being polite and acting like a lady or gentleman. I try to act as a gentleman at all times. Polite people are mannerly. Well-informed people know and follow the basic rules of etiquette. I took some time to learn the rules. While being polite trumps the rules, knowing what to do in any social situation always helps you create positive personal impact.

My friend Sharon Hill, author of *The Wild Woman's Guide to Etiquette,* makes a great point about the difference between manners and etiquette. Sharon says that manners are about kindness and caring about other people. Etiquette is protocol, rules of behavior that you need to learn and use. Manners come from your heart; etiquette comes from your head. Ladies and gentlemen are both well mannered and follow the rules of etiquette.

If you know and follow the basic rules of etiquette, you won't look foolish in social situations. You will be admired for demonstrating class and confidence. Proper etiquette can help you get ahead in business because you will create a positive impression. Sometimes, you won't even know that people are watching, but believe me, someone usually is.

On the other hand, manners distinguish you as a caring person, someone who values every human being. I wrote about this in yesterday's post. Well-mannered people treat every person they meet with a kindness that reinforces the self-worth of the other person. You can know and follow all the rules, but still not be well-mannered. While I think it's important to know and follow the rules, if I had to choose between manners and etiquette, manners would win every time.

Handwritten thank you notes are a great way to distinguish yourself as a lady or gentleman. They demonstrate both good manners and proper etiquette. Here are three tips for writing great thank you notes: 1) Write legibly; 2) Always identify the gift you received – be specific. Your note will be more personal this way; 3) Always mention how you plan on using the gift. You can create all sorts of positive personal impact with thank you notes.

These days there are companies who will do what I call "faux handwritten notes." They take a sample of your handwriting and then use it to create messages that they will send on your behalf. In my opinion, these cards are better than an email, but they still don't substitute for a handwritten note. Two reasons: first, you still have to compose the message and email it to the vendor; and second, while these cards look pretty good, they still don't have the intensely personal feel of a note written by hand.

As with most things, there is one rule of etiquette that I always follow. I always do whatever I can to help the people around me feel comfortable. I do this because I want to be – and be thought of – as a gentleman.

For example, when you are dining with others, you may know that your water glass is on the right and that your bread-and-butter plate is on the left. Other people may not know this. So if someone uses your bread plate, don't say "Hey, that's mine – yours is over there." Just place your roll on your dinner plate. Being right is no excuse for embarrassing someone else.

Remember, friends can help take you where you want to go. Etiquette and manners will help you make those friends and create the life and career success you want and deserve.

The common sense career success coach point here is simple. Successful people are comfortable in all situations. They follow the career advice in Success Tweet 80. "Learn and use the basic rules of etiquette. Social faux pas might not ruin your career, but they certainly won't help it." While being kind and valuing others is more important than knowing and applying the rules, knowing and using the rules will mark you as someone in the know – someone who is an up-and-comer. Take the time to learn the rules. In that way, you'll be able to use them without thinking about them. When this happens, you'll be better able to focus on the conversation and the people around you.

Success Tweet 81

Become a lifelong learner. The half-life of knowledge is rapidly diminishing. Staying in the same place is the same as going backward.

Competence is one of the four keys to career and life success. I discuss it in *Success Tweets* and several others of my books: *Straight Talk for Success; Your Success GPS; 42 Rules to Jumpstart Your Professional Success.* If you want to succeed, you need to develop four basic, but important competencies: 1) creating positive personal impact; 2) becoming a consistently high performer; 3) dynamic communication skills; and 4) becoming interpersonally competent. Tweets 81 – 100 focus on how to become an outstanding performer.

If you want to become an outstanding performer, you need to become a lifelong learner. The other day, I came across a great quote from Louis L'Amour, the great American writer of stories about the old west. I think this quote captures the essence of lifelong learning...

> "There will come a time when you believe everything is finished. That will be the beginning."

I know a lot about career and life success. I've written several books on it. I give lots of talks about it. I've coached hundreds of people – helping them build the life and career success they want and deserve. I write this blog. At one point, I thought I knew it all.

And you know what? Every time I write about life and career success, every time I speak about it, every time I coach someone offering my career advice, I gain a deeper understanding of what it takes to create life and career success

I begin anew every day, doing whatever I can to learn about life and career success so I can pass on this knowledge and wisdom to others. I choose to keep learning. So should you. Pay attention here – this is solid career advice. I've learned that if you don't keep learning, you don't stand still – you fall behind in the game of life. I've also learned that what I learned after I knew it all was some of the best and most important of my learnings.

Thomas Carlyle once said, "What we become depends on what we read after all of the professors have finished with us. The greatest university of all is a collection of books." He lived in the 19th century. If he were alive today, he might have amended his statement to say, "Books and the Internet are the greatest university of all." Today, so many of the great books, as well as other life and career success information, are available on line. The Internet is a great way to access this information. The important thing is to keep learning – how you do it and where you get your information is secondary.

I have a huge collection of books on a variety of subjects. These books are the first place I turn when I am looking for information to post on my blog, when I am working with my career success coach clients, when I am preparing a speech and when I am designing a training program. When I can't find what I'm looking for in my books, I go on line.

My best common sense suggestion for becoming a lifelong learner is simple. Read. Read technical journals. Read trade magazines. Read business publications like "The Wall Street Journal," "Business Week," "Fortune" and "Forbes." If you think they're too stodgy, read "Fast Company."

Read your company's annual report. Read your competitors' annual reports. Read your local newspaper and "The New York Times." Read news magazines like "Newsweek" and "Time." Read business and industry blogs. Read ezines and eBooks. Read books. Reading is the best way to stay up with what's happening in business, in your industry and in the world.

There are other things you can do to keep learning. Attend seminars. Join the major groups or trade associations for your industry. Attend their meetings and participate. Volunteer for committee work. Become known locally in your field. Take a class at your local university. Use your company's tuition reimbursement program to get a free undergraduate or Master's degree.

Your education doesn't stop when you graduate from college or get an MBA, it begins anew. There are many ways to keep learning. Decide which ones work for you, and then follow through. Outstanding performers are competent. They stay competent because they are lifelong learners.

I agree with Albert Einstein who said...

"Wisdom is not a product of schooling but of the lifelong learning attempt to acquire it."

The common sense career success point here is simple. Successful people are outstanding performers. Outstanding performers are lifelong learners. They follow the career advice in tweet 81 in Success Tweets. "Become a lifelong learner. The half-life of knowledge is rapidly diminishing. Staying in the same place is the same as going backward." Lifelong learning is really important to creating the successful life and career you want and deserve. Remember what Louis L'Amour says: "There will come a time when you believe everything is finished. That will be the beginning." Treat each new day as an opportunity to learn. Stay open to new people and new ideas. If you do this, you'll come to realize that you are never finished learning and that what you learn after you know it all is the most valuable knowledge you'll develop.

Success Tweet 82

Learn faster than the world changes. In a world that never stops changing, you can never stop learning and growing.

Lifelong learning is a key to success. In today's fast-paced world, if you don't keep learning, you're not standing still, you're falling behind. One of my favorite quotes from Gandhi nails it when it comes to lifelong learning...

> "Live as if you were to die tomorrow. Learn as if you were to live forever."

He's right. None of us should ever quit learning. I have a thirst for knowledge and do my best to quench it through learning. I try to learn something new every day. Sometimes my learning is trivial, sometimes it is profound. Regardless, I keep on learning.

On days when I feel as if I haven't learned anything, I turn to a little book that I have called, *Live and Learn and Pass It On.* The subtitle is, "People ages 5 to 95 share what they've discovered about life, love, and other good stuff." I usually find something in there that satisfies.

Here are a few of the learnings in the book that have helped me...

> I've learned that if you wait until all conditions are perfect before you act, you'll never act.

> I've learned that if you want to get promoted, you must do things that get you noticed.

> I've learned that 90% of what happens in my life is positive and only about 10% is negative. If I want to be happy I just need to focus on the 90%.

These are little life learnings that I find helpful.

All of the people I know who are committed to lifelong learning have several traits in common. They all...

...Are humble. They admit what they don't know. This is the first step in learning what they need to know.

...Question the status quo. They realize that because something is right today, it may not be right tomorrow. They know that doing things "the way we've always done them" is not good reasoning.

...Are intellectually curious. They truly want to learn and find learning fun, interesting and stimulating. They see life as a journey in which they are constantly learning.

...Are willing to try new stuff. They experiment and see what works. When things work, they use them.

...Are not afraid to fail. They see failure as an opportunity to learn. Just as they incorporate what works into their repertoire, they use failures as stepping stones to other experiments.

...Are tolerant of ambiguity. Learning creates ambiguity. These people are willing to let go of past ways of doing things in order to come up with new ways of doing things in the future. The gap between the past and future can make for an uncomfortable present.

...Focus on staying ahead of the pack. They are early adopters – of new technology and new ways of thinking. They realize that knowledge has a short half-life today. They keep learning to stay ahead.

The common sense career success coach point here is simple. Successful people are outstanding performers. Outstanding performers remain outstanding performers by becoming lifelong learners. They continually expand their knowledge in order to get out in front of the pack and stay there. They follow the career advice in Tweet 82 in Success Tweets. "Learn faster than the world changes. In a world that never stops changing, you can never stop learning and growing." Begin your lifelong learning journey by focusing on your strengths and working to improve them every day. Building on your strengths is easier than overcoming your weaknesses. When you build on your strengths you can make incremental improvements. However, if you have a glaring gap in your skills, address it now. Don't wait to take necessary quantum leaps. What do you need to learn to create the life and career success you want and deserve? How do you plan on learning it? Remember what Ben Franklin had to say, "An investment in knowledge pays the best interest."

Success Tweet 83

Master your technical discipline. Share what you know. Become the go-to person in your company.

I had a big technical learning the other day. I figured out how to podcast. I am planning on turning these Success Tweets blog posts into podcasts. However, I never put in the time it takes to become a proficient podcaster. I promised myself that I would learn to podcast when I began this series of posts. I spent about four hours figuring out how to podcast a couple of days ago. It wasn't all that hard, the information I needed was on the web. Now I know how to podcast – and since knowing is not enough, I've begun doing podcasts of these posts. The URL is simple: http://www.SuccessTweets.mypodcast.com. I hope you check out my podcasts and give me some feedback on them.

Podcasting is an important technical skill for me. I had to learn it if I were to reach my target audience with my common sense career and life success advice. What important technical skill do you need to learn to stay current in your area of expertise? How can you learn it? I suggest you set a deadline for learning this skill, and then do whatever it takes to learn the skill by the deadline.

I am a big fan of SUCCESS Magazine. I read it cover-to-cover every month, always picking up some great success tips – many of which I pass along here. If you're not a subscriber, I suggest you go to www.SUCCESS.com and do so as soon as you finish this post.

A couple of years ago, an issue of SUCCESS had a great story on lifelong learning entitled, "Focusing on Improvement When You've Reached the Pinnacle." It told the story of an American Football coach at the top of his game who reached out to others to keep growing and developing his coaching skills.

The article was about Tom Coughlin, Head Coach of the then Super Bowl Champion New York Giants. Before the next football season began, Mr. Coughlin called Joe Torre and John Wooden. Mr. Torre managed the New York Yankees to three consecutive World Series Championships, and Mr. Wooden won seven consecutive NCAA basketball championships when he was the coach at UCLA. He was a great man who passed away recently.

Mr. Coughlin wanted to learn what to do to motivate a team that had already reached the pinnacle of its sport. Mr. Torre had some interesting things to say:

> "Leading when everyone expects you to win requires that you convince every member of your team that last year doesn't matter. And that's tough to do because all year long they're seeing the words 'defending champions' placed before their names. The only thing that winning last year means is that your opponents are looking forward to playing you. None of them are intimidated by what you did a year ago, and none of them are going to roll over. Your team will have to learn that quickly."

In other words, you can't rest on your laurels. You need to keep on learning and improving. Your past success does not guarantee future success. Things happen quickly in today's business world. If you're not learning, growing and developing your technical expertise, like Tom Coughlin, you're going to fall behind.

Roy Williams, Head Basketball Coach at the University of North Carolina, and winner of a couple of NCAA championships says:

> "It is human nature that once you get to the top, or when it appears that you are better than your opponent, to take a breath and enjoy the moment. What we are trying to teach (the willingness to keep learning and growing) runs counter to human nature... I remind each player that the way you deal with expectations is to focus only on today."

The implication for lifelong learning is simple. No matter how much you know, you can always learn more. Earl Nightingale once said, "If you will spend an extra hour each day of study in your chosen field, you will be a national expert in that field in five years or less." This is great career advice. Focus on today. Spend an hour learning every day. You'll be surprised at the results.

Recently, I saw a great quote from Henry Ford that applies here. "Anyone who stops learning is old, whether at twenty or eighty. Anyone who keeps learning stays young." Another good reason to keep on learning. Don't become old before your time.

The common sense career success coach point here is simple. Successful people master their technical discipline. They follow the career advice in Tweet 83 in Success Tweets. "Master your technical discipline. Share what you know. Become the go-to person in your company." Become the go-to person in your company and industry, like Tom

Coughlin and Roy Williams. Keep learning – even after you've had great success. Follow Earl Nightingale's advice. Spend at least one hour a day studying your chosen field. This extra effort will pay off in the long run. Besides that, as Henry Ford points out, you'll stay young.

Success Tweet 84

Stay up-to-date in your industry. Read industry publications. Know the hot topics for your company, competitors and industry.

I saw a blog post on www.askamanager.blogspot.com a couple of years ago that asked the question, "When hiring, how much does industry knowledge matter?" The answer was "not much." Here are the first two paragraphs of the post...

> When hiring, how much does knowledge of your industry matter? It's a nice bonus, but in most cases it shouldn't be a driving force behind your hiring decisions. But too often I see hiring managers over-valuing this sort of knowledge, and hiring the wrong candidates.

> If you hire someone smart and motivated, they will learn your issue or industry. Hire for the things you can't teach, like intelligence, work ethic, communication skills, integrity, and whatever non-teachable skills the open position truly requires. It may take your new hire a little extra time to get up to speed, but once that happens, he or she will blow away that mediocre candidate whose main advantage would have been starting out with industry knowledge.

The author makes a good point. And it's one with which I agree. Industry knowledge should not be the deciding factor in making hiring decisions. I think it is a nice thing to have.

However, once you have a job, you need to get up to speed in your industry quickly – and more important – stay up to speed.

Here's a personal story. Many years ago, my first job in business was with a large oil company. When I took that job, I decided to learn everything I could about the company and the oil industry. So I read the company's history, and got on the distribution list for all of the industry publications to which my colleagues subscribed.

I took home a stack of magazines every night. I read about trends in petroleum marketing, exploration and refining. I learned about the compliance issues facing the industry – in those days, affirmative action for women was a hot topic. When I joined the company, there were men with whom I worked who had been male secretaries because when they began their careers the company had a policy of hiring no women. As you might expect, environmental compliance was also a hot issue.

I learned about all of these issues, and I went one step further. I befriended coworkers in the Marketing, Exploration, Refining and Compliance areas. I had lunch with them and picked their brains about what Marathon was doing regarding all of the industry issues about which I had read.

Pretty soon, I got a reputation as a knowledgeable young guy. I was working in the Training and Organization Development department, so many people didn't expect me to have the depth of industry knowledge I developed in a relatively short time frame.

One day, I was traveling on the company plane with the VP of Refining. He was making a trip to a refinery we had in Louisiana. I was going to the same refinery to conduct some supervisory training. I engaged him in conversation about something I had read in an industry publication. He had been mentioned in the article.

We got into a fairly deep discussion of the topic. When we were landing he said, "I'm surprised I've never met you. How long have you been with us?" I said "Seven months." He was astonished. He said that I knew as much about the issues as many folks who had been with the company for 10 years. He invited me to visit with him in his office when we returned from the trip.

That visit was the beginning of a great relationship with this guy. He always asked for me when he had training or OD needs. I became a bit of a star because I took the time to become knowledgeable about industry issues.

The common sense career success coach point here is simple. You can build a great reputation in your company by following the career advice in Tweet 84 in Success Tweets. "Stay up-to-date in your industry. Read industry publications. Know the hot topics for your company, competitors and industry." Staying up-to-date doesn't take a lot of effort, especially when so much information is available on line these days. Take a few minutes every day to read at least one industry-related article. You'll find that pretty soon you'll be very knowledgeable about the pressing issues for your company and industry. And, being knowledgeable is a great way to get noticed by the people who can influence your chances for promotion.

Success Tweet 85

Always be on the lookout for new ideas. Find opportunities where others see obstacles.

Henry Ford once said...

> "Obstacles are those frightful things you see when you take your eyes off your goal."

Good one, Henry.

I have a great story about this. It involves a trash can and a hair dryer cord.

In our bathroom at home, the trash can sits under a shelf. Cathy keeps her hair dryer on the shelf. The cord loops down in front of the trash can. Being the frustrated NBA player I am, and also being a normal guy who turns even the most mundane things into sport, I make a game of tossing my used tissues into the trash can. For the longest time, I focused on the hair dryer cord as I tried to swish my tissue into the waste basket. It seems that I hit the cord almost two-thirds of the time, missing my game-winning shot in the 7th game of the NBA Finals.

One day I saw Henry Ford's quote on line. The next day, I focused on the waste basket opening – which is a lot bigger than the hair dryer cord anyway – and I swished the shot; thereby winning the Denver Nugget's first NBA championship. I kept doing this in the days that followed, and I ended up with more NBA championships than Red Auerbach, Phil Jackson, Bill Russell, John Havlicek, Michael Jordan, Scottie Pippin, Kobe Bryant, and Shaq combined. I couldn't miss – all because I kept focused on the goal (the trash can), not the obstacle (the hair dryer cord).

This may sound like a stupid story told by an overgrown adolescent. It's not. It makes an important point. When I tried to avoid the obstacle, I hit it very frequently. When I tried to hit the goal and ignored the obstacle, I began making the shots – achieving my goal. And that's what you need to do, too.

Keep focused on your goals. Don't take your eyes off of them because you'll begin seeing all of the obstacles to overcoming your goals.

Thirty years ago this September, I enrolled in a PhD program at Harvard. I had to overcome quite a few obstacles in the process. First, I had to get accepted. Once I was accepted, I had to figure out how to pay for the privilege of attending an elite university. Then I had to make sure I graduated.

I spent the time necessary and wrote the very best application I could. I got accepted, one obstacle down. I sold my car when I moved to Cambridge. This money, along with grants, student loans, work study jobs and a part-time teaching job at Northeastern University were enough to pay for my education. By the way, I was in my late 40s when I paid off my last student loan.

Graduating became a little more challenging. I left Harvard after I finished my course work, but before I had completed my dissertation. I took a full-time job in New York. Professors advised me against this. They told me that it is very difficult to work full time and write a dissertation. They were right. It took me four and a half years, but I submitted a dissertation that my committee accepted. I kept focused on the goal – the right to call myself "Dr. Bilanich." – Interestingly enough, I never use the title except when I want to get a reservation at a crowded restaurant.

I have too many friends that are ABD – "all but dissertation." These folks wander the earth with a sense of profound incompletion. I promised myself that this was never going to happen to me. I kept my eyes on the goal – even though I had quite a few obstacles thrown at me along the way.

The common sense career success coach point here is simple. Successful people achieve their goals because they stay focused on them. They follow the advice in Tweet 85 in Success Tweets. "Always be on the lookout for new ideas. Find opportunities where others see obstacles." Obstacles often are opportunities in disguise. Successful people see opportunities where others see obstacles. And, as Henry Ford said, "Obstacles are those frightful things you see when you take your eye off the goal." My best career advice here is to keep focused on your goals – whether it's bathroom basketball, or getting a PhD -- and you'll be able to turn obstacles into opportunities.

Success Tweet 86

Stay focused. Don't get distracted. Treat time as the precious commodity that it is. Manage your time and life well.

Success people are focused. They don't let distractions get the better of them. Effective time management is one of the keys to personal organization. If you're like most people, you always have more to do than there is time to do it. I'm pretty good at managing my time, but I do get stressed and overwhelmed occasionally. Time is a very precious and non-renewable resource. When a moment is gone, it's gone forever.

As Stephen Covey says, when you think of your time, all activities fit into one of four categories:

- Not Important and Not Urgent
- Not Important and Urgent
- Important and Urgent
- Important and Not Urgent

Unfortunately, a lot of people spend a lot of time engaged in not important and not urgent activities. Surfing the web is one of the biggest culprits in this area. I, like most people today, search for and find a lot of the information I need on line. I am pretty disciplined, yet I can get caught up following interesting links when I am researching something on the Internet. Following links after you've found what you're looking for is not important and not urgent activity. It is a waste of time and a productivity killer.

Not important and urgent activities can become time traps. These are the kinds of things that you have to do, but in the greater scheme of things, they are not likely to do much to help you become a professional success. These are things like expense reports that must be done within so many days of a trip, weekly staff meetings that you either lead or attend – the types of things that you have to do, but often don't contribute to your larger goals. The trick is to get these activities done in a timely manner, but not to spend a lot of your precious time doing them.

Important and urgent activities are just what they seem. I write this blog five days a week. My blog is a very important marketing tool. It increases my awareness in a very crowded market. It positions me as a career advice expert. And it reinforces my

Common Sense Guy brand. Writing and posting my blog is an important and urgent activity. I do it first thing every day. I'm sure that you have several important and urgent activities on your to do list, too. Do them, and do them well.

Important but not urgent activities are where you get the real payoff when it comes to creating your professional success. It's important to become a lifelong learner. That's why you need to read, join professional organizations and volunteer for projects in your company. You probably don't need to read every day and join all of the professional organizations in your field and industry. These activities are just not that urgent. However, you have to make time for them over the long run. If you don't, you'll find that you are falling behind, not getting ahead or standing still.

Another example – my books serve much the same purpose as my blog. They increase my awareness in a very crowded market; position me as a career advice expert and reinforce my Common Sense Guy brand. I don't need to work on a new book every day. Writing a book is an important but not urgent task for me. I manage this by budgeting at least three hours per week to write. As one book goes into the editing and production process, I get busy writing another. In that way, I never find myself without a forthcoming book.

It can be hard to budget time for important but not urgent activities because they are, well, not urgent. However, important but not urgent activities left unattended will soon become important and urgent and may even become career success crises. My best advice is to focus on your personal set of important but not urgent activities and build some time into your daily or weekly schedule to work on them.

Success Tweet 87

Break large projects into small chunks. They are not so overwhelming that way. Set mini-milestones for yourself.

Jill Koenig, one of my on line friends, posted this bit of wisdom on her Facebook page yesterday…

> "To accomplish big things, you must do the small things. This overcomes inertia. To accomplish the small things, visualize the big picture outcome. This overcomes overwhelm."

That's exactly the kind of career advice I'm talking about in Tweet 87. Small steps and mini-milestones will help you overcome the inertia that can stop you from beginning a big project. At the same time, you need to keep focused on the big picture to avoid being overwhelmed by the sheer number of small tasks involved in completing a big project.

I've written 14 books. Writing a book is a huge project. It can be difficult to get started. I've found that breaking down the writing process into manageable chunks helps me to get started, and keep my momentum. My latest book is called, *Your Career Success GPS: A Common Sense Roadmap for Becoming the Career Success You Are Meant to Be!* I am in the final stages of getting it ready for the printer. In the meantime, you can get a free copy of the eBook at www.CareerSuccessGPS.com. Here's how I went about writing Your Career Success GPS.

First, I created an overall model of career success. This model had four main components:

1. Clarify the purpose and direction for your life and career.
2. Commit to taking personal responsibility for your life and career success.
3. Build unshakeable self-confidence.
4. Get competent in four areas: creating positive personal impact, outstanding performance, dynamic communication and relationship building.

Then I spent time figuring out the career advice that would tell readers exactly what they need to do to apply each of these components to create the life and career success they want and deserve.

Clarity

Create clarity by figuring out what success means to you personally.

Create clarity by creating a vivid mental image of yourself as a success.

Create clarity by determining your personal values.

Commitment

Take personal responsibility for your life and career success.

Set and achieve high goals.

Choose to react positively to the people and events in your life; especially the negative ones.

Self-confidence

Choose to be optimistic.

Face your fears and act.

Surround yourself with positive people.

Find a mentor to help you create your success.

Share your knowledge and wisdom through mentoring others.

Competence

Create positive personal impact by creating and nurturing your unique personal brand.

Create positive personal impact by being impeccable in your presentation of self; in person and on line.

Create positive personal impact by knowing the following the basic rules of business etiquette.

Become an outstanding performer by keeping your skills up-to-date by becoming a lifelong learner.

Become an outstanding performer by learning to manage your time and life.

Become an outstanding performer by living a healthy life-style.

Become a dynamic communicator by demonstrating strong conversation skills.

Become a dynamic communicator by writing clearly and succinctly.

Become a dynamic communicator by mastering public speaking skills.

Build relationships through self awareness. Use this knowledge to better understand others.

Build relationships by paying it forward; give with no expectation of return.

Build relationships by using conflict to strengthen, not weaken, relationships with the important people in your life.

Once I had these 23 ideas down – and this took quite a bit of thinking and work – I was ready to begin writing. Each chapter became a mini-milestone. Writing 23 focused chapters was easier for me than writing a book on such a large and complex topic as career success. You can see the fruits of my labor by downloading and reading *Your Career Success GPS*.

This process works for me, primarily because I break the overwhelmingly large project of writing a book into a series of small steps that are relatively easy to accomplish. That's the beauty of the career advice in Tweet 87.

One more piece of career advice. I always start large projects late in the afternoon. I do this to create momentum. Even though I barely scratch the surface of the project, I get up the next day ready to go because I have accomplished something on the project and have momentum on my side. Try this the next time you are faced with a big project. It works.

The common sense career success coach point here is simple. Successful people are good at taking on and accomplishing big projects. They follow the career advice in Tweet 87 in Success Tweets. "Break large projects into small chunks. They are not so overwhelming that way. Set mini-milestones for yourself." Jill Koenig nails it when she says, "To accomplish big things, you must do the small things. This overcomes inertia. To accomplish the small things, visualize the big picture outcome. This overcomes overwhelm." Small steps in the right direction are the best way to get big things done. One final piece of career advice here: start big projects late in the afternoon. You'll have momentum on your side when you get to work the next day.

Success Tweet 88

Get organized. Organize your time, life and workspace. Sweat the small stuff. Success is in execution. Execution is in the details.

I discussed the importance of managing your time in Success Tweet 88. However, time management, while important, is not the only key to personal organization. The other day, I was looking for something on my office book shelf and I came across one of my favorite booklets. It's called *110 Ideas for Organizing Your Business Life*. Paulette Ensign is the author.

Paulette has packed a lot of common sense advice into this 16-page booklet. I'm going to share my favorite ten nuggets with you here. If you want the other 100, you can purchase the booklet by going to www.tipsbooklets.com.

10 of Paulette Ensign's Tips on Organizing Your Business Life

- Create your own systems based on your common sense needs. Modify whatever you read, hear or see (including these tips) to accommodate your personal requirements.
- Set a toss out date for publications and reports. If you haven't read something by the date, your life has probably continued fine without that information. Today, information comes so quickly that much of it is outdated shortly after you read it.
- Decide if you really need a hard copy of everything you have electronically. Most times a backup disk is fine. You will save money, time and space – not to mention a few trees – by printing a hard copy only when you need it.
- File paper by asking "where would I look for this item?" not "where should I put this item?" The putting part is easy – it's the retrieval that can be difficult.
- Write the date and circumstances of the meeting on each business card you collect. The frame of reference this provides will be very helpful in follow-up conversations.
- Break large projects into short segments. This will keep you motivated to finish the entire project.
- Schedule regular time for reading. Usually lunch time or the end of the day is best for reading. Scheduled time will keep you up on what's happening in your business and life.

- Schedule high brain activities during your peak energy time and low brain, mechanical tasks during your low energy time.
- Use a phone headset to free your hands while you are on the phone. This will facilitate note taking, and finding items important to the conversation.
- Use a conference room, library or unoccupied office to do work where you need to concentrate and be free of interruptions.

These common sense ideas for organizing your time and life are only 10% of the ideas in Paulette Ensign's booklet *110 Ideas for Organizing Your Business Life*. Try them. If they help you become more organized, buy the booklet to become even more organized and productive.

The common sense career success coach point here is simple. Successful people are outstanding performers. Outstanding performers are well-organized; they manage their time, life and stress well. Follow the advice in Tweet 88 in Success Tweets. "Get organized. Organize your time, life and workspace. Sweat the small stuff. Success is in the execution. Execution is in the details." Manage your time and life well by following this advice. Engage in "not important and not urgent" activities like web-surfing in your leisure time only. Complete "not important but urgent" activities quickly and move on. Focus on "important and urgent" tasks. Get them done well and in a timely manner. Create time to work on "important but not urgent" tasks. This will give you a leg-up on your competition and lead to your personal and professional success.

Success Tweet 89

Create your own unique personal organization system based on your needs and what works for you.

When I did a Google search on "personal organization," I came across an article by Roy Posner in which he listed several ways in which you can become better organized. Here are his ideas for becoming better organized:

- Organize the physical things around you — your home, your paperwork and your finances.
- Increase your level of cleanliness and orderliness.
- Be punctual and on time.
- Prioritize to whom your emotions and attention should go.
- Manage your time, your schedule and your work.
- Systematize activities in your life — from cleaning and cooking to bookkeeping.
- Balance your work load during the day.
- Coordinate and organize your communications with others.
- Further organize and distill the knowledge you have in life.
- Delegate work, tasks, and duties to others when appropriate.
- Determine your goals and aspirations.
- Sort out what is truly important to you in life.
- Organize and prioritize your personal values.
- Organize your mind and your thoughts for better thinking and understanding.

Which things on this list give you the most difficulty? What have you done to deal with them? What's worked and what hasn't worked? Please leave a comment sharing your advice with us.

I've found that two pieces of Roy's advice have benefited me greatly over the years. By "sorting out what is truly important to me in my life," and "organizing and prioritizing my personal values," I've been able to create the focus I need to be successful in my life and career.

Early on, I discovered that I value three things above all others: 1) Always do your best; 2) Treat everyone with the dignity and respect they deserve as human beings; 3) Be willing to help others with no strings attached.

Once I came to the understanding that these principles are the ones by which I want to live my life, little things like choosing a career became obvious to me. That's why I became a VISTA Volunteer upon my graduation from college and why I got into the training and development field after I completed my year of service.

It's also why I've expanded my consulting and speaking practice to include coaching. Being a career success coach allows me to work one-to-one with others, helping them achieve life and career success.

What is truly important in your life? What are your personal values? How have you used them to guide your life and career?

The common sense career success coach point here is simple. Outstanding performers are well-organized. They follow the career advice in Tweet 89 in Success Tweets. "Create your own unique personal organization system based on your needs and what works for you." Determining the things that are truly important to you in your life can help you become better organized. Once you are clear on what is important to you, and the personal values by which you want to live your life, it becomes easier to make important life and career success decisions. If you are floundering a bit, go back to basics. Determine what is truly important to you in life. Then choose a set of values that will guide your behavior. Once you do this, a lot of life and career success decisions that may have been perplexing will become clearer to you.

Success Tweet 90

Positive time management is an important habit to develop. Habits are like muscles. The more you use them, the stronger they get.

Here in Colorado, we are required to get our cars checked to ensure that they meet clean air emissions standards before we can renew our license plates. It's a good law, one that helps with the air quality in our beautiful state. It's also a pain in the butt. It requires a trip to an emissions monitoring station and waiting in line for the test. My plates renew in October, so every other October I spend a couple hours getting my car tested. It passed.

The last time I went to get my emissions sticker, Cathy laughed at me as I was leaving the house. I had my briefcase with me, which had my cell phone, a couple of books and a bottle of water. She said I would probably be the only one at the emissions testing facility reading a book. That was OK. I had just received a review copy of Gary Vaynerchuk's new book, *Crush It*. I wanted to read it so I could review it on this blog – and to learn a few things. By the way, *Crush It* is a great book – not just for entrepreneurs.

Carrying a book with me is one of my time management positive habits. Sometimes it's a novel. Most times it's a business or inspirational book. I am in the habit of using spare moments to read and learn. I was able to read the first four chapters of *Crush It* while I was waiting for my emissions test. I also took some notes — ideas that I plan on incorporating into my business. Not a bad use of my time.

I read while waiting for appointment with clients. I read while waiting for my dentist, or doctor – and you know how long those waits can be. I read when I go to get my car washed. I read before a movie if I'm by myself. This is a small habit, but one that allows me to read at least two more books a month than I normally would. That's 24 books a year – and a lot of good ideas to help me grow my business.

Reading spurs ideas. These ideas give me inspiration for this blog. They help me make decisions about my business. They help me clarify my thinking on my passion – helping others create the life and career success they want and deserve. Reading helps me provide better career advice.

Reading in spare moments is one of my most positive habits. What is your most positive habit? If you are thinking that you don't have many positive habits, I suggest you check out Dan Robey's site, www.thepowerofpositivehabits.com. There's a lot to be learned there.

The common sense career success coach point here is simple. Successful people are competent. They set high goals and achieve them. Positive habits will help you reach your goals – but only if you take the time to develop them. Remember the advice in Tweet 90 in Success Tweets. "Positive time management is an important habit to develop. Habits are like muscles. The more you use them, the stronger they get." Reading in what I call "found moments" – the time I spend waiting – is one of my positive habits. I'm amazed at how much I learn just by always having a book with me. The last time I got my car tested for emissions I learned a lot about personal branding by reading the first four chapters of Gary Vaynerchuk's book, *Crush It*. Take the time to develop some positive habits of your own. You'll be surprised at how much they help your productivity.

Success Tweet 91

The better you feel, the better you'll perform. Live a healthy lifestyle. Eat well. Exercise regularly. Get regular checkups.

You have to be in reasonable shape if you want to become a professional success. A reasonable level of fitness will help you deal with the inevitable stress that accompanies creating a successful life and career. Diet and exercise are the keys to living a healthy lifestyle. You don't have to be a fitness fanatic, but you do need to get some exercise and pay attention to what you eat.

I'm not the best role model when it comes to a healthy lifestyle. I've battled weight my entire life. However, as I've gotten older, I've become more serious about living a healthy lifestyle. I exercise more and pay attention to what I eat.

I have found that the US government revised food pyramid provides great guidance on how to eat healthy. Here are some of the highlights. I try to follow these guidelines. If you follow them, you will be doing well from a nutrition standpoint.

Eat at least three ounces of whole grain bread, cereals, crackers, rice or pasta every day. Look for the word "whole" before the grain name on the list of ingredients.

Eat lots of vegetables every day. I'm lucky here. I love vegetables – even brussels sprouts. Dark green and orange vegetables are the best for you. Dry beans and peas are also good for you.

Fruits are also good for you. Raw fruit is the best. On the other hand, it's best to limit your intake of fruit juice. It's often very high in calories and sugar.

Milk is a great source of calcium – something we all need for strong bones. However, whole milk is very high in fat, so it's best to drink low-fat or fat-free milk. Yogurt and cheese are also good sources of calcium.

Eat protein (meat, fish and poultry) in small quantities. Bake, broil, or grill – don't fry – your protein.

The Mayo clinic suggests eating at least three fruits, four vegetables, four to eight servings of grains and pasta, three to seven servings of protein or dairy, three to five servings of fat and no more than 75 calories of sugar a day.

In general, you can eat healthy by eating more fruits, vegetables and whole grains. Reduce your intake of saturated fat, trans fats and cholesterol. Limit sweets and salt. Drink alcoholic beverages in moderation, if at all. Control portion sizes and the total number of calories you consume.

Exercise is the other important component of a healthy lifestyle. It's best if you can exercise for at least 30 minutes five times a week. Fitness experts suggest that, of the 30 minutes, 20 should be spent in some form of cardio exercise, five in stretching, and five in resistance training.

I find that it's best to choose a time to exercise and build your daily schedule around it. Some people like first thing in the morning. Others like the evening. I prefer mid-day. I find that if I exercise around noon, I am less hungry and consume fewer calories at lunch.

Hydration and circulation are important too. Drink plenty of water. It keeps you hydrated and helps combat hunger. If you spend a lot of time at your desk, take a few minutes every hour to get up and stretch. You can do leg lifts and stomach squeezes at your desk. A little bit of activity can give you a burst of oxygen that will energize you and keep you feeling good.

You don't have to become a fitness fanatic to be a high performer. However, eating well and exercising will keep you sharp and on top of your game. It will keep your stress in check. And while a little stress is a good thing, too much stress can knock you out of the game.

The common sense career success coach point here is simple. Successful people are high performers. They follow the career advice in Success Tweet 91. "The better you feel, the better you'll perform. Live a healthy lifestyle. Eat well. Exercise regularly. Get regular checkups." You don't have to be a fitness junky to become a high performer. But if you take care of yourself you'll be more likely to become a high performer, and high performance is a key to creating the life and career success you want and deserve.

Success Tweet 92

Determine your peak energy times. Schedule high brain tasks when your energy is high and low brain tasks when it is low.

A long time ago I learned that my energy is high at the beginning of the day and at the end of the day. My energy is lowest mid day. I schedule myself accordingly.

I reserve the morning for my important and urgent tasks – like writing and posting this blog. I use late afternoons and early evenings to work on my important but not urgent tasks – like writing my books and other thought pieces. Mid-day, I catch up on correspondence, return phone calls, exercise and run errands.

This works for me. I think best and most clearly in the morning and have a bit of a sinker mid-day. My energy and mental acuity picks up again late in the day. This is really helpful, as I get a lot done late in the day when many people are biding their time getting ready to go home.

This schedule works for me. It may or may not work for you. You have to determine your peak energy times and schedule yourself accordingly.

However, no matter how well you plan your day, surprises and interruptions will come along. A couple of years ago, I saw a great article on Success.com by David Allen called, "It's Not About Time." Mr. Allen suggests that too often we focus on managing our time when we should, in fact, be focused on managing ourselves.

> "The savvy know that self management is really an issue of what we do with ourselves during the time we have. Self-management needs to encompass managing our thoughts and emotions, and dealing effectively with our work, family and community relationships. It's about gaining dynamic balance of control and perspective to achieve more successful outcomes and feel more relaxed along the way.

"Self-management is about knowing what to do at any given moment. It's dealing effectively with the things we have to do to achieve our goals and fulfill our purpose. It's also about deciding the importance of the varied and constant information coming at us."

What do you think about David Allen's ideas on self management? I like them. Even though I try to schedule my high brain tasks at the beginning and end of the day, I sometimes end up doing them mid-day when my energy is lowest. I have found that, no matter my preference, sometimes I have to deviate from my preferred schedule to handle matters that are out of my control.

As David Allen says, "self-management is about knowing what to do at any given moment." This means that you cannot become a slave to your to-do list or your personal preferences. No matter how well you plan, you will be faced with new problems and opportunities every day. Sometimes, what I want to do is different from what I need to do. I bet you find this to be true too. My best career advice is to do what you need to, not what you want to, as you go through your day.

Do your best to schedule yourself so that you can deal with high brain tasks when your energy is highest. But when circumstances create different demands, suck it up and do the best you can every moment you have. The problems and opportunities on which you focus at any given moment in time will have a big impact on the level of your performance and, ultimately, your success. Don't be so focused on managing your time that you miss opportunities because they fall outside of your plan for the day.

The common sense career success coach point here is simple. If you want to succeed in your life and career, you need to become an outstanding performer. To become an outstanding performer, you need to become a lifelong learner, set and achieve high goals and be well organized. Self management and time management are two important keys to becoming organized. They are tied to the career advice in Tweet 92 in Success Tweets. "Determine your peak energy times. Schedule high brain tasks when your energy is high and low brain tasks when it is low." But don't become a slave to your to do list or preferred manner of working. As David Allen points out, "Self management is different from time management because it allows you to respond at your best to surprises."

Success Tweet 93

Becoming a high performer is easier if you're physically fit. Increasing your heart rate is a great way to improve your fitness level.

As a career success coach, I advise my clients to live a healthy lifestyle. This means eating right and exercising. You don't have to become a tri-athlete; every little bit of exercise helps. Exercise helps you increase your heart rate. I like to ride my bike to increase my heart rate.

Dan Robey is a friend of mine. He is the author of *The Power of Positive Habits*. I am one of his subscribers. A while back, I received a great email from Dan on brisk walking as a positive habit – and a great way to increase your heart rate. Dan is a generous guy and he always lets me repost his posts here.

Check out what he has to say about the power of brisk walking...

Make "Brisk Walking" A Positive Habit

"Not running, not jogging, but walking is your most efficient exercise and the only one you can safely follow all the years of your life." - Executive Health Organization

Walking as a daily exercise habit can truly be a life-changing positive habit and is one of the most powerful habits for reaching your goal of a healthy trim and fit body. Over the past 20 years, there have been dozens of studies that have proven the benefits of brisk walking.

Thousands upon thousands of people have improved their health and lost weight by the diligent habit of walking. If you think that walking does not provide the same benefits as other more vigorous exercises, think again.

A study published by the New England Journal Of Medicine showed that postmenopausal women who walked regularly lowered their risk for heart disease just as much as women who did more vigorous exercise, such as playing sports or running.

This study suggests that walking is just as good for your heart as heavy exercise. I spoke with study author, Dr. JoAnn E. Manson, Chief of Preventive Medicine at Brigham and Women's Hospital, Professor of Medicine at Harvard Medical School. She said, "The study provides compelling evidence that walking and vigorous exercise provide similar heart benefits, about a 30% to 40% reduction in the risk of cardiovascular disease with 30 minutes per day of either activity."

I also asked her about the benefits of making brisk walking a positive habit, and she responded, "They could surely walk away from heart disease and several other chronic diseases. We have also found that brisk walking for at least 3 hours a week can lower the risk of stroke, type 2 diabetes, and breast cancer.

No pain, no gain, is an outdated notion; exercise doesn't need to be strenuous or uncomfortable. It can be easy and enjoyable. Even though the study consisted solely of women, it is likely that men would experience similar benefits from the positive habit of brisk walking.

Here are additional benefits you will receive from your habit of brisk walking:

Walking burns calories and helps you lose weight and burn excess body fat.

Walking can help to improve your posture.

Walking requires no special equipment or gyms.

Walking can help lower blood pressure and help prevent circulatory and heart disorders.

Brisk, aerobic walking will give you the benefits of other exercises, such as jogging and cycling, but without the risk of injuries.

Walking at night can help promote better sleep.

Dan makes some great points about the benefits of developing a positive habit of brisk walking. Personally, I prefer to bicycle in the summer, and walk in the winter.

A lot of the people whom I coach say that they know they should exercise, but often can't seem to "get around to it." I have come up with the answer to this problem. I have printed several thousand stickers that are round and say "TUIT" in big capital letters. Whenever someone tells me that they know they should do something but can't seem to get around to it, I give them one of these stickers. It is a round TUIT. I tell them that now they can never say that they can't get a around to it anymore, because they have a round TUIT. I have a round TUIT sticker on my computer. I have another one on my bike. They are constant reminders to me to keep up good work and exercise habits.

Would you like a round TUIT? If so, please send me your snail-mail address, and I'll put up to five round TUITs in themail to you – free of charge. Use them for yourself, or give them to your friends who are procrastinators. Just make sure that you get around to living a healthy lifestyle. Elevate your heart rate. Brisk walking is a great way to start.

The common sense career success coach point here is simple. Successful people are outstanding performers. Outstanding performers live a healthy lifestyle. They follow the career advice in Tweet 93 in Success Tweets. "Becoming a high performer is easier if you're physically fit. Increasing your heart rate is a great way to improve your fitness level." My friend Dan Robey, author of *The Power of Positive Habits,* says that brisk walking is a great way to increase your heart rate and one of the most healthy habits you can adopt. I agree, almost everybody can walk. The more you walk, the healthier you'll be. Dan points out that "No pain, no gain, is an outdated notion; exercise doesn't need to be strenuous or uncomfortable. It can be easy and enjoyable." So, like the Nike ads say, Just Do It! Or as this career success coach says, "Get around to it."

Success Tweet 94

Don't take yourself too seriously. Lighten up. It will help you master yourself and become an outstanding performer.

I love the Internet. You can find anything and everything there. I googled "lighten up". I got 1,740,000 hits in less than half a second – 0.42 seconds to be exact. I clicked on a WikiHow called "How to Lighten Up" and found six common sense tips on how to lighten up.

1. Stop assuming you know everything. Nobody knows everything – even in his or her field. When you think you know everything, you become closed to new ideas.

2. Stop exaggerating. Be truthful with yourself about your skills and abilities. Just like you should avoid assuming you know everything, you need to avoid coming across to others as a know-it-all. Knowing it all sets you up for unwanted stress.

3. Let go of things. I love what the WikiHow has to say about this. "Better to be humble and humorous about your journey through life than to be the drama queen of Seriousville." Learn from your mistakes and move on. Don't hold grudges.

4. Laugh. Be willing to laugh at yourself. It may just be me, but I laugh about myself or something I do almost every day. I'm not an idiot, but I do make my share of human mistakes. Instead of getting frustrated, I choose to laugh. Laugh with others. Share their humor. But, never laugh at others.

5. Delegate. This may come as a surprise to you, but you're not indispensible. Someone else can probably do your job at least as well, and maybe better than you. The old saying, "if you want something done right, do it yourself," just isn't true. Figure out what you're holding on to just to satisfy your ego, and then let it go.

6. Stop being so rules-focused. We make lots of rules for ourselves. Things like, "I should do this," or "I should do that." As one of my early mentors told me – "Don't should on yourself. You'll be happier." I couldn't agree more.

I love these tips, and agree with them. I particularly like number 4 – laugh. I think that the ability to laugh at yourself is one of the greatest gifts you can give yourself – and the people around you. Being too serious, beating up yourself over mistakes, causes lots of stress. And it makes you an unpleasant person. No one wants to be around someone who is constantly frustrated by the smallest mistakes.

I heard a story about a teacher the other day. She asked some young children just learning to read if they could identify the animal in a picture she showed them. One little boy said, "it's a frickin' lion." The teacher was upset about his choice of modifiers. When she pointed that out to him, he said, "It is a frickin' lion. It says so right here." The teacher was frustrated, but looked at the picture again and saw that the caption read, "African Lion." Now that's cause to laugh – at yourself and the phonics method of learning to read.

I also like point number 6 – stop being so rules-focused. As I mentioned above, we sometimes create unreasonable expectations for ourselves and these expectations become rules – if only in our head. As I've mentioned above, these rules become "shoulds." "Don't should on yourself" is some of the best career advice I've ever received. Stop thinking that you should do this, or should be so far along in your career, or shouldn't have to do a job you think is below you. The best way to stop letting unnecessary rules govern your life is to stop making up rules to govern you. Don't should on yourself.

The common sense career success coach point here is simple. Successful people work hard at creating the life and career success they want and deserve. But they don't take themselves too seriously. They follow the career advice in Tweet 94 in Success Tweets. "Don't take yourself too seriously. Lighten up. It will help you master yourself and become an outstanding performer." If you want to lighten up, laugh a little more, and don't get too caught up in rules. Or, as one of my early mentors always said, "Don't should on yourself."

Success Tweet 95

Get into a high performance mindset. Don't question yourself. Trust your skills and abilities.

If you want to create the life and career success you want and deserve you have to trust yourself. Trusting yourself is one of the key components of self-confidence. Self-confident people cultivate a high performance mindset, one in which they believe they will succeed at whatever they attempt.

If you read this blog, you know that I am a big fan of The Optimist Creed. Point 4 says,

> "Promise yourself to look at the sunny side of everything and make your optimism come true."

Point 7 says,

> "Promise yourself to forget the mistakes of the past and press on to the greater achievements of the future."

You have to trust yourself to put these two bits of common sense career advice into play. Optimists trust themselves. They trust themselves to do whatever is necessary to meet the goals they set for themselves. They trust themselves to develop the skills they need to meet their goals. They trust themselves to create the life and career success they want and deserve.

There is lots of great career advice in The Optimist Creed. I have prepared a .pdf of it that you can download, print and hang in your office – just like I have done. If you would like a copy of The Optimist Creed, go to http://budbilanich.com/optimist.

Here's a personal example about trusting yourself. I've trained thousands of people in leadership skills, I've led hundreds of team-building workshops, I've coached hundreds of people, helping them create the life and career success they want and deserve. Recently, I decided that I wanted to reach a broader audience – not just the people who work for the Fortune 500 companies who have engaged my consulting and coaching services.

To do this, I needed to make my ideas more widely available via the Internet. Several years ago, I realized that I didn't have a clue about how to prepare, present and market my ideas on the Internet. I trusted my knowledge and wisdom, but I didn't know how to get it to a broader audience. This might have stopped some folks dead in their tracks. But I trust my ability to learn new skills.

First I learned how to blog, and then I committed to blogging five days a week. I've kept that commitment for the past five years. I blog every Monday through Friday, with the exception of two weeks at the end of the year. That's 250 posts every year. Then I learned about social media. I spend about an hour a day on Twitter, LinkedIn and Facebook, sharing my thoughts on life and career success. Finally, I'm continuing to learn about Internet marketing – affiliate programs, membership sites, etc. When I started, I had no Internet marketing skills. Today, I am a bit of an expert. I say this realizing that I need to keep learning and growing in this field.

I trusted myself. I knew I had something of value to give, and I knew I could learn the skills necessary to reach large numbers of people. By the end of this year, I will have launched several information products on the Internet – all because I trusted my ability to learn and my motivation to do new things.

How about you? Do you trust yourself? Do you believe that what you have to offer is important and of high quality? Do you believe that you can learn what you need to know to succeed? I bet you do, or you wouldn't be reading this blog post.

The common sense career success coach point here is simple. Successful people believe in themselves. They follow the career advice in Tweet 95 in Success Tweets. "Develop a high performance mindset. Don't question yourself. Trust your skills and abilities." Trusting your skills and abilities means knowing when you need to learn something new, and then doing whatever it takes to gain that knowledge. Be a self-confident optimist. Trust yourself. Know in your heart of hearts that you will succeed.

Success Tweet 96

Good truly is the enemy of great. Don't settle for good performance. Today, good performance is mediocre. Become a great performer.

In his book, *Good to Great,* Jim Collins hit the nail on the head when he began with the idea that good is the enemy of great. He's right, good is the enemy of great. There are lots of good performers, but only a few great ones. To achieve the life and career success you want and deserve, you need to become a great performer – not just a good one.

Good is seductive. For many of us, it's not too difficult to be good. And good has a nice feeling attached to it. On the other hand, good performance won't get you to the top of the promotion list and keep you off of the layoff list. Great performance will.

But great performance comes with a price. You have to work at it. In *The Success Principles: How to Get From Where You Are to Where You Want to Be,* Jack Canfield of *Chicken Soup for the Soul* fame quotes several great performers on paying the price…

> "If people knew how hard I had to work to gain my mastery, it wouldn't seem wonderful at all." Michelangelo

> "When I played with Michael Jordan on the Olympic team, there was a huge gap between his ability and the ability of the other great players on that team. But what impressed me was that he was always the first one on the floor and the last one to leave." Steve Alford, Head Basketball Coach, University of New Mexico.

> "If I miss a day of practice, I know it. If I miss two days, my manager knows it. If I miss three days, my audience knows it." Andre Previn, Pianist, Conductor and Composer.

> "Talent is cheaper than table salt. What separates the talented individual from the successful one is a lot of hard work." Stephen King, Bestselling Novelist

Here are four people – an artist, a basketball player, a pianist and a writer – all saying the same thing: good is the enemy of great.

Your natural talent might allow you to be good. Great, however, requires determination and persistence.

Here are some interesting ideas about the difference between good and great when it comes to sales. They come from a study done by Herbert True at Notre Dame University.

- 44% of all salespeople quit trying to sell their prospect after the first call.

- 24% quit after the second call.

- 14% quit after the third call.

- 12% quit trying after the fourth call.

Great sales people make the fifth and sixth calls. According to Mr. True, 60 % of all sales are made after the fourth call. And, according to his research, 94% of all salespeople give up after four calls to one prospect. The 14% and 12% of salespeople who give up after the third and fourth calls are probably pretty good salespeople. However, the great salespeople make the fifth and sixth calls – and make more sales.

Recently, I worked for about six months to close a large (for me at least) sale. At first, I seemed to be getting nowhere, but I believed in myself and knew that the services I was selling were valuable to the company to which I was selling them. After six months and way more than six meetings with numerous people, all of whom had some input into the buying decision, I received a signed purchase order for $105,000. I was great – at least when it came to this sale.

My best career advice on going from good to great is to persist. Practice harder, prepare more, make the extra call, rewrite your proposal, rehearse your presentation, and you will find yourself creating the career and life success you want and deserve.

Some of the best career advice on persistence that I've come across comes from Calvin Coolidge, 30th President of the United States...

> "Nothing in this world can take the place of persistence. Talent will not; nothing
> is more common than unsuccessful people with talent. Genius will not;
> unrewarded genius is almost a proverb. Education will not; the world is full of

educated derelicts. Persistence and determination alone are omnipotent. The slogan, "press on," has solved and always will solve the problems of the human race."

The common sense career success coach point here is simple. Successful people are great performers. They follow the advice in Tweet 96 in Success Tweets. "Good truly is the enemy of great. Don't settle for good performance. Today, good is mediocre. Become a great performer." Hard work and persistence are the best ways to become a great performer. If you practice longer, prepare more, make the extra call, rewrite your proposal, rehearse your presentation, you will find yourself creating the life and career success you want and deserve.

Success Tweet 97

Today, do the things others won't do; so tomorrow you can do the things they can't.

I got this one from Jerry Rice an American Football player. He is in the NFL Hall of Fame. When he retired, he held all of the important records a wide receiver could amass. I've never seen anyone better – and I've watched a lot of football over the years. Growing up in Pittsburgh, Sundays meant two things – church and the Pittsburgh Steelers.

Jerry Rice was well known for his commitment to fitness. He worked out harder and longer than any other pro football player. When he was asked the secret of his success, he said, "I am willing to do the things today that others won't do, so I can do things on Sunday that they can't do." In other words, work hard, prepare, commit to taking personal responsibility for your own success.

It's simple, really. Success is all up to you, and me, and anyone else who wants it. We all have to take personal responsibility for our own success. I am the only one who can make me a success. You are the only one who can make you a success. Become willing to do things that others are unwilling to do – and this can be a million little things like keeping your clothes in good repair; shining your shoes; rehearsing your presentation out loud; proofreading your emails, not just relying on spell check; staying up-to-date on your company, your competitors and your industry, building relationships by doing willingly for others.

If you already do these kinds of things, bravo. You're in the minority. Too many people do only what they have to. Successful people always go the extra mile. As Jerry Rice says, they do the things others won't.

Think for a minute. What are the kinds of things that you can do that go above and beyond, that demonstrate your commitment to your own success? Make a list. Then go about doing these things regularly.

Here's a bit of career advice. Stuff happens: good stuff, bad stuff, frustrating stuff, unexpected stuff. Successful people respond to the stuff that happens in a positive way. Humans are the only animals with free will. That means we – you and me – get to decide how we react to every situation that comes up. When you take responsibility for responding positively to people and events – especially negative people and events – you're doing the things that a lot of people won't do. This means that you'll be more successful in the long run.

Personal responsibility means recognizing that you are responsible for your life and the choices you make. It means that you realize that, while other people and events have an impact on your life, these people and events don't shape your life. When you accept personal responsibility for your life, you own up to the fact that how you react to people and events is what's important. And you can choose how to react to every person you meet and everything that happens to you.

The concept of personal responsibility is found in most writings on success. Stephen Covey's first habit in *The 7 Habits of Highly Effective People* is, "Be proactive." My friend John Miller's book, *QBQ: the Question Behind the Question,* asks readers to pose questions to themselves like, "What can I do to become a top performer?" When you ask and answer this question, you'll be on your way to doing the things that other won't do – and getting the promotions and recognition that they can't get.

In my opinion, all of this comes down to two words: activity and persistence. Activity and persistence are my watchwords. I set some very high goals for myself every year. I begin each year in high gear and then I kick it into overdrive. And, I persist until I achieve all of my goals, no matter what. I am committed to activity and persistence.

Mike Litman has some interesting things to say about activity...

> "Activity. Activity. Activity. Too many people are standing still. Too much pondering, too little action. Too much scatteredness, too little focus. Too much talk, too little results. In 2009, commit to a year filled with activity. Be 1% more active each day in your business. Start at 1%.

> "Activity. Activity. Activity. When you stand still too long, moving becomes real tough. Very tough. Every day, do at least one action that moves you forward. What I love best about a lot of activity, is that I get to make mistakes and learn what works. You can do the same. Activity. Activity. Activity. 2009 is about you being more active than you've ever been. Are you in? Are you ready to commit to a year filled with activity?"

Kevin Eikenberry writes to leaders, but his ideas apply to anyone who wants to create life and career success. He says…

> "Let me be blunt. We can create and engage in the best leadership skill training, we can create the best leadership development opportunities, and we can provide coaching and mentoring that is outstanding, and yet, if all of these programs and leadership activities don't include an ongoing persistent process of improvement – a way to instill and inspire persistence – we will fall short of what is possible… Ask yourself today what you can do to create greater persistence in yourself and your organization. Your answer (and the action taken on that answer) will pay you rich rewards."

These guys are right! Activity and persistence will make you an outstanding performer. And they are the key to putting the advice in Success Tweet 97 to work. Activity – even 1% more than you currently do – and persistence – fighting through problems and setbacks – will yield positive results in the long term. But you have to commit to them.

The common sense career success coach point here is simple. Successful people commit to taking responsibility for their life and career success. They follow the career advice in Tweet 97 in Success Tweets. "Today, do the things others won't do; so tomorrow you can do the things they can't." Be willing to put in the time to prepare so that you can create the life and career success that you want and deserve. Successful people are willing to do whatever it takes to succeed. They are active and they are persistent. The law of inertia says that a body in motion tends to stay in motion. That's why activity is so important. Once you get moving, it's easier to stay moving towards your goals. And it's easier to persist in the face of problems and setbacks. To paraphrase Muhammad Ali: "Inside a ring or out, ain't no shame in going down. It's staying down that's shameful." Persistent people don't stay down; they get back up and keep moving. Make activity and persistence your watchwords. You'll amaze yourself with how much you will accomplish, and the life and career success you will create.

Success Tweet 98

Don't worry about getting credit for doing the job. Worry about getting the job done well – accurately and on time.

Harry Truman, 33rd President of the United States, really got it right when he provided this bit of career advice: "It's amazing what you can accomplish if you don't care who gets the credit."

Many years ago I was assigned a joint project with a deadbeat for a partner. This guy was bad. He was a triple threat – not so bright, a big ego and lazy. As the project wore on and we were nearing a deadline, I thought about going to my boss and complaining that he wasn't carrying his weight. I decided not to do so.

I slogged on, got the project done well and on time and submitted it – with his name and mine on the finished product. I was feeling kind of resentful, because I was worried that even though I did all the work, he was getting half of the credit.

A couple weeks later, our boss called me into his office. He said that he wanted to compliment me on the fine job I did on the project. I bit my tongue and said, "Gil and I worked on that project together." My boss said, "I know Gil's work, and I know your work. I could tell that you did all of the work on that project."

I said, "Thanks for noticing." He said, "I assigned you that joint project as a bit of a test. I wanted to see how well you could work with others. I figured you would get frustrated with Gil because I knew he wasn't up to doing quality work on this kind of project. I wanted to see what you would do. You did the work, and didn't rat out Gil. I'm proud of you for that."

We can debate his leadership style here; I don't think it's a good idea to treat the people who work for you as lab rats. But this story makes an interesting point about the career advice in Success Tweet 98. Do your job. Do it well. Don't worry about who gets credit.

It's been my experience that people in positions of authority can identify good work when they see it; and that they can differentiate the work of the people who report to them. If you consistently produce high-quality work and results, you will get your due.

Take it from this career success coach. Focus on getting the job done – well and on time—and you will get the recognition due you in the long run. And creating life and career success is a long run – a marathon, not a sprint. As the old saying goes, "The cream rises to the top."

Delivering high-quality work, consistently and in the long run, will get you noticed and help you create the life and career success you want and deserve. Stay focused on your work, get creative with your ideas. Make sure you cross all of your t's and dot all of your i's and you'll succeed.

The common sense success point here is simple. Successful people deliver high-quality work, consistently and over the long run. They follow the career advice in Tweet 98 in Success Tweets. "Don't worry about getting credit for doing the job. Worry about getting the job done well – accurately and on time." Most leaders recognize the output of the people who work for them. That's why it's important to focus on doing a good job on every job – no matter how small. You'll be building your brand and portfolio in your manager's mind. In the long run, producing consistently high-quality work is the best way to get the recognition due you.

Success Tweet 99

Get the job done with what you have. Don't worry about what you don't have, or would like to have.

I studied journalism as an undergraduate. Journalism is a great major. It teaches you to write. It keeps you up on current events. And most of all, it provides you with the discipline of making deadlines. Bob Farson was my advisor at Penn State. He never accepted a late assignment. He never gave an incomplete in a course. Every journalism student in my day heard his mantra over and over again...

> "There is no late in journalism. You can't put out a blank paper. A good reporter will never have everything he wants for a story. You've got to learn to go with what you've got and do the best job you can with it."

Bob Farson's advice – "go with what you've got" – really stuck with me. I finished my four years at Penn State, got an MA at The University of Colorado and a PhD at Harvard, and never missed a deadline. I never asked for an extension, and I never took an incomplete in a course.

I never worked as a journalist, but my journalism education taught me the importance of getting the job done with what I have – and that, in turn, helped me create the life and career success I so badly wanted.

When it comes to deadlines, I find that people make two types of mistakes: 1) They miss them because they are always looking for that one additional piece of information that will bring everything together perfectly; 2) They get so focused on making them that they don't dig deep enough to find all the information they need to do an outstanding job.

Both are problems. When I say go with what you've got, I mean you need to find the right balance of gathering all the information you need and still making the deadline. Avoid problem number 1 by realizing that you'll never know everything you want to know about a given subject. I've been a career success coach for 20 years, and I still learn new stuff about my field of expertise every day. Avoid problem number 2 by not getting overly focused on the deadline. If you do, you run the risk of not doing as good a job as you can on any given project.

Go with what you've got only after you do an exhaustive information search and make sure that you have all the information you can possibly find and still make the deadline.

In a post earlier this week, I mentioned a great little book: *QBQ: The Question Behind the Question* by my friend John Miller. If you find yourself needing information or materials to get a job done right, don't ask, "Why won't people give me what I need to do my job?" Instead ask yourself, "How can I get what I need to get this job done right and on time?" The answer to that question will put you in charge. You'll be better able to go with what you've got to get the job done well.

The common sense career success coach point here is simple. Successful people meet deadlines. They follow the career advice in Tweet 99 in Success Tweets. "Get the job done with what you have. Don't worry about what you don't have, or would like to have." Take personal responsibility for doing the work with what you have – or getting what you need to do the work well. If you don't have what you need, do whatever it takes to get it. Take personal responsibility for making sure you have what you need to do your job well. Taking personal responsibility for getting the job done – with what you have, not what you want – will set you apart from the pack and put you on the road to the life and career success you want and deserve.

Success Tweet 100

Care about what you do. If you care a little, you'll be an OK performer. If you care a lot, you'll become an outstanding performer.

If you read this blog regularly, you know that I am a huge Pittsburgh Steelers fan. I grew up in Pittsburgh. My dad had Steelers season tickets for many years. He gave them up only because he moved to Florida. He learned to use the Internet at age 70, so he could follow the Steelers on line. He really cares about the Steelers. I'm not that much of a fanatic, but there is no professional sports team more near and dear to my heart than the Pittsburgh Steelers.

On Sunday, February 1 2009, Steelers won the Super Bowl. On Monday, February 2 2009, Mike Tomlin, their coach, noted that because the Steelers were in the NFL playoffs and Super Bowl, he was "a month behind getting ready for the 2009 season. We've got to be thoughtful in how we prepare our football team."

Some may say, "Chill, Mike, savor what you've just accomplished." However, Mike Tomlin knows that outstanding performers don't rest on their laurels. They care about what they do, and they care about their life and career success. High performers always set higher goals and look towards greater achievements. The Optimist Creed urges us to "Press on to the greater achievements of the future."

That's what Mike Tomlin was doing the day after he won the Super Bowl, and that's what all outstanding performers do. They set high goals and meet them. Then they set higher goals and meet them too.

Mike Tomlin is 36 years old. He is the youngest coach to win a Super Bowl. That's pretty impressive. But not to Tomlin. Because he cares deeply about winning he says he expected that kind of success and expects more. On the other hand, he is humble. He realizes that football is a team game. Coaches don't win Super Bowls on their own; neither do players. They need one another...

> "I'm an unrealistic dreamer sometimes. I'm blessed, extremely blessed. I've been around some great people – coaches, players, ownership – and I'm a product of that. That's my story."

And a great story it is. It shows the power of caring about what you do.

I care about helping people create the life and career success they want and deserve. I care a lot. That's why I wrote Success Tweets and I give it away for free. That's why I am writing this series of blog posts explaining each of the 141 tweets in more detail. I care so much about this that I've committed to writing 700 or 800 words every day for 28 weeks. I've also committed to doing a podcast on each of the tweets. I do this because I care. I care a lot about helping you achieve the kind of career success you deserve. And I know that this caring will pay off in me becoming an outstanding career success coach – somebody who gives really great career advice.

When you care you do your very best. This year marks the 50th anniversary of the publication of one of my favorite books: *To Kill a Mockingbird*. There is a passage in that book that has always stuck with me. It's in Chapter 11 and is spoken by Atticus Finch, the father, played by Gregory Peck in the film. He's speaking to Scout, his daughter…

> "I wanted you to see what real courage is, instead of getting the idea that courage is a man with a gun in his hand. It's when you know you're licked before you begin but you begin anyway and you see it through no matter what. You rarely win, but sometimes you do."

It takes courage to care. Because when you care, you put yourself out there. You do your best. And doing your best can be a scary thing. When you care, when you consciously do your best and fail, it is heartbreaking. But at least you have the satisfaction of knowing you did your best.

I remember when I applied to graduate school at Harvard. I decided that I was going to demonstrate to myself how much I cared by writing the very best application I could. I wasn't going to let myself off the hook if I didn't get accepted by saying, "I could have written a better application, but I just didn't spend the time I should have."

When I put my application in themailbox – we still did quaint things like that back in the old days – I was proud of what I had written. I knew it was the very best I could do. I was also frightened because I knew that my best might not be good enough. After all, both of my other degrees were from state schools. Who was I to think that those kind of credentials would get me accepted at Harvard?

I cared about the quality of my application, so I did the very best I could. The story in this case has a happy ending. I was accepted and got my degree. Even if I had not been accepted, I would have been proud of myself because I cared enough to write the best application I could, and I dared enough to admit it to myself.

The common sense career success coach point here is simple. Successful people are proud of what they do. They care. They follow the career advice in Success Tweet 100. "Care about what you do. If you care a little, you'll be an OK performer. If you care a lot, you'll become an outstanding performer." Does your work show that you care? Or does it reflect an "it's good enough" attitude? Take it from a career success coach, if you want to create the life and career success of which you are capable, make sure that how much you care shows through in every single piece of work you do.

Success Tweet 101

All dynamic communicators have mastered three basic communication skills: conversation, writing, and presenting.

The life of a business traveler, especially one like me who travels to New York City regularly, appears glamorous at first glance. People always ask me if I've eaten at famous restaurants like "21" or the latest hot spot they've read about in *Travel and Leisure.*

Most often when I'm in New York and don't have a business dinner, I dine on Chinese food delivered to my hotel room from a local take-out place. Once my fortune cookie read, "Your talents will be recognized and suitably rewarded." I was happy with this fortune, but it made me think.

My talents, your talents, everyone's talents will be recognized and rewarded if we develop and use our communication skills. There are three types of communication skills critically important for career and life success: 1) Conversation skills; 2) Writing skills; and 3) Presentation skills.

You need to develop each of these skills if you want to have your talents recognized. There are a few common sense career success coach points associated with becoming a dynamic communicator.

Become a good conversationalist by listening. Take an active interest in other people and what they're saying. Show them you're listening by asking appropriate follow-up questions to what they say.

Conversation skills enhance your networking ability. Networking is an important but often overlooked communication skill. It is helpful when you are looking for a job, but it is even more important when you are happy with your situation. All people who are a career success build and nurture strong networks.

Networking is an important skill. Successful people have large networks. They have people they can call to help them. They know they can call on these people because these people know they can call on them. That's the real secret of networking – look to help others, not just to find out how they can help you.

Write in a manner that communicates well. In general, this means being clear, concise and easily readable. The best way to make sure your writing is readable is to read it aloud before sending it.

When I was in high school, I was the editor of my yearbook. To raise funds to cover the cost of our yearbook, we sold ads. There were a lot of factories in the town where I grew up. In the past, the yearbook staff had never approached these factories to place ads in the yearbook. I wrote sales letters to all of the plant managers. We got several full-page ads from those letters.

One of the plant managers wrote back, asking if I would come to see him. When I walked in to his office and introduced myself, he was surprised. He told me that my sales letter was so well written that he thought I was the teacher who was the yearbook sponsor. Two years later, I was looking for a summer job after my first year of college. The market was tight. I called this man. He remembered me, and I got a job.

Preparation is the most important key to good presentations. You have to analyze your audience, prepare a talk that gives them what they want, and practice your talk out loud if you want to be a great presenter.

Presentation skills may present the biggest opportunity for getting your talents noticed. Just a few months ago, I did a talk for a local chamber of commerce. As it so happens, the Sheriff's department is a member of this chamber. The Sheriff himself happened to be there that day. He liked my talk. About a week later, I got a call from his training officer. The Sheriff asked him to get in touch with me to conduct some supervisory training for their sergeants. I never would have gotten this business if it weren't for the notice I received from a talk at that chamber meeting.

The Dilbert cartoons often focus on poor communication. I cut out the ones I really like. Here's one from a Sunday paper...

> Dilbert approaches his boss (you know, the one with the tufts of hair that look like devil's horns) and says, "The security audit accidentally locked all developers out of the system." The boss says, "Well, it is what it is."

Dilbert says, "How does that help?" The boss replies, "You don't know what you don't know." Dilbert, obviously frustrated, says, "Congratulations, you're the first human to fail the Turing test." The boss says, "What does that mean?" Dilbert replies, "It is what it is;" to which the boss says, "Why didn't you say so in the first place?"

There really is such a thing as a Turing test. Dictionary.com defines it as follows: "A test proposed by British mathematician Alan Turing, and often used as a test of whether a computer has humanlike intelligence. If a panel of human beings conversing with an unknown entity (via keyboard, for example) believes that that entity is human, and if the entity is actually a computer, then the computer is said to have passed the Turing test."

This is pretty funny. It is also kind of sad as it is indicative of the lack of communication in today's business world. Scott Adams, Dilbert's creator, really gets it when it comes to workplace communication problems.

*Beyond Bullsh*t*, by UCLA Anderson School of Management Professor, Samuel Culbert, is an interesting little book. Professor Culbert defines bullsh*t in the following way.

> "It is telling people what you think they need to hear. It may involve finessing the truth or outright lying, but the purpose is always self serving. And while I appreciate the role of some b.s. in keeping the corporate peace, it makes people feel beaten up, deceived – even dirty. When people talk straight at work, companies make out better because the best idea usually wins. In contrast, when people are bullsh*tting, they hide their mistakes and the company suffers. Straight talk is the product of relationships built on trust."

Phrases like "it is what it is" are not straight talk. They are part of the inexplicable jargon that has overtaken us. Dynamic communicators say what they mean, in an easily understood manner. Effective communicators don't show off their large vocabularies. Instead, they choose words that are the most easily understood and still get across their point.

Dynamic communicators eschew, I mean don't use, jargon. They avoid meaningless phrases like "it is what it is" to explain something. They use the simplest words possible to get across their ideas. And they don't bullsh*it. They say what they mean. Follow these four rules in conversation, writing and presenting, and you'll become known as a dynamic communicator.

The common sense career success coach point here is simple. Successful people are dynamic communicators. If you want to become a dynamic communicator, follow the career advice in Tweet 101 in Success Tweets. "All dynamic communicators have mastered three basic communication skills: conversation, writing and presenting." You don't have to be a career success coach to know that if you're a great conversationalist, a good writer and an outstanding performer you will reach your career success goals. Successful people communicate well. The career advice here is simple. Develop your communication skills if you want to create the life and career success you want and deserve.

Success Tweet 102

We're all in sales. You have to sell yourself every day. You need to become a dynamic communicator to sell your ideas.

In a post I did on lifelong learning in mid 2009, I stressed the idea that successful people pay attention to information that may seem as if it has little relevance to them – they know that they might learn something that will help them create the career success they deserve.

Today's post is about the information in a book that you might be tempted to overlook if you're not a sales professional – or if you haven't read the post on lifelong learning I mentioned above.

How to Win a Pitch, a very interesting book by Joey Asher, might seem like a book meant only for sales professionals. But it's not. Some of my best career advice is that we're all in sales, as we have to sell ourselves every day. We have to create positive personal impact to get people interested in us, and then we have to be good communicators to sell our ideas.

Joey presents five common sense fundamentals for becoming a persuasive communicator...

1. Focus your message on the business problem.
2. Organize your message around three memorable points.
3. Show passion.
4. Involve your audience in your presentation.
5. Rehearse… Rehearse… And Rehearse Again.

I like Joey's points – even if he has five instead of three. Just kidding. The important idea is to focus on a minimal number of points. Joey has five fundamentals for becoming a persuasive communicator. I have four keys to career and life success: Clarity, Commitment, Confidence and Competence. The fact that my four keys begin with the letter "C" makes it even easier for people to remember them. In my case, this was a happy coincidence. I don't suggest trying to force alliterations or acronyms. If your subject matter lends itself to them – great go with it. If not, don't force it.

I love Joey's career advice about passion. He is 100% correct when he says that your voice is your first key to passion. It's OK to sound as if you're excited – you should be excited about the points you're making.

I learned this the hard way. I once lost a job I really wanted because I didn't let my passion for the job show through in the interview. Ironically, I made a conscious decision to act in a laid-back manner in the interview – you know, "We're both professionals here. I'm calm. I know myself. No sense in over hyping it." As it turns out, I was one of two finalists for the job. The recruiter told me that the hiring manager liked my skills and experience more than the other guy, but he hired the other guy because he showed more passion and drive. I've never made the mistake of not letting my passion show through again.

By nature, I am a passionate guy. I care about what I do. After that hard lesson, I let this passion show through, when I'm selling and when I'm doing my work. I have found that it's hard to care too much. And, if I'm going to fail, I'm going to fail showing how much, not how little, I care. Joey Asher and I urge you to do the same.

I agree with Joey on the importance of rehearsals. As I often say – only half jokingly – "Preparation makes up for a lack of talent. That's how I've gotten as far as I have in my life and career." Prepare, prepare, prepare and you'll become a better communicator.

The common sense career success coach point here is simple. Successful people are dynamic communicators. Dynamic communicators have mastered three critical skills: conversation, writing and presenting. They follow the career advice in Tweet 102 in Success Tweets. "We're all in sales. You have to sell yourself every day. You need to become a dynamic communicator to sell your ideas." Dynamic communication hinges on your ability to sell yourself. Once you realize that, regardless of your job title, you are a salesperson and that you need to constantly sell yourself and your ideas you'll be ahead of the game. In *How to Win a Pitch*, Joey Asher suggests that successful sales people have mastered five fundamental skills: 1) Focus your message on the business problem; 2) Organize your message around three memorable points; 3) Show passion; 4) Involve your audience in your presentation; 5) Rehearse... Rehearse... And Rehearse Again. This is great career advice. Become an expert in these five fundamental skills, and you'll be on your way to creating the life and career success you want and that you deserve.

Success Tweet 103

Speak from your heart. Show that you care about yourself and the people with whom you are speaking.

Occasionally I see a presentation that is really great. That was the case a while back. I was at a meeting at a very large pharmaceutical company. This company is working hard to adapt to its changing business environment. They are in the midst of massive organizational change.

Nat Ricciardi is a senior leader at this company. He embodies all of the five keys to success that I discuss in my book *Straight Talk for Success*. He is self-confident. He creates positive personal impact. He has been an outstanding performer over his entire 38-year career. He is a dynamic communicator and one of the most interpersonally competent people I know.

I was at a meeting where Nat was the last person on a very busy agenda. He took the stage and immediately won over a tired audience. He had to stop because he ran into the dinner hour. But he stayed at the venue, eating dinner with the meeting participants. After dinner, he continued with a Q&A session. He didn't finish until he made sure that he'd answered every last question.

Nat delivered a dynamic presentation for a variety of reasons. He knew his material. He knew his audience. He was able to present his thoughts in a manner that addressed the audience's concerns. It helped that he was a senior executive presenting to a group of employees in a company that is in the midst of massive change.

However, there was one thing that put Nat's presentation over the top. He spoke from his heart.

It was clear to everybody in the audience that Nat not only knew his material, but that he really cared about what he was saying and how what he was saying impacted them. He told personal stories about his life and career. The strength of his talk was his willingness to share his humanity with the audience.

Nat Ricciardi is a great speaker and a dynamic communicator because he always speaks from his heart – whether he is speaking to one person or an audience of several hundred. He is truly genuine. You can't fake his genuineness. When you are in his presence, you know that you are with somebody who cares about what he does, and who cares about the people around him.

And that's the common sense career success coach point here. If you want to become a dynamic communicator, follow the career advice in Tweet 103 in Success Tweets. "Speak from your heart. Show that you care about yourself and the people with whom you are speaking." Make sure that the person with whom you are in conversation or the audience to whom you are speaking knows that you care about them as much as you care about what you are discussing or the information you are presenting. Here's some important career advice. Give people a glimpse of you as a person. Share your stories; your triumphs and failures, as well as your thoughts and feelings on your topic. Show that you care – about yourself, your material and the people to whom you are speaking — and other people will hang on your every word.

Success Tweet 104

Learn to handle yourself in conversation. A brief conversation with the right person can greatly help – or hinder – your career.

I've been looking over the transcripts of my old Internet radio show. I had some pretty interesting guests who said some pretty interesting things. Debra Fine, author of the best seller, *The Fine Art of Small Talk,* was one of my guests. We discussed how to become a good conversationalist.

Here is part of what Debra had to say...

Bud: What are some icebreakers or conversation starters that shy people – or anyone—can use to get a conversation going?

Debra: Don't be afraid to dig deeper. When you say to them "how's work?" they're going to say "pretty good" or "good" or "great" or whatever. Dig in deeper, let them know you're sincere with one more question, "So, what's been going on with work, Bud, since the last time we talked?" or if you say to somebody, "how were your holidays?" and they say "great," say "well, what did you do over the holidays that you enjoyed the most?" Let them know you are sincere, when you are sincere, when you have the time.

We say to our friends, "how are you, Bud?", "great", you got to follow up with something like, "Bud, bring me up-to-date – what's been going on in your life since the last time I saw you?" Now Bud knows I really want to know how he is, otherwise "how are you" means "hello". That's all it means. My own husband will walk into the house and say "how was your day?" and I'll say "pretty good" because my guess is my husband doesn't really want to know how my day is and this is my second husband, Bud, okay? And he doesn't want to know. But if he digs in deeper, I'll know that he was interested.

Okay, so that's just one tip. We don't want to become FBI agents; that's why that one following question is important, but no more after that. You don't want to do one of these numbers, "Bud, what do you do?" So, what's your answer to that, Bud?

Bud: Well, I'm a consultant, speaker, and right now, an Internet radio show host.

Debra: And, Bud, it sounds like you have an accent from back east, so what part of the country are you from?

Bud: Pittsburgh.

Debra: Look at what just happened. I said "what do you do, Bud?" and you said consultant, etc. and I said it sounds like you have an accent, like you're from back east or something and you responded to that. I became an FBI agent. That was the point of that little shtick. If you're going to start with "what do you do?" stay on topic.

Bud: You make a great point here. People get uncomfortable if you jump around in conversations because it gets them off balance, they don't know what's coming next. So if you begin a conversation by asking somebody about their job or career, ask a follow-up question about their job or career. I think this is tremendous advice — making sure that you follow up with a question that's on target, not something that goes off in another direction.

Debra: And I'm saying to you to make it an open-ended question. "Tell me about it, describe that for me, how was that like for you, how did you come up with that idea?" Everybody's got to use an open-ended question if at all possible so you can open up the conversation. Do we have a couple more minutes for another tip?

Bud: Yes, we do.

Debra: Okay, let's talk about the most common response to the question, "what's been going on in your life?" Do you know what most of us say to "what's been going on?"

Bud: Not much.

Debra: Exactly. That's exactly right. We say "not much" or "nothing." And I bet you would have said "not much" if I asked you that question because that's what first came out of your mouth just now when I asked that, and yet you told me I believe during a break that you're going to New York tomorrow.

I think there's a lot going on and "not much" is just a bunch of bologna, right? And that's how it is for all of us. We've all said "not much" and what we really mean is "there's so much going on, I can't possibly think of what it is so I'll just say not much". That's what we mean. There's just too much going on to think of what to say.

Now, if you're just walking down the hall and don't have time to stop and chat, a one-word answer like that is fine and dandy. But, if you'd like to connect at an annual conference when someone says to you "what's been going on?" please have an answer. It doesn't have to be an elevator speech, just an answer, "well, we just introduced flex time at our company and that's been a huge burden, but I feel like we've seen the worst of it, and we're going to get through it."

Now I have something to talk about with you, flex time. Like, how did you set it up, how does that impact you? Do you get three days off a week? I mean, give me something, it doesn't have to be mushy, it doesn't have to be about your divorce. Just give me something.

If you said to me, "Debra, how have you been?" I might say "well, I became an empty-nester this year and it's really been a whole new experience, and not a sad one, a good one and I've really enjoyed it." Now, did I brag about my kids? No. Did I go on and on about how perfect and gorgeous and wonderful they are? Absolutely not. I just let you know something about myself that I'm willing to talk about. If you're not interested, you'll go, "oh, Debra, good for you, let's talk about that contract… what do you think…?" You don't want to chit-chat, that's fine. Let's get down to the business at hand.

Bud: I think that's really great and that you're absolutely right. The point you're making here is that if you do go to an event and you're somebody who is not naturally able to roll things off the tip of your tongue, be prepared, because somebody's probably going to say to you, "what's going on, what's happening?"

Debra: Yes, and you get something else when you do this, Bud. You become a three-dimensional person. If you sell insurance, then you're a sales person who sells insurance. But if I ask you "how was your weekend?" and you say "it was pretty good, we went to the theater and saw Dr. Doolittle and it wasn't as bad as all the reviews said," you just became more than an insurance salesman, you became a human being in my mind. By saying that you went to a musical you became three-dimensional. You are not just a sales person; you are now a human being. Human beings go to shows called Dr. Doolittle.

Does that make sense? "How was your weekend?" "I worked in the garden, I played on my volleyball league, I finished a good book, I'm finishing my basement." That's all you have to say. You don't go on and on about it. Just give me a sentence.

Bud: A small bit of self-disclosure can be helpful and make it easy. Let me try to summarize… (A) When you enter a networking situation, put yourself out, introduce yourself to somebody. (B) When somebody introduces themselves to you, be three-dimensional. Do a little bit of self-disclosure. Be willing to say something about yourself.

Debra: Right.

Bud: One last thing, what do you do when all of a sudden there's dead silence in a conversation?

Debra: Well, you better be prepared. The worst time to think about something to talk about, Bud, is when there's nothing to talk about. So my rule for myself, and I wrote a book about it, is if I'm going to take you out to lunch and you're a customer or client, I've got two to three things in the back of my head ready to go just in case we have nothing to talk about. Maybe it's current events. Maybe it's something I already know about you. You have a wife, her name is Cathy, she used to be a flight attendant. Do you understand? Have some questions in the back of your head, to be able to keep conversations moving when there's that huge awkward silence. You've got to be prepared. It's not a big deal to be prepared. It takes one whole minute. It's not like a Yoga class.

That's some great common sense on becoming a great conversationalist from Debra Fine, author of *The Fine Art of Small Talk*.

The common sense career success coach point here is clear. Successful people are dynamic communicators. Dynamic communicators are great conversationalists. Great conversationalists know how to begin conversations and keep them going. They follow the career advice in Tweet 104 in Success Tweets. "Learn how to handle yourself in conversation. A brief conversation with the right person can greatly help – or hinder –

your career." Questions are a great way to open conversations. Use open-ended, not yes or no, questions. Follow up with a comment or a question that follows in the same vein. When someone asks you a question, become three-dimensional by being willing to disclose something about yourself as a person. If you know who you are going to be seeing, think back to the last time you saw that person. Think about what you discussed. Keep these things in the back of your mind. They can help you prevent awkward silences in your conversation.

Success Tweet 105

Conversation tips: be warm, pleasant, gracious and sensitive to the interpersonal needs and anxieties of others.

How you start conversation is very important if you want to be seen as warm, pleasant, gracious and sensitive to others. Several years ago I read an eBook by Dennis Rivers called, *Cooperative Communication Skills for Success at Home and at Work*. I came across the eBook in my files the other day. Chapter 2 really caught my attention. It is entitled, "Explaining Your Conversational Intent and Inviting Consent." Dennis makes some common sense, but seldom seen, points about conversation skills in it. In summary, he says, "Make sure that you tell the other person what type of conversation you want to have. Ask him or her if he or she is ready to have this type of conversation at that time."

Check out some of what he has to say...

> In order to help your conversation partner cooperate with you and to reduce possible misunderstandings, start important conversations by inviting your conversation partner to join you in the specific kind of conversation you want to have. The more the conversation is going to mean to you, the more important it is for your conversation partner to understand the big picture. If you need to have a long, complex, or emotion-laden conversation with someone, it will make a big difference if you briefly explain your conversational intention first and then invite the consent of your intended conversation partner.

> Why explain? Some conversations require a lot more time, effort and involvement than others. If you want to have a conversation that will require a significant amount of effort from the other person, it will go better if that person understands what he or she is getting into and consents to participate. Of course, in giving up the varying amounts of coercion and surprise that are at work when we just launch into whatever we want to talk about, we are more vulnerable to being turned down. But, when people agree to talk with us, they will be more present in the conversation and more able to either meet our needs or explain why they can't (and perhaps suggest alternatives we had not thought of). Many good communicators do this explaining intent/inviting consent without giving it any thought. They start important conversations by saying

things such as: "Hi, Steve. I need to ask for your help on my project. Got a minute to talk about it?" "Maria, do you have a minute? Right now I'd like to talk to you about... Is that OK?"

When we offer such combined explanations of intent and invitations-to-consent we can help our conversations along in four important ways:

First, we give our listeners a chance to consent to or decline the offer of a specific conversation. A person who has agreed to participate will participate more fully.

Second, we help our listeners to understand the "big picture," the overall goal of the conversation-to-come. Many scholars in linguistics and communication studies now agree that understanding a person's overall conversational intention is crucial for understanding that person's message in words and gestures.

Third, we allow our listeners to get ready for what is coming, especially if the topic is emotionally charged. (If we surprise people by launching into emotional conversations, they may respond by avoiding further conversations with us or by being permanently on guard.)

And fourth, we help our listeners understand the role that we want them to play in the conversation: fellow problem solver, employee receiving instructions, giver of emotional support, and so on. These are very different roles to play. Our conversations will go better if we ask people to play only one conversational role at a time.

To be invited into a conversation is an act of respect. A consciously consenting participant is much more likely to pay attention and cooperate than someone who feels pushed into an undefined conversation by the force of another person's talking.

It's not universal, but to assume without asking that a person is available to talk may be interpreted by many people as lack of respect. When we begin a conversation by respecting the wishes of the other person, we start to generate some of the goodwill (trust that their wishes will be considered) needed for creative problem solving. I believe that the empathy we get will be more genuine and the agreements we reach will be more reliable if we give people a choice about talking with us.

The common sense career success coach point here is simple. Successful people are dynamic communicators. Dynamic communicators follow the career advice in Tweet 105 in Success Tweets. "Conversation tips: be warm, pleasant, gracious and sensitive to the interpersonal needs and anxieties of others." Inviting people to participate in a conversation and getting their agreement before jumping in is an important, but often overlooked conversation skill. People who are invited to join a conversation and choose to do so are more likely to be better participants. If you want to become an excellent conversationalist, take a few minutes to explain why you want to have a conversation. Ask the other person if he or she has the time and is willing to participate in a conversation on that topic. Your conversations will be better and more productive if you follow this simple common sense advice.

Success Tweet 106

Demonstrate your understanding of others' points of view. Listen well and ask questions if you don't understand.

My friend, Pamela Culpepper, gave me an interesting book a couple of years ago: *Turning to One Another: Simple Conversations to Restore Hope for the Future.* Margaret Wheatley is the author. Dr. Wheatley is an alumna of one of my alma maters – the Harvard Graduate School of Education (we both did our doctoral work there) and the author of one of the most innovative leadership books I've ever read, *Leadership and the New Science.* If you haven't read it, I suggest that you check it out.

In *Turning to One Another*, Dr. Wheatley outlines six points for effective conversation. Notice how, in one way or another, all six focus on being a better listener.

1. Acknowledge one another as equals.
2. Stay curious about one another.
3. Recognize that we need each other's help to become better listeners.
4. Slow down to have the time to think and reflect.
5. Remember that conversation is the natural way for humans to think together.
6. Expect it to be messy at times.

Here is my take on these six common sense points.

1. Acknowledge one another as equals. You cannot have a good conversation if you don't recognize one another as equals. Regardless of your hierarchical relation to the other person – if he or she is your boss, peer or subordinate – remember that we are all human beings. As such, we are entitled to respect and dignity. Talk with people, not to them and you'll be surprised at the quality of your discussions.
2. Stay curious about one another. People are fascinating. I have had some of the most interesting conversations with limo and cab drivers. Often they are immigrants. It's interesting to hear their take on life in the USA. Be curious about the people you know, too. People are always growing and changing. When you express your curiosity you'll be bound to find out new and interesting things about old friends and acquaintances.
3. Recognize that we need each other's help to become better listeners. Help others listen. Think before you speak. Speak clearly. Ask them questions;

answer the questions they ask you. Remember, communication in general and conversation in particular is a process fraught with potential misconnects. So listen hard to others and make it easy for them to listen to you.

4. Slow down to have the time to think and reflect. When you slow down, you do indeed have time to think. Don't be afraid to pause and reflect on a question. This shows the other person that you are carefully considering your response – not just saying the first thing that comes to mind. Other people will appreciate you for your thoughtfulness, not knock you for not being quick or clever enough.

5. Remember that conversation is the natural way for humans to think together. I love this one – "conversation is the natural way for humans to think together." The idea of "thinking together" is great career advice. The world would be a better place if we all "thought together" instead of thinking separately and trying to convince others that our thoughts are better than theirs. Since this is the season, I would love to see political debates where the candidates worked together to develop an approach to handling a problem or issue – instead of watching them advance their ideas while taking swipes at the other person's ideas.

6. Expect it to be messy at times. Conversation is messy. That's OK. In fact, I think it's great. Some of the best ideas come out of messy conversations. The willingness to get into the mess and slop around is what frees your creativity.

I really like *Turning to One Another*. It provides some great career advice on conversation and listening. If you're interested in becoming a better conversationalist – and you should be – pick it up, read it and think about what Dr. Wheatley has to say. More important, put her ideas to use.

The common sense career success coach point here is simple. Successful people are great conversationalists. They follow the advice in Tweet 106 in Success Tweets. "Demonstrate your understanding of others' points of view. Listen well and ask questions if you don't understand." Listening takes a little bit of work, but it is worth it in the long run. It will help you become a dynamic communicator and build solid relationships that will fuel your life and career success. Remember Meg Wheatley's six points for conversation success. They are great career advice. 1) Acknowledge one another as equals; 2) Stay curious about one another; 3) Recognize that we need each other's help to become better listeners; 4) Slow down to have the time to think and reflect; 5) Remember that conversation is the natural way for humans to think together; 6) Expect it to be messy at times.

Success Tweet 107

Become an excellent conversationalist by listening more than speaking. Pay attention to what other people say; respond appropriately.

If you want to become a dynamic communicator, you need to develop three skills: conversation, writing and presenting. The Merriam Webster Dictionary defines the word "dynamic" as, "Marked by continuous and productive activity." In many ways, this is a good definition for an effective conversation. In a conversation, two types of activities occur simultaneously: speaking and listening. In good conversations, both of these are continuous and productive. In plain English, when you're in a conversation, if you're not speaking and providing information, you need to be listening and receiving it.

In other posts I've pointed out that asking good questions is an important way to become known as a great conversationalist. But to take full advantage of the questions you ask, you need to really listen to the answers and respond appropriately.

Here are my top seven tips for becoming a good listener – and conversationalist.

1. Look the other person in the eye when he or she is speaking. This demonstrates that you are engaged with him or her.
2. Listen to understand what the other person is saying – not to plan your rebuttal.
3. Listen really hard when the other person begins by saying something with which you don't agree.
4. Know the words that trigger your emotions. Don't get distracted by them.
5. Be patient. Some people take longer than others to make their point. Don't interrupt.
6. Ask clarification questions when you don't understand.
7. Repeat what you have heard the other person say – to make sure you got it right, and to show him or her that you were listening.

If you use these seven tips in conversation, you will become known as a great conversationalist and a dynamic communicator.

The common sense career success coach point here is simple. Successful people are competent. Dynamic communication is an important key success competency. If you want to become a dynamic communicator, you have to become a good conversationalist. To become a good conversationalist, follow the career advice in

Tweet 107 in Success Tweets. "Become an excellent conversationalist by listening more than speaking. Pay attention to what other people say; respond appropriately." Learn to listen well. Listening, like a lot of career success advice, is just common sense. Show the other person you are engaged. Focus on understanding, not on rebutting points with which you don't agree. Don't get distracted by words that trigger your emotions. Ask clarification questions to ensure you understand what is being said. Repeat what you've heard. Most of all, get in the habit of listening more than speaking.

Success Tweet 108

Live people take precedence over phone calls. Continue in-person, face-to-face conversations, rather than answering your cell phone.

I am really sorry that Women's Edge Magazine is no longer with us. I used to find a lot of great career advice and wisdom in its pages. The January 2008 issue of Women's Edge made two great quotes that relate to the career advice in Success Tweet 108.

- "Communicate respect in every encounter with every person, regardless of position or background." Robyn Hall, Raleigh Police Department
- "Listen and speak at the same time, meaning that you actively engage people with your full attention." Judy Fourie, J. Fourie & Company

These are two pieces of great common sense career success advice. They will help you become known as an interpersonally competent person.

Focusing on live people – rather than your electronic gadgets – is the best way to demonstrate your respect for others. Respect is the key to building strong relationships with the people in your life – not just those who can do something for you, but everyone you meet. Cathy, my wife, is a good example of this. She makes friends with everyone, because she treats everyone with respect. The dry cleaner, pharmacy clerks, mailman, paper delivery guy, our housekeeper, all love her because she treats them with the respect they deserve as fellow human beings. She is genuinely interested in them as people. This interest communicates her respect for them.

Many people show a lot of respect for people above them in the hierarchy, and little respect for those below them. This is too bad. Often people below you can do as much or more for you than those above you. But that's not the point. The point is that they're people too, and as such, are entitled to your respect.

The Optimist Creed has some great things to say about respect. It encourages us to, "Promise yourself to make all your friends feel as if there is something in them...and to give every living creature you meet a smile." If you want a copy of The Optimist Creed to hang in your office, go to http://BudBilanich.com/optimist.

The second quote is interesting for what it has to say about human interaction. I like the idea of "listening and speaking at the same time." In other words, as you engage someone, listen very carefully to what he or she has to say so you can respond appropriately. What you say should be directly related to what he or she has just said. This demonstrates that you are listening. It also demonstrates that you value what he or she says – a great way to show someone that you respect him or her.

Being fully engaged means that you shut out the distractions of the world and focus your attention on the person with whom you're having a conversation. People tell me that I seem to never answer my cell phone. This is true. I tell people that my cell phone is not a good way to contact me because it is usually off. My cell phone is usually off because I am often in conversations with my clients. I don't want the distraction of a ringing or vibrating cell phone when I'm trying to concentrate on another person and what he or she is saying.

The two quotes at the beginning of this post are complementary. One of the best ways to show others that you respect them is to engage them. One of the best ways to engage people is to listen to what they say and respond appropriately. If you keep these two pieces of common sense in mind as you meet people, you'll be on your way to becoming known as an interpersonally competent person.

The common sense career success coach point here is simple. Demonstrate your respect for other people by paying attention to them and what they have to say. Follow the career advice in Tweet 108 in Success Tweets. "Live people take precedence over phone calls. Continue in-person, face-to-face conversations, rather than answering your cell phone." Focusing on live people – rather than your electronic gadgets – is the best way to demonstrate your respect for others. Respect is the key to building strong relationships with the people in your life – not just those who can do something for you, but everyone you meet.

Success Tweet 109

Use the 2/3 – 1/3 rule. Listen two-thirds of the time; speak one-third of the time. Focus your complete attention on the other person.

Listening to others and then responding appropriately is one of my first rules for becoming an outstanding conversationalist. I always urge my career success coach clients to do three things when they are in conversation: 1) Ask lots of questions; 2) Really listen to what the other person is saying; 3) Respond appropriately; Laugh if the person says something funny. Commiserate if the person reveals something that is sad. Make sure the other person knows you are tuned in and paying attention.

Most people like to talk about themselves. That's why listening is so important. You can gain a reputation as a great conversationalist – even if you don't say much. Listening is that important. That's why the 2/3 – 1/3 rule is such great career advice.

Of course, adding your thoughts to the conversation doesn't hurt – as long as you keep them focused on what the other person is saying. If you absolutely need to change the subject, let him or her know. Say something like, "I understand and appreciate what you're saying. If we're done with that topic, I need to speak with you about something else. OK?" In that way, you're demonstrating your respect for the other person.

In her great book, *CEO Material*, my friend Debra Benton has a lot to say about listening and conversation. Here is a small sample…

> "The best way to influence others is with your ears. If you listen in a way that causes people to feel heard, you'll hear things right the first time, maintain the self-esteem of others, build better relationships, see nuances.

> "Shut out other people and distractions, and stop thinking about what anyone else is thinking or your response. Take off your headphones, stop texting, turn off your cell phone, put away your Blackberry. Don't doodle; fidget with your hands, arms or fingers; squirm; body rock; or get up and move around (like you have ADD). Instead, lean forward, tilt your head a little, give some eye contact, and maybe throw in a brow furrow, don't glance around or act bored, disbelieving, or disagreeing. Just listen to the person who is talking, remember what he or she says, and say some of it back to that person later.

"Don't quit listening if you don't like what you're hearing. Pay attention to complete information. Try to make sense of the data, even if you don't agree. Not every misguided opinion needs to be corrected by you. Pick your battles, as they say. You'll create calm for both of you — and the other person will more likely listen to you also."

That is not only great advice on listening. It's great career advice as well.

The common sense career success coach point here is simple. Successful people are dynamic communicators. Conversation skills are one key to becoming a dynamic communicator. Follow the career advice in Tweet 109 in Success Tweets. "Use the 1/3 – 2/3 rule. Listen two-thirds of the time; speak one-third of the time. Focus your complete attention on the other person." Listening is at the heart of being a good conversationalist. If you want to become known as a good conversationalist, do three things: 1) Ask lots of questions; 2) Really listen to what the other person is saying; 3) Respond appropriately. If you make sure the other person knows you are tuned in and paying attention, you'll be able to conduct a productive conversation with just about anyone you meet, become known as a dynamic communicator, and be on your way to the life and career success you want and deserve.

Success Tweet 110

Remember and use people's names. Look for common ground with the people you meet. Find out about them, their hobbies and passions.

If you want to create the career success you want and deserve, get good at networking. Learn how to engage others quickly and leave a positive, lasting impression. Dressing well and paying attention to your appearance is a great start. However, great networkers know that looking good is only one piece of the puzzle.

The second piece is simple: Remember people's names. Check out what Dale Carnegie has to say about remembering names...

> "If you remember my name, you pay me a subtle compliment; you indicate that I have made an impression on you. Remember my name and you add to my feeling of importance."

This is great career advice.

Shakespeare also chimes in on the importance of remembering other people's names...

> "What a disgrace it is to me to not remember thy name."

That's true too. We disgrace ourselves when we don't remember other people's names. It shows that we value them very little. I work hard at remembering people's names and using them.

If you read my blog, you probably know that I went to Penn State. Joe Paterno was the football coach when I arrived there in 1968. He's still the coach today. Joe is quite a guy, and he is good with names.

Several years ago, I was in New York. It was the day after the ESPYs had been held at Radio City Music Hall. I was walking along Sixth Avenue when I came face to face with Joe Paterno. He had won an ESPY the night before.

I looked him in the eye, and said "Joe." He stopped. I introduced myself – "Bud Bilanich, class of '72." He said, "How are you doing, Bud?" Our conversation lasted about 10 minutes. Joe probably used my name at least 10 times in that conversation.

He said things like, "You know Bud…", and "When was the last time you were in State College, Bud?, and "What are you doing in New York, Bud?"

I know that he was repeating my name so that he could remember it. And at the same time, I felt good about the fact that a famous football coach not only took the time to chat with me on a cold windy street corner in New York, he went out of his way to remember and use my name.

Remembering people's names is an important networking tool. People who are a career success are good at networking. They know how to engage others quickly and leave a positive, lasting impression. Dressing well and paying attention to your appearance is a great start. However, great networkers know that looking good is only one piece of the puzzle. Remembering people's names is the second part of the puzzle.

Here are my four best ideas on becoming a great networker…

> ***Stay focused on the person with whom you are in a conversation***. Many people let their eyes wander – especially at networking events. When you do this, you are sending a message to the person with whom you are speaking that he or she is less important than someone else you might spot in the crowd. It's not only polite, it's good business sense to focus on the person in front of you. Exchange business cards before you move on to speak with someone else.

> ***Listen and respond appropriately to people you meet.*** Maintain eye contact. Ask questions if you don't understand what they say. Paraphrase what they say to make sure you understand. Above all, respond appropriately – don't take the conversation in a new direction until the topic under discussion has been exhausted.

> ***Build relationships with people you meet by being helpful.*** Take the initiative. Give them leads that may help them. Last week, Helen Whelan, CEO of SuccessTelevision.com, sent me an email letting me know about a public relations opportunity. I thanked Helen and followed up on the opportunity. I also sent it to two people I know who may be better suited than me. Why? Because I wanted to strengthen my relationships with them – and what better way to build strong relationships than by giving something of value to other people.

Learn from as many people as you can. Everybody has something to offer. With some people you have to dig a little more deeply than with others. Regardless, treat every conversation as a learning opportunity. The more you listen, the more you'll learn.

The common sense career success coach point here is simple. Successful people create positive personal impact. Networking is a great way to create a powerful lasting impression. When you are networking, follow the career advice in Tweet 110 in Success Tweets. "Remember and use people's names. Look for common ground with the people you meet. Find out about them, their hobbies and passions." Besides remembering people's names, you will create positive personal impact in networking situations if you: 1) stay focused on the person with whom you are engaged in conversation; 2) listen and respond appropriately; 3) build relationships by being helpful; and 4) learn from as many people as you can.

Success Tweet 111

Become a clear, concise writer. Make your writing easy to read and understand. Use simple, straightforward language.

Clear, concise writing is one of three important communication skills. Here are four enemies of clear, concise writing.

- Too many words.
- Passive voice.
- Polysyllabic (big) words.
- Jargon and cliches.

In this post, I'll show you how to avoid these problems.

Too Many Words

I write in a pretty straightforward, clear manner. However, when I reread my writing, I usually find that I need to cut, rather than add words. Here are some sentences that I've picked out of some of the business correspondence I've received lately. All of them have too many words. Below, you will find the wordy sentence, followed by my suggested rewrite.

Wordy Sentence: At this point in time, we should, or perhaps I should say we must, proceed to examine our policy of sales incentives.

Rewrite: We need to examine our sales incentive policy now.

Wordy Sentence: I was unaware of the fact that your device could be used for security purposes.

Rewrite: I didn't know your device could be used for security.

Wordy Sentence: The reason I failed to reply is that I was not apprised of the fact until yesterday that somehow the report had been unavoidably delayed.

Rewrite: I didn't reply because I didn't know until yesterday that the report was delayed.

You can see that I was able to cut down the length of each sentence without changing the meaning. If you want to become a clear, concise writer, work hard at eliminating unnecessary words. Carefully read what you write, and ruthlessly cut any words that don't add to your message. You should use the exact number of words you need to accurately and completely get your message across – no more, no less.

Passive Voice

The active voice is always better than the passive voice. It is more forceful and direct. Here are some examples that illustrate my point.

Passive Voice: Plans for the conference will be made by my assistant.

Active Voice: My assistant will plan the conference.

Passive Voice: An error has been discovered by our staff.

Active Voice: Our staff discovered an error.

Passive Voice: The mistake in billing was rectified by the supplier posthaste.

Active Voice: The supplier corrected the billing mistake quickly.

Polysyllabic Words

Sometimes, it's tempting to show off your vocabulary. Unfortunately, when you're showing off, you're probably not doing a good job of communicating. When my niece graduated from college, I gave her a copy of my just published book, *Straight Talk for Success*. I told her that I was trying for an "avuncular hip" tone, and asked her for her feedback once she read the book.

She looked at me and said, "What does avuncular mean?" I said, "Uncle-like." She said, "Why didn't you just say so?" She had a great point. She's no dummy, graduated magna cum laude and has gone on to some great career success early on. However, she didn't know what the word "avuncular" meant. Whose problem was that? Mine. I should have used the most easy to understand word; in this case that was two words, "uncle-like."

I don't watch a lot of TV, but I used to enjoy *Law and Order* – especially when Jack McCoy was the Assistant DA. "Hubris" was one of Jack's favorite words in his jury summations. I remember watching some shows where he used this word and wondered why he didn't say "arrogance." They mean the same, and more people are likely to know the word "arrogance" than know the word "hubris."

Several years ago, I read Stephen King's book, *On Writing*. He is a big proponent of small, easy to understand words. To illustrate his point about small words, he shared a passage from John Steinbeck's **The Grapes of Wrath** – one of my all time favorite novels.

> "Some of the owner men were kind because they hated what they had to do, and some of them were angry because they hated to be cruel, and some of them were cold because they had long ago found that one could not be an owner unless one were cold."

That's a 50-word sentence with 39 one-syllable words and 11 two-syllable words. If you've read the book, you know how well this writing explains the lives of itinerant workers during the great depression. The career advice here is simple. Read over what you write, strike the polysyllabic (I mean big) words, and you'll communicate better.

Jargon and Cliches

Finally, eliminate jargon and clichés from your writing. Don't assume that everyone who will read what you write is as up on jargon as you are.

You might not believe me when I say that I don't watch a lot of TV, as I have another great example from a TV show. If you spend any time on the Internet – especially Twitter – you know what the expression "wtf?" means. Cathy really likes the show, Modern Family. It won a couple of Emmys this past year. I think it is pretty funny too.

In one of the episodes, the father was trying to show his teenage daughters that he was pretty cool and with it. He said something like, "I know about these Internet abbreviations…. omg – Oh My God, lol – laugh out loud, wtf – why the face?" Remember, some of your readers may be as clueless about things you take for granted as the father on Modern Family.

Cliches are another problem for clear writing. If "it goes without saying," don't say it in writing. When you say, "To be perfectly honest..." I wonder if you're usually not honest in what you say. Read your writing carefully for clichés. Cut them.

The common sense career success coach point here is simple. Follow the career advice in Tweet 111 in Success Tweets. "Become a clear, concise writer. Make your writing easy to read and understand. Use simple, straightforward language." Reading what you write is the key to following this career advice. When you read your writing, look for words that you can eliminate and for ways to use the active, rather than passive voice. If you put these two common sense pieces of career advice to work, your writing will improve greatly.

Success Tweet 112

Explain jargon as you go along; or provide a glossary at the end of the document. Better yet, avoid jargon if at all possible.

A couple of years ago, the Money section of USA Today had an interesting article called, *Do Foreign Executives Balk at Sports Jargon*?

Author Del Jones began by saying, "English may be the international language of business, but foreign executives who are fluent in it find themselves at a loss unless they master conversational horsehide and the vocabulary of other US sports." "Conversational horsehide", by the way, is jargon for the ability to use baseball terms in conversation.

She wrote about how baseball jargon has infiltrated business conversation in the USA. As we are getting close to the baseball playoffs and World Series, I thought I'd use her article to illustrate how much we use sports jargon in the USA and how this can have a negative impact on our ability to communicate both in writing and conversation.

People who are not familiar with US sports – and that includes a lot of people born in the US – suffer from sports jargon overload. Del Jones article was very entertaining, and it had an important message for anyone who wants to become a good communicator – use jargon, especially sports jargon, as little as possible in everyday conversation and business writing.

I agree. I learned this lesson the hard way. I was conducting a workshop in Europe that I had conducted very successfully in the US. The workshop began with a baseball analogy – one has to go from first to second to third base before scoring a run. While most of the people in the European audience understood the concept and the reference, many were upset that an American would use a uniquely American example when conducting a workshop in Europe.

Paula Shannon, a Senior VP with Lionbridge, a Massachusetts-based company with 4,000 employees in 25 countries, knows what I'm talking about. She says, "The Hail Mary (American football jargon) is my favorite example of bad jargon. You can establish your American-centricity, and risk a religious offense at the same time."

The common sense career advice here is simple. In order to become a great communicator, limit your use of jargon. Converse, write and present in easily and universally understood terms. Be precise in your use of language.

Having said that, I am going to post the baseball/business dictionary Ms. Jones included in a sidebar to her article – just because I think it's fun...

Baseball – Business Dictionary

Manufacture a run

Baseball: Scoring without power, or even a solid hit. For example, a walk, followed by a stolen base, an error and a squeeze play. Also called small ball.
Business: Succeeding via hard work; growing sales without a blockbuster product.

Late innings

Baseball: The seventh, eighth and ninth innings of a baseball game.
Business: Late stages of a project; an old product seeing sales eroding due to a competitor's new product.

Step up to the plate

Baseball: Take your turn at bat, often in an important situation.
Business: Confront a problem, make a crucial decision, go the extra mile when it's safer or more convenient not to.

Pickle

Baseball: A rundown, catching a runner stranded between bases.
Business: Getting into trouble with little chance of escape.

Can of corn

Baseball: A fly ball that is easy to catch.
Business: A decision or action that is a no-brainer; a product that sells itself.

Ducks on the pond

Baseball: Runners on base.
Business: A situation with a good chance of success.

Curve

Baseball: A pitch that breaks before it gets to the plate.
Business: Anything unexpected.

All bases covered

Baseball: Fielders doing their job and positioned on relevant bases so the team can get an out.
Business: Being prepared for every contingency.

Mop up

Baseball: When a mediocre relief pitcher is used because the outcome of the game is certain.
Business: When employees have to remain on projects after star employees have moved on to bigger and better things.

Homer, dinger, tater

Baseball: Home runs of various types.
Business: Major accomplishment.

O-fer

Baseball: When a batter goes hitless.
Business: Slump with poor results.

If you're a baseball fan, you may disagree with some of the definitions in this dictionary. And that is one of the reasons I've included it here – to include a graphic depiction of the problem with jargon.

I remember reading a column in an airline in flight magazine on jargon. Even though it's been several years, I still remember this column. The author began by saying that he has a folder of memos with obtuse language that he has collected over the years. He shared one memo that a friend sent to him. I was so struck by the language that I saved it on my hard drive. The guy who wrote the memo said he was going to "map the handoffs and all processes in a combined swim lanes uber-process." I'm pretty hip to a lot of business jargon as I see it every day. However, I must admit that "swim lanes uber-process" is a new one on me.

As I'm writing this, I'm reminded of an IBM commercial I saw a while back. A guy walks into a large, dimly lighted conference room where he sees no tables and chairs and about twenty people lying on the floor. He says, "What are you guys doing?" Someone answers, "We're ideating." He says, "What's that?" Someone responds, "Coming up with new ways of doing things." He says, "Why don't you just call it that?"

Interestingly enough, the word ideating sounds a lot like a made-up word to me. I expected spell check to flag it. It didn't. So I guess I am behind the times on some of my business jargon. Even so, I think saying that you're "Coming up with new ways of doing things," is much more clear than saying that you're "Ideating." But what do I know?

The common sense career success coach point here is simple. Jargon causes communication problems. Successful people follow the career advice in Success Tweet 112. "Explain jargon as you go along; or provide a glossary at the end of the document. Better yet, avoid jargon if at all possible." Don't assume that everybody who reads what you write will be as familiar with jargon as you. Make your writing clear, concise and readable – that means as little jargon as possible.

Success Tweet 113

Write clearly and simply: short words and sentences, first person, active voice. Be precise in your choice of words.

Good writing will set you apart and put you on the road to personal and professional success. Unsuccessful people are poor writers. They are unclear. They ramble. Their emails, letters and reports are a series of long sentences filled with big words that don't really say anything. You can't catch people's attention by writing this way. You need to write in a clear, crisp, concise manner.

I try to write like a journalist. I use short sentences with a simple subject-verb-object structure. My writing may read a little staccato-like, but it communicates. People tell me that they can understand my points and the reasoning behind them. And that's what I want when I write.

Your objective in writing at work is to communicate – not to impress others with your vocabulary. In a recent post I mentioned the time I was speaking with my niece about my book "Straight Talk for Success" at her college graduation party; I said that I'd tried for an "avuncular hip" writing style. She said, "What does that mean?" I replied, "Avuncular means uncle-like. I wanted to sound like a hip uncle to people reading the book." She came back with a great question: "Why didn't you just say so?"

She was right. Everybody knows what "uncle-like" means. A lot of people, including magna cum laude graduates like my niece, don't know the word "avuncular." I was just showing off my vocabulary by using that word. As a result, I didn't communicate effectively.

Write with your reader in mind. Sometimes it's a good idea to read aloud what you've written to get a feel for how it will sound to your reader. Write in short, simple sentences. Use the simplest words you can to get across your point, while still being accurate. Write fast. Get your thoughts on paper or the computer screen as quickly as you can. Then edit and rewrite until you've said exactly what you want to say. One of my first bosses always told me that rewriting is the secret to good writing.

Spelling counts, too. Correct spelling does two things for you. First, it shows that you have a good command of the language. Second, and more important, correct spelling demonstrates that you respect both yourself and the reader. Misspelled words stand out like sore thumbs to readers.

Don't just spell check your documents. Proof them. Spellcheck often won't pick up improper usage in words like "your" and "you're," "hear" and "here," and "their" and "there."

The same holds true for punctuation. Make sure that you know how to properly use periods, question marks, commas, colons, semicolons, exclamation marks, quotation marks and apostrophes. If you're not sure about punctuation rules, spend a little time on the Internet learning proper usage.

I like the Poynter Institute for good information about writing. While the information on their site www.poynter.org is aimed at journalists, there is a lot of very helpful information about writing and editing there – especially in the article in "Tip Sheets" which can be found by clicking on the "Reporting, Writing and Editing" button.

This brings me to the Bafflegab Thesaurus. I first saw the Bafflegab Thesaurus back in the 1970s. It's made a comeback lately, only this time it's called "Buzzwords for Business Writing." Whatever you choose to call it, it's very clever, and it points out just how much jargon has taken over business communication and how few people write clearly and simply.

Here's how it works. When you're stuck in your writing, the Business Writing Buzzword Generator helps you create phrases that will make you sound as if you know what you're talking about, even if – no, especially when – you don't.

It's simple. Think of any three-digit number, then select the corresponding buzzword from each column and you're done.

COLUMN I	COLUMN II	COLUMN III
0. Integrated	0. Management	0. Options
1. Heuristic	1. Organizational	1. Flexibility
2. Systematized	2. Monitored	2. Capability
3. Parallel	3. Reciprocal	3. Mobility
4. Functional	4. Digital	4. Programming
5. Responsive	5. Logistical	5. Scenarios
6. Optional	6. Transitional	6. Time-phase
7. Synchronized	7. Incremental	7. Projection
8. Compatible	8. Third-generation	8. Hardware
9. Futuristic	9. Policy	9. Contingency

The creator of the Business Buzzword Generator provides this example...

> "The three-digit number 257 produces 'systematized logistical projection.' You can drop this phrase into almost any report. It has a ring of decisive, knowledgeable authority. Of course, no one will have the remotest idea of what you're talking about. But that's OK. The important thing is, they are not about to admit it."

Realize that I'm joking here. While "systematized logistical projection" may sound good, it really means nothing. The best writers use small words, simple sentences, and the active voice. Never use this buzzword generator in your business communication. But you can have fun reading the writing of some people who appear to have used it.

The common sense point here is simple. Successful people are dynamic communicators. If you want to become a dynamic communicator, you need to develop your writing skills. Follow the career advice in Success Tweet 113. "Write clearly and simply: short words and sentences, first person, active voice. Be precise in your choice of words." Writing is not difficult if you write in a manner that communicates well. In general, this means, being clear, concise and easily readable. Use short sentences and the smallest word that communicates exactly what you want to say. Write with your reader in mind. Read your writing aloud before sending it. This will help you get a feel for what your reader will experience.

Success Tweet 114

Use the active voice in your writing. Say "I suggest we do this," rather than "It is suggested that…"

When you use the active voice, your writing and you come across as strong, forceful and self-confident. If you need a grammar refresher, in the active voice the subject of the sentence does something. Go back to the tweet. In the first example, "I" is the subject of the sentence. To continue with the example, I does something, he or she suggests doing this…

Think of the title of the Marvin Gaye song, "I heard it through the Grapevine." It is in the active voice. I (the subject) heard (the verb) it (the object).

The passive voice is just the opposite. In the passive voice, the target of the action is the subject. In some cases, this makes no sense. No one would be likely to write, "It through the grapevine I heard." The passive voice tends to use more words, and can confuse the reader. And, you can come across as a weasel when you use the passive voice.

I'm old enough to remember the Iran-Contra affair. When speaking about it, President Reagan said, "Mistakes were made." The problem with this sentence is that it begs the question of who made the mistakes. This sentence would be stronger if it read, "I made a mistake." Or, "This administration made a mistake." Of course, in this case the active voice may not have been the best to use politically.

As I'm writing this, I think I may be over-complicating things. The English Department at Purdue University does a good job of providing examples of the active and passive voice…

Active Voice: The dog bit the boy.

Passive Voice: The boy was bitten by the dog.

Active Voice: Scientists conducted experiments to test the hypothesis.

Passive Voice: The hypothesis was tested in experiments conducted by scientists.

Active Voice: Over one-third of the applicants failed the entrance exam.

Passive Voice: The entrance exam was failed by over one-third of the applicants.

Active Voice: The committee is considering the bill.

Passive Voice: The bill is being considered by the committee.

When you write in the active voice – especially when you use the first person "I" – you come across as strong, forceful and self-confident. Your writing is clear. It communicates better.

In conclusion, it is suggested by this writer that the active voice should be used in your writing. Just kidding. I'll give a copy of the eBook version of my book, *I Want YOU…To Succeed* to everybody who rewrites the sentence immediately preceding this one in the active voice. Please share your rewrites as a comment.

The common sense career success coach point here is simple. If you want to write well and clearly, follow the career advice in Tweet 114 in Success Tweets. "Use the active voice in your writing. Say 'I suggest we do this,' rather than 'It is suggested that…'" The active voice is almost always more clear. It makes your writing easier to understand. And, when you write in the active voice you come across as self-confident and in command of your subject.

Success Tweet 115

Become an excellent presenter. Careers have been made on the strength of one or two good presentations.

Darren Hardy is the Publisher of SUCCESS Magazine. I love SUCCESS. It is full of very useful and usable information every month. If you aren't already a subscriber, go to www.success.com as soon as you finish reading this post and do so. A subscription to SUCCESS will put you on the road to the life and career success you want and deserve.

Darren also sends very informative emails to subscribers. A while back he posted a great piece covering his best tips for delivering dynamite presentations. He was gracious enough to allow me to repost it here...

Darren Hardy's 10 Tips for More Compelling Presentations:

1. Prepare. Nothing beats great preparation. I usually write out a presentation word for word, then I reduce it to a skeleton outline, then bullet points, then just key words on paper in case I need to quickly glance down at trigger words to guide me along, but I will rarely use the notes. Just going through the process is my process for learning the presentation.

2. Know your audience. Find out the demographic mix of the audience. Find out who the key players are so you can use their names during the presentation. Understand core aspects about their company, cause, products, ideals, etc. Understand the trends, competition and key issues that the audience faces. If they know you know who they are in the first few minutes, they will be your ally for the rest of the presentation.

3. Sell it. Not necessarily you or what you are promoting, sell your presentation. Open up with an attention getter. Imagine the format of an infomercial. Explain the grand benefits they are going to get by listening raptly to the information you are about to share.

4. Package it. Tell them what you are going to tell them (through benefits, outcomes, the difference this information will make in their lives), tell them (deliver the goods), then tell them what you told them (post-sell the benefits so they know you have just given them great value).

5. Be entertaining. Yes, you need to be informative and enlightening, but you are talking to humans—they are bored easily. If people are entertained, they are engaged and are more apt to actually listen to what you are saying.

6. Be visual. I think in pictures, so I talk in pictures. I use visual aids and talk in word pictures and metaphors. People seldom recall words, but they do remember pictures.

7. Tell stories. I am not a natural storyteller. I have to force myself to break off and tell a story, but the best speakers, lecturers and influencers the world has known were all great storytellers. Collect them and get good at telling them. BUT, make sure they are relevant to the point you are making. I dislike gratuitous storytelling for stories' sake in a keynote. I can read a book or go to a movie for that. Make sure the story is on point.

8. Overdress. My grandmother taught me this. People look at you before they listen to you. How you show up communicates 80 percent of whether someone should (or will) listen to you or not. During the first 5 minutes people will assess you up and down and draw all sorts of conclusions. Make sure the conclusions they draw are: professional, polished, credible and sensible (at least). Whatever you think the dress code will be, dress at least one or two steps above it. There is nothing worse than being underdressed—it's disrespectful. You are going to be onstage; people expect that you respect that position and dress UP for it.

9. Be Yourself. Don't try to be Zig Ziglar or Tony Robbins. Me? I don't like beating on my chest and yelling, having the crowd jump up and down on their chairs, run around the stage or drop to my knee for dramatic effects. You will never see me do that; it's not me. My best advice for you is to be you. Be onstage as you are offstage. Be real, authentic and communicate through your true feelings and conviction—it is from that place you can be persuasive, rousing and influencing.

10. See the 'O.' I always spend a few minutes before each keynote visualizing the presentation and the audience response: the rapt attention, the awe-inspired looks on their faces, their laughing and having a good time, then the rousing standing ovation at the end. It helps me get into the 'zone' and raise my emotional energy before getting started.

Knowing your audience is Darren's second presentation tip. It is an important step in creating a memorable presentation that will get you noticed by the right people. I saw a Dilbert cartoon a couple of years ago that reinforces the importance of audience analysis for creating and delivering great presentations. Pay attention, the lesson to be learned here is some great career advice.

In the first panel, the boss says, "Dilbert is our next presenter." Standing in front of a screen with a PowerPoint slide projected on it, Dilbert says, "Thanks for coming to my presentation. I put in a lot of time creating it. I hope you'll like it and find it informative. First, I'm going to run a little slide show and do a humorous rap to accompany it. Then you'll all get a chance to participate. I'll give you funny hats and you'll put together some skits. And then we'll have fireworks in the atrium of our building."

The last panel shows the members of the audience. One of them says, "Can you cut it short, we allowed only three minutes for your talk."

I know this sounds absurd, but one of my career success coach clients experienced an eerily similar situation. His boss's boss asked him to prepare a presentation on what his department does. This talk was going to be for the Executive Committee of his company – the 12 most senior people in the entire company – and this was a big company, over $20 billion in sales, so these were very important people.

He saw this as a huge opportunity – for himself and his department. The presentation was a month in the future. He spent most of that month working on the talk, developing about 70 nice-looking slides with animation and a brief video. There were no funny hats and fireworks, but the presentation had a lot of very cool graphics. He practiced again and again, making sure that he had it down pat. The talk lasted about 90 minutes.

The day before he was supposed to do the talk, his boss's boss asked him to come to his office to do a run through of the talk to make sure that things would go smoothly the next day. He, his boss and the big boss went into a conference room. He hooked up his computer to the projector and began previewing his carefully thought-out talk. After about seven minutes, the big boss said, "How many more slides do you have?"

My client said, "I'm just getting started, I have about 70 slides total."

The big boss said, "That's way too many. They only want a 10-minute overview of what your department does. You need to revise your talk and cut down the number of slides."

My client spent the rest of the day and most of the evening revising his talk, cutting out the graphics and animation.

When he and I next got together for a career success coach discussion, he was really frustrated. He explained the situation to me and complained about the big boss. "He never told me that all they wanted was a 10-minute overview of what we do. I wasted a lot of time putting together this presentation."

I said, "Did you ever ask him how long the talk should be?"

He said, "No. I just assumed that the Executive Committee would want a very thorough understanding of what our department does."

And that is the crux of the problem. My client missed a really important step in developing a powerful presentation. He did no audience analysis. He assumed his audience would be as interested in his topic as he is. In this case, he failed to realize that the senior people in the company wanted a quick look at his department – not an in-depth review of everything they do and how they do it. If he had taken the time to ask the big boss a few simple questions, he wouldn't have wasted his time developing an in-depth presentation. He didn't really want to hear it, but this was the best career advice I could give him.

Analyzing your audience is an important first step in developing any presentation. Here are a few simple questions you should ask and answer before you begin developing any presentation…

- Who is my audience for this presentation?
- Why are they there?
- What do they want or need to get from my talk?
- How much do they know about my topic?
- Are they familiar with any jargon I might use?
- What is their general attitude towards me and the information I'll be communicating?

These questions will help you develop and deliver the kind of presentation that will meet your audience's needs, help you shine as a presenter, and get you on the road to the life and career success you want and deserve.

The common sense career success coach point here is simple. Successful people are competent communicators. Presentation skills — along with conversation and writing skills — are among the communication skills you have to master if you want to become a life and career success. Follow the career advice in Tweet 115 in Success Tweets. "Become an excellent presenter. Careers have been made on the strength of one or two good presentations." Audience analysis is the first step in developing a compelling presentation. You have to understand your audience's wants and needs before you can develop a great talk. Take a few minutes to think about your audience before you begin developing any presentation. If you do, you'll be more likely to deliver a great talk that will get you noticed in a positive way.

Success Tweet 116

Presentations are opportunities to shine. Don't let stage fright rob you of your opportunity. Get control of your nerves.

The other day, I was at a workshop and one of the speakers was clearly nervous. He began his talk by telling the old story about the survey that asked people to name their greatest fear. Public speaking came in first, by a large margin. Death was fourth. So, if you believe the results of this survey, most people would rather die than stand up and give a talk. He was one of them. He urged us to be kind to him because he was nervous doing this talk.

He was suffering from what is known by a number of names: presentation anxiety, stage fright, the jitters. Whatever you call it, presentation anxiety can be the death knell for an otherwise great talk. We all get nervous before a talk, but being nervous doesn't have to mean you'll do a bad talk. Presentation anxiety is a response to fear of doing a poor talk. It shows up in a number of ways: blushing, shaking, stuttering. At its worst, it will lead you to feel as if you're not making sense, or worse yet, to lose the thread of your talk.

I make speeches for a living, and I get nervous before every one of them. In fact, if I'm not a little nervous, I start to worry that I will be flat and deliver an unenthusiastic talk. Over the years, I've developed a few tricks that I use to calm my nerves before a big presentation and make them work for, not against me. Check them out...

Practice your talk out loud. This will help you get comfortable with your material and your delivery.

Think good thoughts. Imagine yourself succeeding beyond your wildest dreams. Imagine that you will get a standing ovation for your talk. This is what visualization is all about.

Get there early. In this way, you'll be able to set up your computer and run through your slides one last time.

Greet people as they arrive; exchange a few words with them. This will help you make a good first impression with members of the audience. It will also help you get control of your nerves, because you'll feel more comfortable speaking to a group of people you know rather than a group of strangers.

Take a deep breath before you begin. This will calm you, help center you, and give you enough air to get through your opening.

Move. When you begin your presentation, move around. Use body movement to help release some of your nervous energy. Don't get trapped behind the podium. It can inhibit you from releasing your energy.

Just chat with the audience. Think of your presentation as a conversation. There might be 10, or 25, or 100 people in your audience. But in terms of real communication, there are only two people in the room: you and a single listener.

Tell stories to illustrate your main points. People like listening to stories and they tend to remember points illustrated by stories.

Ask questions during your talk. This will help you build a dialogue and a participatory feeling. I try to make at least one-quarter and as much as one-half of my talk a discussion with the audience. In this way, it's less of a speech and more of an expanded conversation with every person in the room.

Don't worry if you make a mistake. To begin with, most people won't realize that you made a mistake. Second, realize the audience is with you. They've all been there and know that presenting can be nerve-wracking. Most people in the audience will be pulling for you to do a good job.

Last week I met a guy named Ron Balagot. He shared his eBook, *Public Speaking Fear Conquered: Your Fearless Presenter Within Unleashed,* with me. This is the perfect book for you if you suffer from fear of public speaking. Its career advice is terrific! You can get a free copy at http://www.publicspeakingtipsforyou.com. You owe it to yourself to download this eBook.

The common sense career success coach point here is simple. Successful people are dynamic communicators. They understand the career advice in Tweet 116 in Success Tweets. "Presentations are opportunities to shine. Don't let stage fright rob you of your opportunity. Get control of your nerves." Presentations are opportunities to shine – to demonstrate that you are a dynamic communicator. Stage fright is the biggest enemy of presentation success. Don't let stage fright rob you of your opportunity to shine. One good presentation can make a career. Presentations are the best ways to get noticed and have your name at the top of the list when promotional opportunities come up. There are several ways to deal with presentation anxiety: be prepared, know your stuff cold; think of your talk as a conversation with the audience; tell stories to illustrate your points. However, there is one piece of advice that trumps all when it comes to delivering dynamic presentations: practice, practice, practice!

Success Tweet 117

Presentation steps: 1) Determine the message; 2) Analyze the audience; 3) Organize the information; 4) Design visuals; 5) Practice.

If you want to become a dynamic communicator and career success, you need to become an excellent presenter. Presentations are an important communication tool. Many careers have been made on the strength of one or two good presentations.

A lot of people suffer from presentation anxiety. Public speaking can be frightening, although it doesn't have to be. Presenting is like any other process, there is a series of logical steps to follow. The five steps to effective presentations in the Tweet have served me well for over 35 years.

In this post, I'll be sharing the material I cover in a three-day workshop on presentations skills. Breaking the presentation process down into the five easily manageable steps listed in the Tweet is the best way I know to get over presentation anxiety. Let's look at them in some detail.

1. Determine your message.
2. Analyze your audience.
3. Organize your information for impact.
4. Design supporting visuals.
5. Practice, practice, practice.

Ask yourself these questions to help you determine your message:

- What do you want or need to communicate?
- What information does the audience need?
- Why do they need it?
- At the end of the presentation, what should the audience: Understand? Remember? Do?

Determine the best way to communicate your message by analyzing your audience. Ask yourself these questions:

- Who is the audience for this presentation?

- Why are they attending?
- What is their general attitude toward you and the topic?
- What is their knowledge level on this topic?

Use the golden rule of journalism: "Tell them what you're going to tell them, Tell them, Tell them what you told them" to organize your information.

- Begin at the end. Prepare your presentation ending first. This is helpful, because it keeps you focused on where you're going.
- Prepare your presentation beginning. A good beginning has two things: a hook, and an outline of your talk.
- Fill in the blanks with your content.

Design visuals to support and enhance what you are saying. Good visuals support the points you are making, create audience interest, improve audience understanding, save you time – a picture is worth a thousand words, and they are memory aids.

Practice, Practice, Practice. There is an old saying, "practice makes up for a lack of talent". Prior to getting in front of an audience, say your presentation out loud – several times. Listen to yourself. Consider videotaping yourself. If you don't have the equipment, practice in front of a mirror, or your spouse, or your dog or cat – just practice.

The common sense career success coach point here is simple. Successful people are competent. Dynamic communication is an important career success competency. Dynamic communicators present with impact. Many people are frightened by the idea of standing in front of a group of people and doing a talk. Unfortunately, presentations can make or break your success. You can conquer your fear of public speaking by following the career advice in Tweet 117 in Success Tweets. "Presentation steps: 1) Determine the message; 2) Analyze the audience; 3) Organize the information; 4) Design visuals; 5) Practice. If you follow the career advice in these five steps – especially number 5, practice – you'll become a confident, successful presenter and a career success.

Success Tweet 118

Presentations are easy to create. Write your closing first, your opening next. Then fill in the content. Practice. Practice. Practice.

Writing your presentation closing first is some of the best presentation and career advice I can give you.

People remember two things about your talk: how you begin and how you finish. They remember how you finish because that's the last thing they hear. You want to finish strong, reinforcing and highlighting the main points you want people to remember. That's one reason for writing your closing first.

Another reason for writing your closing first is because it will help you map out the rest of your content. You'll probably have more information than you need for any presentation you make. If you write your closing first, you can use it to help you decide what information to leave in and what to leave out of your presentation.

For example, when I do my talk "How to Create the Life and Career Success You Want and Deserve" I always end by saying something like…

> And there you have it, my best advice on how to create the life and career success you want and deserve.
>
> It comes down to Four Cs: clarity, commitment, confidence and competence.
>
> If you want to create a successful life and career, you have to
>
> a) Clarify the purpose and direction for your life and career.
>
> b) Commit to taking personal responsibility for your life and career success.
>
> c) Build unshakeable self-confidence.
>
> d) Get competent in four areas: creating positive personal impact, outstanding performance, dynamic communication, and relationship building.

Hopefully, you know more about how to create the life and career success you want and deserve now than an hour ago. But, like the US Steel pencils my dad would bring home from work used to say, "Knowing is not enough." You've got to use the information you learned here today if you are going to create the life and career success you want and deserve."

When I was writing this talk, I wrote this closing first. I began by listing the key points I wanted to make – in this case the 4 Cs of Success. Any time I was wondering if I should include a specific piece of information in the talk, I asked myself, "Does this information reinforce the point you want people to remember about this talk?" If the answer was "yes," I left it in. If "no," I took it out.

OK, got it about writing your closing first? Good. Now let's talk about writing your opening second.

You want to accomplish two things in your presentation opening: 1) Capturing the audience's attention, and 2) Giving them some idea of what you will be covering in your talk.

When I do my talk, "How to Create the Life and Career Success You Want and Deserve" I always begin by saying something like...

Hello and thank you for coming. Today, I want to dispel one of the biggest myths about life and career success. And that myth is, "good performance is enough to create the life and career success you want and deserve." Good performance not only is not enough, it is merely the price of admission in today's highly competitive world.

If you want to create a successful life and career, think C – no, think 4 Cs...

Clarity, Commitment, Confidence and Competence.

If you want to create a successful life and career, you have to:

a) Clarify the purpose and direction for your life and career.

b) Commit to taking personal responsibility for your life and career success.

c) Build unshakeable self-confidence.

d) Get competent in four areas: creating positive personal impact, outstanding performance, dynamic communication and relationship building.

Over the next hour, I'm going to tell you more about each of these four Cs and show you how to put them to work to create the life and career success you want and deserve…

See what I mean? I captured the audience's attention by telling them that I was going to explode a myth about life and career success. Then I shared the myth. Then I outlined what I was going to cover in the next hour.

This format is the golden rule of journalism: Tell them what you're going to tell them. Tell them. Tell them what you've told them.

By writing your closing first and your opening second, you've done two of these: you've told your audience what you're going to tell them, and you've recapped what you've told them. Filling in the content becomes pretty simple once you've completed these two steps.

The common sense career success coach point here is simple. If you want to create dynamic presentations that communicate and get you known as a high performer, follow the career advice in Tweet 118 in Success Tweets. "Presentations are easy to create. Write your closing first, your opening next. Then fill in the content. Practice. Practice. Practice." Writing your closing first gives you the direction you need to create a dynamic presentation. Writing your opening next helps you capture the audience's attention and gives you an outline for creating the rest of your content. I learned this bit of career advice early in my career – way back in 1973 – and have used it ever since. If you use it, you'll be on your way to creating the life and career success you want and deserve.

Success Tweet 119

Discipline yourself to prepare for presentations. Practice out loud until you are totally in sync with what you're going to say.

Many people fear making presentations. That's why they're not very good at them. I subscribe to James Malinchak's ezine. It's always full of interesting anecdotes. A couple of days ago, James told a very interesting story about a conversation he had with Michael Jordan. He posed the following scenario to Michael...

> "It's Game 7 of the NBA Finals and your team is playing on the road at your opponents' place. There's 00:01 second left on the clock and your team is losing by 1 point. You're at the free-throw line to shoot two shots. This is literally win or lose time, and the ball is in your hands. If you make both free throws, your team wins their first ever championship. If you miss both, your team loses the championship. How would you feel?"

Michael Jordan's response...

> "That's easy! That situation wouldn't bother me because I would have already disciplined myself to make sure I had already prepared for success in that, or any other situation!"

James went on to say...

> "Not the answer I was expecting, but it's very profound when you think about those two words that most would rather simply skim over: 1) Disciplined; and 2) Prepared. The more I thought about those two words, the more I began to realize just how important they are for becoming a successful speaker, author, trainer or coach! Most people are not disciplined to prepare themselves for success."

James is on to something here. Disciplined preparation is the key to becoming a dynamic communicator. I teach my coaching clients a five-point model of presentation success. The fifth point is "practice, practice, practice." I suggest practicing your talk out loud using your visuals. I suggest doing this as many times as it takes to become 100% comfortable with what you are going to say and how you are going to say it.

When I say this I am often met with frowns and a lot of excuses about not having the time to do the kind of preparation I suggest.

And that's why many people suck at presenting. In Michael Jordan and James Malinchak's words, they don't have the personal discipline to prepare for a successful presentation. And without disciplined preparation it's basically impossible to do a good presentation.

Cathy and I were in Florida last year to celebrate our niece, Morgan's, wedding. Cathy was hosting a bridesmaid luncheon. The night before the luncheon, she practiced the welcoming talk she was going to give at the luncheon at least five times. And you know what? It got better every time she practiced it. She practiced one more time the morning of the luncheon, and she had it down cold. She disciplined herself to prepare for her talk. She was ready to do it. And she gave a killer talk. Good for her.

Cathy often accompanies me when I travel. If I am doing a talk the next day, she knows my ritual before going to bed. I will practice my talk – out loud – at least twice, and as many times as it takes for me to feel that I have it perfected. It takes a little bit of time to practice like this, but the audience applause and, more important, my feeling of satisfaction after delivering a great talk are worth it.

The common sense point here is simple. Successful people are dynamic communicators. Dynamic communicators are good presenters. They follow the career advice in Success Tweet 119. "Discipline yourself to prepare for presentations. Practice out loud until you are totally in sync with what you're going to say." As Michael Jordan and James Malinchak point out, disciplined preparation is a key to success in any endeavor – from basketball to business. Disciplined preparation is especially important to becoming a great presenter. If you want to become a great presenter, discipline yourself to prepare for your talks by practicing – out loud and with your visuals – until you are totally in sync with what you are going to say and how you are going to say it.

Success Tweet 120

Practice presentations. You can control your nerves by practicing out loud. The more you practice, the less afraid you'll be.

By now it should be pretty clear that I think that practicing your presentations – out loud – is the most important presentation success tip. I've mentioned practice in the last five success tweets.

Here's a recap of why I think it is really important to practice your presentations out loud.

Practicing your presentations out loud...

- Calms your nerves. When you practice several times, the presentation is familiar and comfortable to you. This makes you less nervous.

- Helps you edit your talk for impact. There is nothing like saying it out loud to show you the rough spots in your presentation. Once you identify these rough spots, you can correct them before you're in front of an audience.

- Helps you get better. The more times you repeat a talk out loud, the better it gets. It's almost impossible to be over-prepared. Practice does indeed make perfect.

These three reasons should convince you that it's important to practice your talk out loud. Yet, I am always amazed that so many people don't take the time to practice. They have some great excuses...

- It takes too much time.

- I know what I'm going to say, I don't need to practice.

- I feel foolish talking to myself.

- I won't get any better.

- I've done this talk a million times, I don't need to practice.

And I say, "WRONG!!!"

Practice is the main ingredient of any successful presentation, not funny slides and animation – practice.

Thomas Edison is famous for saying, "Many people miss opportunity because it comes dressed in overalls and looks like work." I am semi-famous for saying, "Most people know the right thing to do in most situations, their common sense tells them. They don't use their common sense for a bunch of bogus reasons."

So don't come up with bogus reasons for not practicing your presentations out loud. If you want to become a dynamic communicator, and create the life and career success you want and deserve, you have to practice your talks – out loud. That's some of the most important career advice I can give you.

The common sense career success coach point here is simple. If you want to be able to deliver dynamic presentations, you have to follow the career advice in Tweet 120 in Success Tweets. "Practice presentations. You can control your nerves by practicing out loud. The more you practice, the less afraid you'll be." Besides controlling your nerves, you'll get better each time you practice. Trust me on this one, time spent practicing a presentation is time well spent.

Success Tweet 121

Get genuinely interested in others. Help bring out the best in everyone you know. Others will gravitate to you.

This post is the first of 20 on relationship building – the final life and career success competency. Relationships are an important key to creating the life and career success you want and deserve. None of us can do it alone. We all need other people if we are going to succeed in our careers.

It's difficult -- if not impossible – to build strong, mutually beneficial relationships with the people in your life if you don't display a genuine interest in others. Show others that you care about them as people. Do small things like remembering the name of their spouse and children, asking about their family, learning about their interests outside of work. You don't have to become best friends with everybody at work, but it helps tremendously if you take the time to know them as whole people, not just work colleagues.

For years, I've made it a habit to remember other people's birthdays and send them an ecard. It's easy to do. There are any number of online sites that will allow you to store people's birthdays. They will even send you a reminder a week before. It's a small thing – and one which is hardly ever reciprocated – but people are always pleased when I remember their birthdays. Remembering people's birthdays is just one small way that you can follow the career advice in Success Tweet 121 – get genuinely interested in others.

A couple of years ago, I hosted an Internet radio show on which I interviewed some very interesting people. Judith Glaser was one of them. Judith is an executive and organizational coach. She has worked with many fortune 500 companies... names you all know: Pfizer, JP Morgan Chase, Clairol, IBM, Citibank, Pepsico, Verizon, among others. Judith is the best-selling author of, *Creating We*, one of Fortune Magazine's forty best business books in 2005.

She and I discussed *Creating We* and the thinking behind it in some detail. Here's an excerpt from that conversation. I particularly liked what Judith had to say about our "vital instincts". Judith says that we all have a vital instinct to bond with others. Demonstrating a genuine interest in others is a great way to begin the bonding process.

Judith: If you focus on the team level and the individual units aren't learning how to bond, then we've missed what creates the ongoing energy and momentum from making something happen.

Bud: When you say individual units, you're talking about the…

Judith: People

Bud: The people who make up an organization, whether it's a 20-person organization, or a 20,000-person organization?

Judith: Yes.

Bud: You talk about vital instincts in your book, and can you talk a little bit about that?

Judith: I had a most amazing "ah-ha" that came to me somewhere in the beginning or middle of the first year when I was trying to articulate what this was all about. The backdrop to this is that I wrote a business dictionary in 1986 so I had to come up with 3,500 new business terms that weren't in the mainstream dictionary. That's how I actually got my name Benchmark for Benchmark Communications.

In the process, words became a fascination for me, and I said, "what if there was no word yet that existed to explain what it was that was driving human beings to be together and to be successful together?" In that pursuit, I came up with the term "vital instincts." I decided that human beings have vital instincts that are alive all the time when we feel trust and when we are in a good relationship with someone. When this trust is broken and we become a fearful and distrusting person, there is a loss, or the cutting of those vital instincts. This interruption of communication with someone is actually what causes people to fight and want to survive or focus only on their own self-interest.

Bud: So if I get this right, we all have a need to trust other people and have a bonding need, a need to be in relationships with people?

Judith: Yes.

Bud: And when we struggle in relationships – whether it's in our marriages, our friendships or at work, it usually means that someone severed that trust that was the glue in the bond, or at least created the impression that the trust was severed?

Judith: Exactly, when people feel that trust has been severed they will go to someone else to build a new bond or to secure the bond that they have for safety and being in a relationship and being in a healthy communication.

So let's say you and I have a fight and all of a sudden our bond is broken. I then feel a need to re-secure that bond with someone else, so I turn to him or her and I say, "you know that Bud guy, can you believe what he just did to me?" And then all of a sudden I have a new friend who's now helping me. If you watch animals, it's licking wounds.

Bud: So vital instincts, at their core, really are a bond. We all seek to have relationships with other human beings. Sometimes we develop relationships that don't work so well and can be harmful to an organization because the bonding results from you and your other person talking about how bad I am, to use your example.

Judith: Exactly. And that's what we say when an organization is dysfunctional – that's what we're talking about. And by the way, vital instincts are so powerful and so important that if we don't have them, if we take children and leave them in the forest for example, without human contact, they do not grow beyond, they're called feral, they don't grow beyond being animals.

And so this instinct for bonding is also what leads to the ability for human beings to grow and develop parts of their brain that enables them to socialize and enable them to innovate and enable them to contribute.

Bud: Let's talk about conventional wisdom. Just how do we get along – what do we need to do to work well together and build strong relationships?

Judith: I've come to believe that creating "we" is not just getting along and working with each other. I really focus on getting down to the basics. If two human beings can sit down with each other, and they can talk about what a strong relationship would look like and then they can talk about what they need to give each other to create that; then they can talk about what they're going to do if they fall out of it, so that they can continually get back into it. Then we have something that talks about how people can stay in that "we" and in that bonding relationship.

Bud: So relationship building – bonding if you will – is dealing with people in a straight-forward, open manner. I think that a lot of what you're saying, and I think a lot of people who are listening to you are saying, "What she's saying makes sense" and it really does.

Judith: Thank you.

Judith Glaser's ideas about vital instincts are important for anyone who aspires to be an interpersonally competent person and a life and career success. Interpersonally competent people have the ability to build strong bonds with the people in their lives – and the ability to repair and strengthen those bonds when they are threatened. Pick up a copy of *Creating We*. I think you'll find it to be interesting and stimulating reading.

The common sense career success coach point here is simple. You can't become a life and career success all on your own. You need to build strong, mutually beneficial relationships with other people. Follow the career advice in Tweet 121 in Success Tweets. "Get genuinely interested in others. Help bring out the best in everyone you know. Others will gravitate to you." It is easier to create strong relationships when you bond with others. Judith Glaser calls bonding a "vital instinct" of all human beings. And, as she astutely points out, bonding is based on trust. Build relationships by being a person worthy of others' trust. Becoming genuinely interested in others is the first step in the trust building process and some great career advice.

Success Tweet 122

Keep confidences and avoid gossip. Don't embarrass others by repeating what they share with you – even if it isn't in confidence.

A couple of years ago I received a press release from *Randstad USA* that I saved. The press release focused on a study they did that identified the *Top 7 Pet Peeves in the Workplace*. Here they are, with the percentage of people who identified each pet peeve.

1. Gossip – 60%
2. Other's poor time management skills – 54%
3. Messiness in communal spaces – 45%
4. Potent scents – 42%
5. Loud noises – 41%
6. Overuse of electronic personal communication devices in meetings – 28%
7. Misuse of email — 22%

Why should you care? Because all of these pet peeves are things to avoid if you are going to have positive personal impact and create the life and career success you want and deserve.

In this post, I want to focus on gossip. The same day that I received the press release, I got an email from Gary Ryan Blair, The Goals Guy. He has a special report out called *Gossip, Rumors and Innuendo: Understanding Gossip and How to Control It!* You can purchase it by going to www.goalsguy.com. Click on "Store", then "Special Reports".

Gary likens gossip to workplace violence.

> "To many people, the idea of "workplace violence" connotes the physical harm that one may do to another. However, there is another form of workplace violence that is just as dangerous and insidious, and this is workplace gossip, rumors, and innuendo. While your first inclination may be to consider the way we talk as not being violent , the fact remains, our words in the context of gossip, rumors, and innuendo often lead to hurt, pain and suffering."

He's right. I know there's an old saying, "Sticks and stones may break my bones, but words can never hurt me." This is something that mothers tell their children to help them deal with the inconsiderate things kids say to one another. Unfortunately, it's not true.

Gossip can have a very debilitating effect on another person. Interpersonally competent people just don't do it. People with positive personal impact just don't do it. Gossip serves no good purpose, other than to hurt the person who is the subject.

The book, *As A Gentleman Would Say*, offers some great advice about gossip.

> "When a gentleman is asked to substantiate a rumor… He does not say: 'Let me put it this way: I'm not going to say yes, I'm not going to say no.' 'I think I know the truth, but I better not say it.' 'Don't you have any better way to waste your time?'
>
> But he does say: 'I don't know the truth about that, so I'd prefer not to say anything.'

Breaking confidences is another way to kill workplace relationships. I always suggest to my career success coach clients to avoid revealing anything said to them – even if the person who says it doesn't ask you to hold his or her remarks in confidence.

When I was a young guy, I had two mentors: my boss, the VP of HR, and a client, the VP of Marketing. I liked and respected each of them. And I wanted them to like and respect one another. One day, my boss mentioned that she found the VP of Marketing to be somewhat aloof and difficult to get to know.

This bothered me, so in a conversation with the VP of Marketing, I mentioned that my boss found him a little aloof and hard to get to know. I wanted the two of them to like each other. And, I thought that together they could really do some great things for the company. Boy, was that a mistake!

The VP of Marketing (my client) called the VP of HR (my boss) and complained that she was talking behind his back, and that if she had a problem with him, he wished that she would take it up with him. As soon as she got off the phone, my boss called me into my office and proceeded to let me know in no uncertain terms that she didn't appreciate me violating her confidence.

I was shocked. To begin with, I was surprised that she thought of her comment about the VP of Marketing as confidential. Second, I was surprised that he was upset enough to call her to complain.

I apologized to my boss. She then said something that I remember exactly to this day. "That's OK you made a mistake. Everybody is entitled to make a mistake now and then. But trust me on this, you'll never make the same mistake three times. I expect you to learn from it the first time. If you make the same mistake two times, there will be no third time because you'll be gone."

That's how I learned how to keep confidences, even if I thought they weren't told to me in confidence. The best career advice I can give you on this is to never do or say anything that will embarrass your boss, your colleagues, or other people in your company. Stay silent.

The common sense career success coach point here is simple. Follow the advice in Tweet 122 in Success Tweets. "Keep confidences and avoid gossip. Don't embarrass others by repeating what they share with you – even if it isn't in confidence." Gossip not only hurts other people, it makes you smaller. People with positive personal impact don't gossip. The old saying, "Extraordinary people talk about ideas, average people talk about events, and little people talk about other people," is true. Be an extraordinary person. Don't gossip or share things told to you in confidence. Treat most things that aren't common knowledge in your company as being told to you in confidence.

Success Tweet 123

Use every social interaction to build and strengthen relationships. Strong relationships are your ticket to success.

I have found that little things make for strong relationships. In other words, sweat the small stuff because it's the small stuff that will help you build and maintain strong, lasting, mutually beneficial relationships with the people who can help you create the life and career success you want and deserve.

A couple of years ago, I had an opportunity to preview a great DVD on relationship building called, *Little Things Mean a Lot.* The DVD is based on the work of Brigid Moynahan, founder of The Next level Inc. She is a well-known and highly recognized speaker and trainer.

Ms. Moynahan says that when it comes to relationships, it's important to sweat the small stuff. She says that we send micro-messages in all of our interactions with other people. Micro-messages are the signals we send to one another through our behavior. While micro-messages are often small, their impact can be enormous.

Micro-messages can help or hinder your relationship-building efforts. Micro-affirmations help you build and maintain strong relationships. Micro-inequities hinder your ability to build and maintain strong relationships.

These are important concepts that deserve a closer look.

Not surprisingly, micro-affirmations are micro-messages that we send to other people that cause them to feel valued, included, or encouraged.

Micro-inequities are micro-messages that we send to other people that cause them to feel devalued, slighted, discouraged or excluded.

Here's some great career advice. Consciously avoid micro-inequities and consciously send micro-affirmations.

Ms. Moynahan puts a diversity spin on her work. While I agree that moving from an organizational culture based on micro-inequities to one based on micro-affirmations will build a more inclusive – and thereby productive and profitable – organization, I also believe there are life and career success lessons to be learned here.

Ask yourself, "When do I feel excluded, disrespected and devalued?" In most of these cases, you have been the recipient of a micro-inequity. The way you feel when you experience a micro-inequity is the way others are likely to feel when you engage in micro-inequity behavior. That means you should refrain from using these behaviors in your interactions with others.

Then do just the opposite. Ask yourself, "When do I feel included, respected and valued?" In most of these cases, you will have been the recipient of a micro-affirmation. Work hard to incorporate behaviors that are micro-affirmations into your daily interactions with others.

In short, when you focus on sending micro-affirmations and avoiding micro-inequities, you will be better able to build solid, lasting relationships with the people in your life. And strong relationships are an important key to your personal and professional success.

The common sense career success point here is simple. Successful people are competent in four areas: 1) creating positive personal impact; 2) consistent high performance; 3) dynamic communication; and 4) interpersonal competence. Interpersonally competent people build strong relationships with the important people in their lives. They follow the career advice in Tweet 123 in Success Tweets. "Use every social interaction to build and strengthen relationships. Strong relationships are your ticket to success." Build and strengthen relationships by sweating the small stuff. Focus sending positive micro messages – the small things that show another person that you value him or her. Avoid "micro-inequities" – behaviors that demean people in small ways. Instead, focus on "micro-affirmations" – behaviors that encourage others and build their self-esteem.

Success Tweet 124

Everyone has something to offer. Never dismiss anyone out of hand. Take the initiative. Actively build relationships.

Successful people have a deep respect for the dignity of each individual. It doesn't matter if the person in front of you is the President of the United States, your boss, a co-worker, a taxi driver, a security guard or the housekeeper at your hotel.

Cathy, my wife, is the best example of someone who values every person she meets. She is friends with everyone – the pharmacy techs where we get our prescriptions, the couple who own the dry cleaners where we do business, the supermarket checkout people and baggers, the servers at the restaurants we frequent, and on and on and on.

Cathy is genuinely interested in these people. She knows their names, their spouses' names and their kids' names. She inquires about their lives. She knows about their vacations, what grades their kids are in school and lots of other things about them – all because she values them as individuals and takes the time to get to know them. She is one of the least judgmental people I know.

If you want to create the life and career success you deserve, take a lesson from Cathy. Pay attention to the people around you. You will learn a lot and your life will be richer for it. Don't judge people by what they do. Get to know others as individuals. You'll be surprised at what you learn.

I have had some very interesting conversations with taxi drivers in New York City. These days, most of them are immigrants. They love this country and are well-informed about it. When I get into a taxi, most often the driver is listening to NPR or an all-news station. I have had some great conversations about local and national politics, the state of the US economy, and sports with taxi drivers.

In Denver, I occasionally use a car service to go to and from the airport. This service is a cooperative. The members of the coop are all immigrants from Ethiopia. They were all political refugees. They love this country and are willing to discuss it in depth. I love my rides to and from the airport with them.

And, I learned something very interesting. Ethiopia was a Catholic country until the schism in 1066. The Ethiopian Church sided with the Eastern Church in Constantinople and broke with Rome. I was raised Catholic, but my father's parents were Orthodox Christian, or Russian Orthodox as we called them. In that tradition they celebrate Christmas on January 7 because they use a different calendar.

I remember having two Christmases when I was young. I always got a small present on January 7. Imagine my surprise when a guy from Africa told me that he couldn't drive me to the airport on January 7 because he chose to stay at home and celebrate Christmas with his family. This led to a very interesting discussion on how Ethiopia participated in the schism. When the Ethiopian community in Denver was building a new church, Cathy and I were some of the donors.

See what I mean about treating everyone as if he or she has something to offer? I never would have learned some valuable information about how similar the life experiences of a black guy from Ethiopia were to my own growing up had I not taken the time to engage this person in conversation.

The common sense career success coach point here is simple. Successful people follow the career advice in Tweet 124 in Success Tweets. "Everyone has something to offer. Never dismiss anyone out of hand. Take the initiative. Actively build relationships." Following this career advice will help you create the life and career success you want and deserve. More important, it will lead to a richer and fuller life. When you engage people, when you expect to find them to be interesting, you will open yourself up to a world of ideas that will not only help your career success, but will also help you succeed as a person.

Success Tweet 125

Get to know yourself. Use your self knowledge to better understand others and build mutually beneficial relationships with them.

Interpersonally competent people know themselves, have the ability to build and maintain strong mutually beneficial relationships with others, and are able to resolve conflict in a positive manner.

Today, I'd like to focus on the first point – knowing yourself. There are quite a few instruments on the market that help you get to know yourself. I am most familiar with the *Myers Briggs Type Indicator (MBTI)* and the *DISC*. Both of these are based on Jungian psychology and provide you with an easy to understand framework for getting to know yourself.

I believe that we can all benefit from gaining a better understanding of ourselves – what turns us on, what turns us off, what motivates us, etc. However, I think that the real benefit is less knowing yourself than in using the framework to know other people. If you understand other people — what turns them on, what turns them off, what motivates them – you are in a better position to build positive, constructive relationships with them.

I'll use myself as an example. The MBTI measures preferences along four continuums:

- Extraversion (E) – Introversion (I)
- Sensing (S) – Intuiting (N)
- Thinking (T) – Feeling (F)
- Judging (J) – Perceiving (P)

I am a slight introvert – that means that I get my energy from within, as opposed to extraverts who get their energy from other people. I prefer a lot of solitary activities: reading, writing, watching movies, riding my bike. I get recharged by being by myself. On the other hand, Cathy, my wife, is a high extravert. She gets her energy from being around other people.

She frequently drives me to, and picks me up from the airport. When I come home from a trip, I most often want to relax and look out the car window as we drive home. I'm an introvert. I recharge my batteries by getting quiet and going within myself. Cathy is an extravert. She wants to talk. She enjoys having me home so we can interact.

When I get into the car after a trip, I get myself into a conversational mode. I ask about Cathy, and what she did while I was gone. I listen to what she has to say. I tell her about my trip – whom I saw and what I did. I do this because I love her, and want to do my part to make our relationship as strong as it can be. I use my knowledge of myself, and my knowledge of her to act in a manner that will strengthen our relationship.

Here's another example. One of my clients is a strong S and strong J. I am a strong N and strong P. He likes things to be very organized and predictable. I am more comfortable going with the flow.

One day, I arrived at his office in the late afternoon. I was going to facilitate a team-building session for his leadership team the next day. He asked me what I planned on doing in our meeting. I explained it to him verbally. He said, "Do you have an agenda?" I responded that I'd just told him what I was planning on doing. He said, "I heard you, but I'd like to see the agenda." I told him I had no written agenda. He was unhappy with this. So we spent 15 minutes putting what I had told him I planned to do in the meeting on paper.

You might think this is pretty silly. But there is an important lesson here. He has high needs for structure, and an agenda is a way to structure a meeting. I am very comfortable having a rough idea of what I'm hoping to do and accomplish in a meeting and then going with the energy in the room as the meeting unfolds. This works for me – but not my client.

The career advice here is simple. He's the client; I have to adapt my preferred style of leading a meeting to his needs, or I am unlikely to be successful in building a long-term, mutually beneficial relationship with him. It was up to me to recognize our differences and to adapt my behavior to something that will make him comfortable – not the other way around.

The common sense career success coach point here is straightforward. Successful people understand themselves. They follow the career advice in Tweet 125 in Success Tweets. "Get to know yourself. Use your self knowledge to better understand others and build mutually beneficial relationships with them." They use their understanding of themselves to compare and contrast their needs and wants with the people around them. In this way, they adapt their behavior to the other person – making it easier to build strong relationships. The next time you run into someone who looks at the world differently from you, see what you can do to adapt your communication style and behavior to his or her style. If you do this, I guarantee you'll be on your way to building a better, stronger relationship with that person.

Success Tweet 126

Self awareness is the first step in building relationships and resolving conflict.

You need to be interpersonally competent to build strong relationships. In 1988, researchers at the Department of Psychology at UCLA suggested that there are five dimensions of interpersonal competence...

1. Initiating relationships.
2. Self-disclosure.
3. Providing emotional support.
4. Asserting displeasure with others' actions.
5. Managing interpersonal conflicts.

Self-awareness was not one of the interpersonal competence factors identified by the UCLA researchers in 1988. On the other hand, the first three – initiating relationships, self-disclosure and providing emotional support — are ways to build and nurture relationships. The last two – asserting displeasure with others' actions, and managing interpersonal conflicts — are ways to resolve conflict in a positive manner.

I believe that self-awareness is the foundation of interpersonal competence. Self-awareness is the first step in building positive relationships and in resolving conflict in a positive manner. Self-aware people understand how they are similar to, and different from other people.

They use this insight to help them do things like initiate relationships with a variety of people; determine how much they should disclose about themselves at various points in a relationship; and determine the appropriate amount of emotional support they should offer others. Self-aware people also use their knowledge of themselves and others to determine when and how to assert their displeasure with another person's actions, and to manage and resolve interpersonal conflicts.

If you understand yourself, you can better understand others. I'll use myself as an example. I prefer to think things through before I make my position on an issue known. There are several people I know who "think out loud," meaning that they reach a position on an issue by talking about it. When I am with one of these people, I join them in thinking out loud. I know that if I don't, decisions are likely to get made while I am thinking through my position silently.

Here's another example. I make intuitive leaps. My mind goes from A to B to F. A lot of people I know process information sequentially. Their minds go from A to B to C to D to E to F. When I am with these people, I don't blurt out my intuitive leaps. When I have one, I go back and fill in the B to C to D to E before I come out with F. In this way, I am better able to get my point across to my sequentially thinking colleagues and clients.

One more: I am happy to leave my options open, and to change my mind somewhat late in the game. I know a lot of people who don't feel comfortable with this. They have strong needs for closure. Once a decision is made, they want it to stay made. When I'm dealing with these types of people, I ask myself if the change I am proposing will make a real difference. If not, I don't propose it. If I think it is necessary, I bring it up. However, when I do, I am very clear that I am revisiting a decision that has already been made, that this might be frustrating to other people, but that I think it is necessary to rethink the decision – and then I give very specific reasons for wanting to revisit the decision and how such a conversation can yield better results.

The common sense career success coach point here is simple. Successful people build strong relationships with the important people in their lives. They follow the career advice in Tweet 126 in Success Tweets. "Self-awareness is the first step in building relationships and resolving conflict." You can build solid relationships by taking the initiative, sharing information about yourself, being emotionally supportive, and sharing your feelings about behavior to which you have a negative reaction in order to resolve conflict positively. However, relationship building begins with self-awareness. Understanding yourself and how you are similar to, or different from others, is great career advice and the foundation of all relationship building.

Success Tweet 127

Pay it forward. Build relationships by giving with no expectation of return. Give of yourself to build strong relationships.

This tweet reminds me of an inspirational movie I sent to my subscribers a while back. It's called the 100-0 principle. The principle is simple. The best way to build solid relationships is to take 100% responsibility for them. You can see this movie by logging on to http://flickspire.com/1sst/TCSG/HundredZero. Check it out. It is a great movie that you'll want to share with your family, friends and coworkers. You have not only my permission, but my encouragement, to do so.

In 2009 I participated in a writing project with my colleagues at the Creating WE Institute. We published a little book called, *42 Rules for Creating WE*. The rules were short essays that contained a lot of great career advice. I contributed three rules. One was called, "There is No Quid Pro Quo in WE." This rule goes directly to the idea of paying it forward described in Tweet 127. I'd like to share the career advice in this essay – with a few minor edits – with you here.

> WE is built on relationships; the idea that we are all connected, and that through a WE-centric, rather than a traditional I-centric approach, our collective wisdom grows and evolves. This kind of thinking creates stronger organizations and societies. It fosters mutual shared respect for the unique contribution every person is capable of making. Solid, lasting, mutually beneficial relationships are at the core of WE. Giving with no expectation of return is a great way to create these types of relationships.

> This is a quid pro quo world: you do for me and I'll do for you. While there is nothing wrong in reciprocating a good deed or a favor, there is a fundamental problem with quid pro quo. It is reactive not proactive. Too many people wait for others to go first. They adopt the attitude, "When and if you do for me, I'll do for you." This scarcity mentality is not conducive to creating WE, or building strong relationships. When you come from a scarcity mentality, you focus on holding on to what you already have. This can prevent you from receiving what you might possibly get.

On the other hand, giving with no expectation of return comes from a proactive abundance mentality. When you give with no expectation of return, you are acknowledging the abundance of the universe. You are demonstrating faith that the good you do will benefit others close to you and the world at large – and that good things will come back to you.

Giving with no expectation of return is ironic. I have found that the more I give, the more I receive; often from unlikely sources. But that's not my reason for giving – and I hope it is not yours. The best reason for giving is the basic joy of making a difference in other people's lives and in creating a WE-centric world.

I love the Liberty Mutual Insurance "responsibility" ads. They are a very visual demonstration of the ideas behind creating WE – especially giving with no expectation of return. You've probably seen them.

They begin with someone going a little out of his or her way to do something that benefits others; picking up a piece of trash, opening a door for another person who's hands are full. Another person observes this and goes out of his or her way for someone else. The cycle repeats several times during the ad. The message is clear. We are all better off when we help each other.

Giving without expectation of return not only helps you create a WE-centric culture, it helps you build strong partnerships. Larry Agresto is a WE-centric guy. He says, "Truly successful people never compete, they network and leverage their relationships by providing value and giving more than they receive."

In the end, giving with no expectation of return comes down to your mentality – scarcity or abundance. If you come from a scarcity mentality, you will live by quid pro quo, and perpetuate the I-centric status quo. If you come from an abundance mentality, you will give with no expectation of return and begin to create a WE-centric world and create the kind of strong, mutually beneficial relationships that will help you create the life and career success you want and deserve.

I choose abundance and paying it forward. I agree with Winston Churchill, who once said, "We make a living by what we get, we make a life by what we give."

When you give with no expectation of return you will get a good life. You'll also get a better world; one in which we all look out for one another.

The common sense point here is simple. Successful people are adept at building strong relationships. They understand and use the career advice in Tweet 127 in Success Tweets. "Pay it forward. Build relationships by giving with no expectation of return. Give of yourself to build strong relationships." Paying it forward is the opposite of quid pro quo. When you go first – give of yourself to help someone else, with no expectations of return – you are laying the foundation for a successful relationship. When you wait to reciprocate a good deed by another person, you are engaging in quid pro quo behavior that usually results in lost relationship opportunities. Do yourself a favor, follow this career advice when it comes to relationship building – pay it forward. Check out the 100-0 movie by going to http://flickspire.com/1sst/TCSG/HundredZero/

Success Tweet 128

When meeting someone new ask yourself, "What can I do to help this person?" You'll build stronger relationships by thinking this way.

"Give with no expectation of return" is one of the suggestions I make to my career success coach clients when it comes to building strong relationships. "Pay it forward" is the main advice in Success Tweet 127. I follow both of these pieces of career advice myself. That's one of the reasons I write this blog – to help people create the life and career success they want and deserve.

A while back, I did a blog post in which I highlighted Linda Salazar's great book, *Awaken the Genie Within.* I didn't know Linda at the time, only what she wrote. I wrote the post because I loved the book and thought it has some great life and career success advice.

I sent Linda an email telling her about the blog post. I attached one of my career success books.

As it turns out, Linda thought that that my post helped her too. I received this email from her the day after I published the post...

> Bud,
>
> I am deeply touched by your blog write up that includes so much information about my book. You are obviously a man who walks his talk and you should know you have engrained yourself deep in my heart because there are not a lot of people in the world who do that.
>
> Thank you so much. And I would like to reciprocate on my blog when I've gotten at least half-way through your book. I started it last night and am enjoying it greatly.
>
> Understand this is not because I have to! This is truly because I want to and that's just the way it is!
>
> What's so wonderful is the detail you give about yourself and your life at the start of the book – a perfect way to get to know the author before delving into his book – gives it such a personal touch.

Have a wonderful day and I'll be in touch.

Blessings,

Linda

Pretty cool, right? I was trying to help readers of this blog create career success by writing about Linda's book – you really should get it and read it. Linda saw my post as helpful to her. She took the time to write me a very nice note, and offered to reciprocate on her blog.

Linda and I now have a relationship – one that can benefit both us of personally and professionally – all because I mentioned her book in one of my blog posts. That's the power of giving with no expectation of return. I bet you've had experiences like this. Please share them in a comment.

The common sense career success coach point here is clear. Successful people are interpersonally competent. Interpersonally competent people build strong relationships by giving with no expectation of return. They follow the career advice in Tweet 128 in Success Tweets. "When meeting someone new, ask yourself, "What can I do to help this person?" You'll build stronger relationships by thinking this way." Here is some great career advice. The next time you meet someone new, ask yourself, "What can I do to help this person?" Most people ask the opposite question, "How can this person help me?" By thinking "how can I help" first, you'll be better able to build strong relationships that will pay off and help you create life and career success. Way back on January 20, 1961, in his inauguration speech as President of the United States, John Kennedy said, "Ask not what your country can do for you. Ask what you can do for your country." These words – with a slight twist — are true today and will help you become a life and career success. Ask not what others can do for you. Ask what you can do for others.

Success Tweet 129

There is no quid pro quo in effective relationships. Do for others without being asked or waiting for them to do for you.

I was in Phoenix for some business a couple of years ago. On that trip, I did something that I do too seldom. I put on my bathing suit, took my iPod and did nothing but sit by the pool listening to music for an hour.

I have several Eagles songs on my iPod. I know that it's become fashionable to bash the Eagles these days, but I was a fan years ago and am still a fan today. "Desperado" is my favorite Eagles song. It came up on the shuffle. As I was listening, I was struck by the following words...

> "And freedom, oh freedom well, that's just some people *talking.*
> *Your prison is walking through this world all alone."*

These lyrics are right on. You are putting yourself into a self-imposed prison if you choose to go it alone. We all need other people in our lives if we're going to grow, flourish and succeed. This is true in your personal life, as well as your career and professional life. That's why building and nurturing strong relationships is one of the keys to creating the career and life success you want and deserve.

How do you build strong relationships? Simple. Give with no expectation of return. Don't think "quid pro quo." Think "how can I help this person?"

This is the third tweet in a row that deals with the idea of paying it forward, of giving with no expectation of return, of avoiding a quid pro quo mentality. If you're getting the idea that I think these ideas are some powerful career success advice, you're right.

> This is a quid pro quo world: you do for me and I'll do for you. There is a fundamental problem with quid pro quo. It is reactive not proactive and comes from a scarcity mentality. Too many people wait for others to go first. They adopt the attitude, "When and if you do for me, I'll do for you." This scarcity mentality is not conducive to building strong relationships. When you come from a scarcity mentality, you focus on holding on to what you already have. This can prevent you from receiving what you might possibly get.

On the other hand, paying it forward, giving with no expectation of return, comes from a proactive abundance mentality. When you pay it forward, give with no expectation of return, you are demonstrating faith that the good you do will benefit others – and that good things will come back to you.

I believe this with all my heart.

Here is a humorous example to drive home this point. I was in New York a couple of weeks ago. I was entering the subway when I saw a homeless guy standing on the landing. I usually don't give money to individual homeless people, preferring to support the local organization that provides services to the homeless, The Denver Rescue Mission.

But there was something about this guy that made me pull out a dollar and give it to him. He thanked me, I smiled and continued down the steps.

All of a sudden I hear, "Psssst." I look up and he has opened a gate, which he was standing in front of. He says, "Come on, you can get in for free through here." I had my MetroCard in my hand, but I went back up the steps and through the gate he was holding open. It costs $2.25 to ride the NY subway. I got a ride for a dollar because I gave it to this homeless guy.

I know that I displayed some questionable ethics in this case, beating the NY Transit Authority out of a fare, but that's not the point. I did something for someone who, I thought, could do absolutely nothing for me, and I got an immediate return of over 125%.

I don't recommend you go about giving money to every homeless person standing just outside the subway, but I do think that this story illustrates the power of giving with no expectation of return.

The common sense career success coach point here is simple. Successful people build and nurture strong relationships with the important people in their lives. Giving with no expectation of return is a great way to begin building relationships. Follow the career advice in Tweet 129 in Success Tweets. "There is no quid pro quo in effective relationships. Do for others without being asked or waiting for them to do for you." Don't think quid pro quo. Don't wait for someone else to make the first move. Be willing to go first. Put yourself out there and do what you can for others. You'll be demonstrating your relationship-building skills and your interpersonal competence. Take the first step today. Find someone for whom you can do something – then do it. You'll be surprised at what you might get from a selfless act – maybe even a free subway ride.

Success Tweet 130

Be generous. By giving with no expectation of return, you'll be surprised by how much comes back to you in the long run.

When my book, *Straight Talk for Success,* first came out I did a big launch campaign that resulted in it becoming an Amazon.com bestseller. A few months before the launch, I settled on April 22 as my launch date; mostly because the timing was right. When I looked closer at my calendar, I saw that April 22 happens to be Earth Day. I can remember participating in teach-ins at Penn State on the very first Earth Day in 1970.

I decided that there was some karma involved here. Since I had chosen April 22 without knowing it was Earth Day, I thought it would be nice for me to make a symbolic gesture and donate 10% of my net proceeds from book sales that day to an organization that supports the environment. I knew the perfect one.

I am a member of Volunteers for Outdoor Colorado, an apolitical environmental organization. Their mission is to "motivate and enable Colorado citizens to be active stewards of Colorado's public lands, thereby creating enthusiastic and beneficial stewardship of Colorado's natural and cultural resources." They are my favorite environment related non-profit. They do great work. I was happy to help them out by donating a part of the money I made on book sales that Earth Day.

I called Ann Baker Easley, VOC Executive Director, and told her what I had in mind. I was expecting a "thank you." I got that, and much more. Ann put me in touch with Piep van Heuven, VOC Deputy Director of Development and Communication. Piep included a message about my book launch in the VOC newsletter, and sent an email to their membership on the day of the book launch, asking them to purchase a copy of *Straight Talk*.

What started off as a philanthropic endeavor on my part turned into a partnership. And, it proved my point about giving with no expectation of return. I approached VOC thinking that I could help them by making a small contribution. They embraced my idea, and took it one step further. So now, we are partners. I think this is great.

This doesn't always work. Prior to my book launch, I participated in a book launch campaign for another author. When I asked her to return the favor, I got an email saying, "I am not participating in any book launch promotions just now. I am laser focused on building my business using Facebook."

In other words, "Kiss off, Bud." But that's OK. I helped her with her successful launch, and many other people – some very unexpected — are helping me with mine. In my experience, for every experience where my help is not reciprocated, there are two or three more like my experience with Volunteer for Outdoor Colorado.

Recently, I have partnered with a new non profit: the Go For It! Institute. Go For It! teaches kids seven keys to life success...

- **KEY 1: I Have a Positive Attitude!** Learn what attitude is; what aspects of your life are controlled or directed by your attitude; how to determine your attitude at any given moment; specific strategies to make a positive attitude a permanent habit in your life.
- **KEY 2: I Believe in Myself!** Understand the nature of human potential through a simple process of identifying your personal talents and abilities; developing academic strengths and personal interests to create personal fulfillment and economic opportunities for your future.
- **KEY 3: I Build Positive Habits!** Understand the process of how habits are created; learn to identify and remove self-defeating habits; create habits that will make all aspects of your life easier and more successful.
- **KEY 4: I Make Wise Choices!** Learn the dramatic relationship between any current circumstances in your life and the choices that created these; develop a personal proactive plan for desired outcomes through conscious, wise choices.
- **KEY 5: I Set and Achieve Goals!** Recognize the difference between a wish and a goal; make a commitment, plan and take action; recognize completion.
- **KEY 6: I Use My Creative Imagination!** Learn to adapt a technique professional athletes use to extend their physical ability, to accelerate problem solving and goal achievement in *all* areas of your life.
- **KEY 7: I Am Persistent!** Track progress; develop the focus and determination required to succeed; create an attitude of gratitude as the access to fulfilling your dreams, link the *Seven Keys to Success* together in everyday life.

I like these seven keys and I like the people at Go For It! who are spreading the word to young people, parents and teachers all across the USA. These are smart people who give generously of themselves to help kids – our future. I am proud to be one of their partners. I am launching a new website on which I will sell career advice books and other career success materials I have developed. I will donate a percentage of my profits to the Go For It! Institute. In this way, you'll be able to help them by helping yourself.

The common sense career success coach point here is clear. Successful people build and nurture strong relationships with the people in their lives. One way they do this is by giving with no expectation of return. Follow the career advice in Tweet 130 in Success Tweets. "Be generous. By giving with no expectation of return, you'll be surprised by how much comes back to you in the long run." Often, when you give with no expectation of return, you'll be surprised by what comes back to you. But that's not the important reason for it. Give with no expectation of return to help others and to build strong, mutually beneficial relationships with the important people in your life.

Success Tweet 131

Be happy to see others succeed. Use the success of others to motivate you to greater success.

A while back in a post I did on optimism and self-confidence, I mentioned a quote in which a guy by the name of Ambrose Bierce bashed optimism – and I am an incurable optimist. I advocate optimism as a way to create self-confidence and career success

Anyway, Ambrose defined optimism as, "The doctrine that everything is beautiful, including what is ugly, everything good, especially the bad, and everything right that is wrong... It is hereditary, but fortunately not contagious."

I come across quotes from Mr. Bierce frequently. Check out this one: "Calamities are of two kinds: misfortunes to ourselves, and good fortune to others." Both of these quotes are really cynical. I wondered what kind of guy would produce them.

So I decided to learn something about Ambrose Bierce. As it turns out, he was called "Bitter Bierce" by his contemporaries. And I can see why. First he bashes optimism, then he suggests that human beings see the good fortune of others as a personal calamity.

Ambrose Bierce is an interesting character. He was born in 1842, and served in the Union Army during the Civil War. No one knows for sure, but it is thought that he died in 1914. In 1913, he traveled to Mexico to get involved with the revolution going on there.

He joined Pancho Villa's army in Juarez. On December 26 1913, he posted a letter to a friend from Chihuahua. That was his last correspondence. Wikipedia says, "Several writers have speculated that he headed north to the Grand Canyon, found a remote spot there and shot himself, though no evidence exists to support this view. All investigations into his fate have proved fruitless, and despite an abundance of theories his end remains shrouded in mystery. The date of his death is generally cited as '1914?'". His disappearance is one of the most famous in American literary history."

In 1906, Ambrose Bierce published "The Cynic's Word Book." The title was changed to "The Devil's Dictionary". It is a book of satirical definitions of English words. Ambrose was clever, I'll give him that. I often see quotes from this book online, including the one that inspired today's post: "Calamities are of two kinds: misfortunes to ourselves, and good fortune to others."

But I digress. I wish he were around today, because I would like to ask him where he got his bleak view of human nature. He defines politeness as, "The most acceptable hypocrisy." In another quote, he defines perseverance as, "A lowly virtue whereby mediocrity achieves an inglorious success."

Do you know any people like Ambrose Bierce? If you do, hold them at arm's length. While you may find them to be witty and entertaining at first, they will drag you down in the long run.

People like Ambrose Bierce may be clever, but their views are incompatible with becoming self-confident, creating positive personal impact, building strong relationships and becoming a life and career success. Successful people look for, and usually find, the best in others. They are polite because it is the best way to build strong relationships. They are willing to extend themselves to help others, even when they can see no immediate return to them for so doing.

If you read this blog regularly, you know I am a big fan of The Optimist Creed. Point 6 says,

> "Promise yourself to be just as enthusiastic about the success of others as you are of your own."

This is 180 degrees from the Ambrose Bierce quote that I cited at the beginning of this post and from his life view in general. Successful, self-confident, optimistic people aren't jealous or upset by the success of others. They are genuinely pleased when they see others succeed. They use others' success as an inspiration. They use it to motivate themselves to achieve their own life and career success.

If you would like a copy of The Optimist Creed that you can frame and hang in your workspace, go to http://budbilanich.com/optimist.

The common sense career success coach point here is clear. Successful people are self-confident, create positive personal impact, interpersonally competent and adept at building strong relationships with the people around them. In part, they build these relationships by being genuinely pleased about the success of others. They are neither jealous, nor petty. They are happy to see others succeed. They follow the career advice in Tweet 131 in Success Tweets. "Be happy to see others succeed. Use the success of others to motivate you to greater success." Successful, self-confident people use the success of others to motivate themselves to greater success. They aren't jealous. They are happy to see others succeed, if for no other reason than others' career success can be a springboard for their own life and career success.

Success Tweet 132

Trust is the glue that holds relationships together. The more you demonstrate trust in others, the more they will trust you.

Building relationships comes down to two words: trust and abundance.

When you trust others you are willing to put yourself out there – to give with no expectation of return, to act in a non quid pro quo manner. Recently, I did a blog post in which I mentioned a chapter I wrote in *42 Rules for Creating WE* called, "There is no quid pro in WE". In that post, I pointed out that while there is nothing wrong with returning the favor when someone does you a good turn, waiting for others to help you is not a good idea when it comes to building relationships. Successful people are willing to put themselves out there – to pay it forward.

Paying it forward takes trust, but it is great career advice. Trust yourself to do for others with no guarantee of return. Trust that others won't take advantage of you. Trust in the universe in that the good you put out will come back to you in unexpected ways. Trust is the glue that holds relationships together. The more you demonstrate trust in others, the more they will trust you.

Abundance is also important in building relationships. People who come from an abundance mentality see life as a non-zero sum game; a perspective that holds that we can all be winners in the game of life. They realize that there is enough for all of us – enough money, recognition, success, the things that people who come from a scarcity mentality see as in short supply. People who come from a scarcity mentality see life as a zero sum game; if you win, I have to lose and vice versa.

I choose trust and abundance because I have seen them work in the real world – and I find that I am happier with myself when I am trusting and come from a place of abundance. What do you choose – trust and abundance, or mistrust and scarcity? The choice you make can have a huge impact on your ability to build relationships and create the life and career success you want and deserve.

The common sense career success coach point here is simple. Successful people are competent at building strong, mutually beneficial relationships with the important people in their lives. They follow the career advice in Tweet 132 in Success Tweets. "Trust is the glue that holds relationships together. The more you demonstrate trust in others, the more they will trust you." A trusting attitude and abundance mentality are the best way to build relationships. When you trust yourself, others and the universe, you will approach life from an abundance mentality. You'll be willing to give of yourself with no expectation of direct return. This world view will make it easier for you to build and maintain the relationships that will help you create the successful life and career you want and deserve.

Success Tweet 133

Resolve conflict positively. Treat conflict as an opportunity to strengthen, not destroy, the relationships you've worked hard to build.

Successful people resolve conflict in a positive manner. No matter how interpersonally compent, or how easy-going you are, you will inevitably find yourself in conflict. People will not always agree with you, and you will not always agree with others.

I know a little bit about conflict resolution. It was the topic of my dissertation at Harvard. Way back in the 1970's, Ken Thomas and Ralph Kilmann developed an instrument to measure a person's tendencies when in a conflict situation.

They came up with five predominant conflict styles: Competing, Collaborating, Compromising, Accommodating and Avoiding. Their research suggests that all five are appropriate depending on the situation.

As a career success coach however, I have found that the Collaborating style is the best default mode. When you collaborate with others to resolve conflict, you focus on meeting both your needs and the needs of the other person. I like this style because it helps you bring together a variety of viewpoints to get the best solution.

When you collaborate, neither person is likely to feel as if he or she won or lost. Also, collaborating with the person or persons with whom you are in conflict creates the opportunity for you to work together to build a solution that best addresses everyone's concerns.

Successful people are adept at resolving conflict in a positive manner. Collaboration is the best choice of the five most common handling styles. When you collaborate with others – especially those with whom you are in conflict – you not only are likely to resolve your conflict in a positive manner, you will strengthen your relationship with the other person. It's a win-win.

When I work collaboratively with someone, I focus on our similarities, not our differences. This creates a bond that not only helps us get through our conflict, but helps us strengthen our relationship, and strong relationships lead to career success.

As I mentioned in the paragraph above, my favorite method for dealing with conflict is counter-intuitive. By definition, conflict is a state of disagreement. When I'm in conflict with someone, however, instead of focusing on where we disagree, I focus on where we agree.

This is a great way to not only resolve conflict positively, it helps strengthen relationships. And, as we all know, conflict often leads to a deterioration of relationships. So to me this approach is a no-brainer. First, you get to resolve conflict positively. Second, you strengthen your relationships. Third, you improve your chances of becoming a life and career success.

I look for any small point of agreement and then try to build on it. I find that it is easier to reach a larger agreement when I build from a point of small agreement, rather than attempting to tear down the other person's points with which I don't agree.

Most people don't do this. They get caught up in proving their point. They hold on to it more strongly when someone else attacks it. If you turn around the discussion and say, "Let's focus where we agree, and see if we can build something from there," you are making the situation less personal. Now the two of you are working together to figure out a mutually agreeable solution to your disagreement. You're not tearing down one another's arguments just to get your way. Try this. It works.

President Obama demonstrated this in his first speech to a joint session of Congress. As he was winding up his talk, he said...

> "I know that we haven't agreed on every issue thus far, and there are surely times in the future when we will part ways. But I also know that every American who is sitting here tonight loves this country and wants it to succeed. That must be the starting point for every debate we have in the coming months, and where we return after those debates are done. That is the foundation on which the American people expect us to build common ground.
>
> "And if we do — if we come together and lift this nation from the depths of this crisis, if we put our people back to work and restart the engine of our prosperity, if we confront without fear the challenges of our time and summon that enduring spirit of an America that does not quit – then someday years from now

our children can tell their children that this was the time when we performed, in the words that are carved into this very chamber, 'something worthy to be remembered.' Thank you, God bless you, and may God bless the United States of America."

Regardless of your political views, the President is right on with this one. When you come together with the people with whom you are in conflict by identifying some small point on which you agree, you are putting yourself in the position to begin building a resolution to the conflict – one that is likely better than either side's opening position. And, by working together, you'll be strengthening your relationship. This will facilitate even more effective conflict resolution down the road. Look for common ground. When you find it, build on it. You'll find that this is a great way to resolve conflict in a manner that enhances, not destroys relationships.

Be assertive, not aggressive in resolving conflict. Here's a true story. Frontier flight 862, Denver to Phoenix. I get on late because I'm on standby for an earlier flight. I have a middle seat, 14B. When I arrive at row 14, there are women sitting in seats A and C. I say hello, stow my bags, and get into my seat.

The woman in 14A smiles at me, looks at the book I have in my hand, and says, "That looks like an interesting book." I'm reading Laura Lowell's book, *42 rules of Marketing*. We chat a minute about the book and then lapse into some general conversation.

Her name is Cheryl Munsey, and as it turns out, Cheryl and I know a few people in common. And she's very personable. We chat the whole time the plane is taxiing and through take-off.

As soon as the plane is in the air, the woman in 14C rings the flight attendant call button. The flight attendant comes on the loudspeaker and says, "We are still in our ascent. Will the person who rang his or her call button turn it off until we reach our cruising altitude? Leave it on only if it's a real emergency."

14C leaves the light on. I'm worried that she might be ill. The flight attendant struggles down the aisle. When she arrives at our row, 14C says, "I need a pair of headphones. These people are talking too much and driving me crazy." As she is saying this, she is removing ear plugs.

I feel bad. I tend to speak softly in crowded, enclosed places like airplanes and was surprised that our conversation was annoying her – especially when she was wearing ear plugs. I say to 14C, "I apologize if we were annoying you. I didn't realize we were speaking so loudly." She says, "I was trying to sleep," and puts on the headphones that she got from the flight attendant.

Not a minute later, she rings the call button again. When the flight attendant comes back, she says, "I need another pair. These earphones aren't drowning out these people." I thought this was kind of peculiar, as Cheryl and I were stunned by what happened and really hadn't said anything since her original comment that we were speaking too loudly.

All of this should just go into one of those irritating, bizarre moments in life files and be forgotten. However, it makes a point about personal responsibility, interpersonal competence and life and career success.

The woman in 14C never told Cheryl and me that we were disturbing her sleep. Instead, she chose to complain to the flight attendant about our conversation. It came across to both Cheryl and me as a pretty hostile gesture. We both wondered why she just didn't ask us to speak more softly. That's what an interpersonally competent person would have done. That's what someone who was taking responsibility for herself and her needs would have done.

It's called being assertive. Assertive people stand up for their rights, but do it in such a way as not to offend other people. Passive people let others trample on them and don't stand up for their rights. Aggressive people get what they want, but at the expense of others. In this case, 14C was being aggressive.

There are two common sense career success coach points here: one, take responsibility for yourself. Tell people how you feel. Don't let others do things that make your life unpleasant. And two, stand up for yourself in an assertive, non-aggressive way. Follow the career advice in Tweet 133 in Success Tweets. "Resolve conflict positively. Treat conflict as an opportunity to strengthen, not destroy, the relationships you've worked hard to build." Conflict can destroy relationships – and it can strengthen them. When you find yourself in conflict with another person, choose to see it as an opportunity to strengthen your relationship with them. The career advice here is simple. Resolve conflict by acting in a positive, proactive and assertive manner.

Success Tweet 134

Settle disputes and resolve differences quickly. Don't let them drag on. Engage the other person in meaningful conversation.

An article that appeared in the Wednesday, May 9 2007 Business Day section of *The New York Times* made this point ever so clearly.

> "On March 23, *Andrew N. Liveris*, the chief executive of **Dow Chemical**, wrote a scathing performance review about one of his top lieutenants.

> "'I expect to see that your negative body language when you disagree with a course of action is eliminated,' he wrote to the executive, Romeo Kreinberg, who ran the $21 billion performance plastics and chemical business portfolio. 'Frankly, your recent behavior was the last straw and I will not allow such destructive behavior to be repeated.'

> "Mr. Liveris gave Mr. Kreinberg three months to change his behavior. Otherwise, he warned, 'I will have no choice but to sever your links with Dow.'"

From the sounds of it, Mr. Kreinberg is a poster boy for a lack of interpersonal incompetence. "Negative body language"…"destructive behavior" – it would have been fun to be a fly on the wall in the meetings that led up to Mr. Liveris' review of Mr. Kreinberg's performance.

In my experience, people who are so blatantly unaware (or uncaring) of the impact of their behavior on others, very seldom end up running $21 billion businesses. Most never make it past the level of individual contributor or first-level manager.

There is some simple, but powerful common sense career advice here. If you can't build and maintain strong relationships with the people in your organization; and if you can't learn to deal with conflict in a positive manner, you are unlikely to become a career and life success.

Successful people realize that they have to continue working with the people with whom they find themselves in conflict. They accept decisions that go against them graciously. They pitch in and help make decisions work; even if they argued strenuously against those decisions before they were made.

Successful interpersonally competent people avoid "negative body language" and "destructive behavior" – for the good of their company, and the good of their careers.

By the way, Mr. Liveris fired Mr. Kreinberg three weeks later for a non-related issue – being "involved in unauthorized discussion with third parties about the potential acquisition of the company."

The common sense career success coach point here is simple. Successful people follow the career advice in Tweet 134 in Success Tweets. "Settle disputes and resolve differences quickly. Don't let them drag on. Engage the other person in meaningful conversation." Don't let your body language show how negatively you feel about a decision or other person. Don't engage in destructive behaviors – actions that damage your reputation, your relationships and your company. Instead, address differences head on. Resolve them quickly and move on. Treat people with whom you disagree with dignity and respect.

Success Tweet 135

Be a consensus builder. Focus on where you agree with others. It will be easier to resolve differences and create agreement.

The July 2009 issue of SUCCESS Magazine had an interesting interview with Patrick Lencioni, author of, *The Five Dysfunctions of a Team.* I'm an admirer of Patrick's writing. I particularly like what he has to say about teams and teamwork. Fear of conflict is one of the team dysfunctions he discusses in the book and interview in SUCCESS.

And, if you read this blog with any regularity, you know that I am a big fan of SUCCESS Magazine. I read it cover-to-cover every month and usually blog about one or two of the articles in each issue. If you're not a subscriber, I suggest you go to www.success.com and do so now.

Here's what Patrick Lencioni has to say about conflict and disagreement...

> "The fact is that great teams argue. Not in a mean-spirited or personal way. But they disagree, and passionately, when important decisions are made. They argue about concepts and ideas and avoid personality focused, mean-spirited attacks. So many of us have been raised to avoid conflict and disagreement that we try to compromise and reach artificial consensus, and that only leads to mediocrity."

Successful, interpersonally competent people are not mean-spirited. They don't attack others. They do, however, voice their disagreement with another's ideas in a positive manner. They use conflict to find better, more creative solutions to their differences with others.

I always encourage people who are in conflict to do something that is counter intuitive – focus on where you agree, not where you disagree. When you find yourself in conflict with another person, it is natural to focus on your differences. However, this approach tends to lead to digging in your heels and looking for support for your position. The more you do this, the less open you are to hearing what the other person has to say. Conflict resolution becomes a zero sum, win/lose game.

On the other hand, if you actively look for and find places where you agree, you can jointly create a solution that satisfies both of your needs. Here is an example.

When we bought our house, we had a conflict with the seller over the closing date. This was happening at the end of the year. The seller, who was also the builder, wanted to close by December 31. We were not planning on moving until February 1. Due to some ambiguous language in the contract, the situation was becoming quite contentious.

Finally, I said to the builder, "John, you want to sell this house. We want to buy it. I'm sure we can work out a closing date that suits us both." At that point, the tone of our discussions changed. We were working together to solve a problem – not arguing over December 31 and February 1 dates. Even though we both ended up giving a little, neither of us felt that we had given up on our position. We were able to resolve our conflict positively.

The common sense career success coach point here is simple. Successful people are interpersonally competent. Interpersonally competent people resolve conflict positively, with little damage to their relationships. They follow the career advice in Tweet 135 in Success Tweets. "Be a consensus builder. Focus on where you agree with others. It will be easier to resolve differences and create agreement." Conflict can be destructive to relationships and it can kill your career success. But when you work to resolve conflict positively, you strengthen your relationships. Strong relationships make it easier for you to resolve future conflicts and build your career success. Focusing on points of agreement, however small, is the best way to resolve conflict positively. Focusing on where you agree puts you in a position to jointly create a mutually satisfying solution to a conflict, as opposed to win/lose negotiation, in which one person wins and the other loses.

Success Tweet 136

Be responsible for yourself. No one can "make you angry." Choose to act in a civil, constructive manner in tense situations.

Your values are your personal guide for day-to-day living. They are the best way to take responsibility for yourself. They help you make decisions in your everyday life. Values ground you – providing direction for decision making in ambiguous situations. Because I'm in business for myself, I have two sets of values – one set guides my personal life; the other, my professional life. They are complementary, but have slightly different foci.

My personal values are...

- Always do my best.
- Treat all people with the respect and dignity they deserve as fellow human beings.
- Help others wherever and whenever I can – with no strings attached.
- Use my common sense.
- Be a supportive and loving husband.

My business values are...

- I believe we too often make things more complex than they really are. I help my clients simplify the complex, and develop and implement common sense solutions to their problems and issues.
- I believe in human potential. I assist my client organizations and the individuals in them to use applied common sense to achieve their full potential.
- My clients pay a premium for my services. Therefore, I provide them with extraordinary value-added services in order to justify their faith in me.
- My clients trust me. They openly discuss their hopes, fears, problems and opportunities with me. This trust is sacred. I will not violate it.
- All of my customers are unique. I honor this uniqueness. I don't sell one-size-fits-all consulting, coaching or speaking services. I am diligent about gaining a complete understanding of each client's unique needs before I suggest a course of action.

I use these values as a guide for my day-to-day living. I do my best to conduct myself in a manner that is consistent with them. Several months ago, I did a blog post in which I mentioned an argument I had with my dad. I let myself get angry over a trivial matter. After I calmed down, I called my dad to apologize. I did this because one of my personal values is, "Treat all people with the respect and dignity they deserve as fellow human beings."

By raising my voice and arguing, I was not conducting myself in accordance with one of my personal values – so I had to do something (apologize) to rectify the situation. This value of treating people with respect and dignity is so ingrained in me that I had a feeling of unease for the two days it took me to apologize for losing my temper.

That's the way values work. They become so much a part of you that when you act in a manner inconsistent with them, you feel a little off and uncomfortable. This discomfort led me to do what I needed to do to fix the problem I had created.

Just last week I had an experience that gets at what I'm talking about here. I sent an email to a group of people with whom I have an affinity asking if they would like to join me as a joint venture partner. Several said "yes." I received a response from one person that was an email with a subject line that said REMOVE. There was no body in the text.

I sent this person a very nice email in which I apologized for bothering her, assured her that I would not contact her again and attached one of my eBooks as a sign of good will. I received a rather condescending response to the second email – offering me coaching on email etiquette. We traded two more emails discussing this issue.

I finally figured out that this person had a strong need to have the last word in this correspondence. I chose to terminate the conversation – and let her have the last word. By letting her have the last word, I was following the career advice in Tweet 136. "Choose to act in a civil, constructive manner in tense situations."

I still think that I was the aggrieved party in this situation, but in the long run it doesn't matter. I took responsibility for not extending a conflict situation that was of little or no importance by letting the other person have the last word – something that seemed important to her.

The common sense career success coach point here is simple. Successful people are clear about what they want out of their lives and careers. They define what success means to them, personally. They create a vivid mental image of their success. And they develop a set of personal values that guides their day-to-day life. They follow the career advice in Tweet 136 in Success Tweets. "Be responsible for yourself. No one can 'make you angry.' Choose to act in a civil, constructive manner in tense situations." Your values are guides to decision making in ambiguous situations. They provide you with the guidance you need as you go through life. Take a few minutes to think about what's important to you. Write it down. Then live your life by these values. You'll be on your way to a successful life and career.

Success Tweet 137

Do your job; give credit to others for doing theirs. Everyone likes to work with people who share the credit for a job well done.

As I was searching the net for some inspiration on what to write about in this tweet, I came across a piece by Susan Heathfield on About.com called, *Play Well With Others at Work*. Successful, interpersonally competent people are able to build strong relationships with the people with whom they work – this involves both working and playing well with others at work. Here is an edited version of what Ms. Heathfield has to say about playing well with others at work.

These are the top seven ways you can play well with others at work. They form the basis for effective work relationships. These are the actions you want to take to create a positive, empowering, motivational work environment for people.

- Suggest solutions to the problems you identify and raise. Identifying problems is easy. People who provide thoughtful solutions to the problems and challenges they raise earn the respect and admiration of their coworkers and bosses.
- Don't ever play the blame game. You alienate everyone around you. Yes, you may need to identify who was involved in a problem. You may even ask the Deming question: what about the work system caused this failure? But, not taking responsibility for problems you create and publicly identifying and blaming others for failures creates enemies. These enemies will, in turn, help you to fail. Interpersonally competent people realize that they need allies at work.
- What you say and what you do matters. When you talk down to someone, use sarcasm, or sound nasty, other people are likely to hear you. We are all radar machines that constantly scope out our environment. In one organization a high level manager said to me, "I know you don't think I should scream at my employees. But, sometimes, they make me so mad. When is it appropriate for me to scream at the employees?" Answer? Never. This goes for people who aren't in leadership positions too. It's never appropriate to raise your voice to a colleague or coworker.
- Never blind side people. Interpersonally competent people keep their colleagues in the loop. They discuss problems with the people directly involved before discussing them with others. Interpersonally competent people do not

ambush others. They know that if they do, they will never build effective work alliances. And without alliances, you never accomplish the most important goals.

- Keep your commitments. When you fail to meet deadlines and commitments, you affect the work of other people. Always keep commitments, and if you can't, make sure the affected people know what happened. Provide a new due date and honor the new deadline.
- Share credit for accomplishments, ideas, and contributions. It's very rare to accomplish a goal or complete a project with no help from others. Take the time, and expend the energy, to thank, reward, recognize and specify contributions of the people who help you succeed. This is a no-fail approach to building effective work relationships.
- Help other people find their greatness. Every person has talents, skills, and experience. If you help people harness their best abilities, you benefit them and your organization immeasurably. Personal growth and development benefits everybody. Compliment, recognize, praise, and notice contributions. You don't have to be a manager to help create a positive, motivating environment.

If you carry out these seven actions regularly – especially number 6, "Share credit for accomplishments, ideas and contributions," you will become known as someone who plays well with others. And, you'll develop effective work relationships. You'll become interpersonally competent. Colleagues will value you. Bosses will believe you are a team player. You'll accomplish your work goals, and you may even experience fun, recognition, and personal motivation. Work can't get any better than that.

The common sense career success coach advice here is simple. Successful people follow the career advice in Tweet 137 in Success Tweets. "Do your job; give credit to others for doing theirs. Everyone likes to work with people who share the credit for a job well done." Pay attention to Susan Heathfield's advice when she says, "Share credit for accomplishments, ideas, and contributions. It's very rare to accomplish a goal or complete a project with no help from others. Take the time, and expend the energy, to thank, reward, recognize and specify contributions of the people who help you succeed. This is a no-fail approach to building effective work relationships." If you follow this career advice, you'll be on your way to not only building strong work relationships, but to the life and career success you deserve.

Success Tweet 138

We all make mistakes. Own up to yours. You'll become known as a straight shooter, honest with yourself and others.

For this post, I'd like to return to one of my favorite documents: The Optimist Creed. If you would like a copy of The Optimist Creed suitable for framing, please go to http://budbilanich.com/optimist.

The Optimist Creed

Promise Yourself:

To be so strong that nothing can disturb your peace of mind.

To talk health, happiness and prosperity to every person you meet.

To make all your friends feel that there is something in them.

To look at the sunny side of everything and make your optimism come true.

To think only of the best, to work only for the best, and to expect only the best.

To be just as enthusiastic about the success of others as you are about your own.

To forget the mistakes of the past and press on to the greater achievements of the future.

To wear a cheerful countenance at all times and give every living creature you meet a smile.

To give so much time to the improvement of yourself that you have no time to criticize others.

To be too large for worry, too noble for anger, too strong for fear, and too happy to permit the presence of trouble.

In this post, I'd like to delve into the seventh point: "Promise yourself to forget the mistakes of the past and press on to the greater achievements of the future."

Let's begin with a quote from Ann Landers:

> "If I were asked to give what I consider to be the single-most useful bit of advice for all humanity, it would be this: expect trouble as an inevitable part of life and when it comes, hold your head high, look it squarely in the eye, and say 'I will be bigger than you. You cannot defeat me'."

I like what Ann Landers has to say here because it is a bit of a reality check. She's right, trouble – and setbacks and failure – are an inevitable part of life. Self-confident people look trouble squarely in the eye and move forward. They are not cowed by their failures, rather they embrace them and use them to move towards their goals. They also own up to their mistakes. In this way, they become widely trusted. And trust is the glue that holds together all relationships.

If you read this blog somewhat regularly, you probably know that I am a big tennis fan. A couple of years ago, I saw two great matches at The Australian Open, the first major tennis tournament of the year.

James Blake, one of the two best American men tennis players at the time, won a great five-set match on Friday night. He lost the first two sets to Sebastien Grosjean. Then he won the next three to win the best of five-set match. He was down four games to one in the fourth set, but won in a tie break. He was gritty.

To put it in terms of The Optimist Creed, James Blake was able to "forget the mistakes of the past and press on to the greater achievements of the future." In this case, the past was the first two sets of the match. Also, to win, James Blake had to honestly evaluate his play in those first two sets and make some changes.

Roger Federer, on the other hand, was the best player in the world at that time. He still is very good. He had a terrible match against Janko Tipsarevic on Saturday afternoon of that Australian Open. He made 64 unforced errors and lost 16 of 21 break points. If you follow tennis, you know that this is a recipe for losing.

However, Mr. Federer won the match in five sets. Afterwards he said, "He (Mr. Tipsarevic) was just going for his shots and kept making them. In the end, I just tried to block out all the chances I missed." The Optimist Creed shows up again. By blocking out "all the chances I missed," Mr. Federer was able to win the match.

I believe that James Blake and Roger Federer won these matches because of their self-confidence, their optimism, and as Ann Landers says, their ability to "look it (trouble) squarely in the eye, and say 'I will be bigger than you. You cannot defeat me'." They also owned up to their mistakes and made the changes in their games that they needed to do to win their matches. By the way, Lleyton Hewitt did the same thing in his five-set match against Marcos Baghdatis.

The common sense career success coach point here is simple. Follow the career advice in Tweet 138 in Success Tweets. "We all make mistakes. Own up to yours. You'll become known as a straight shooter, honest with yourself and others." Successful, self-confident people realize that mistakes are part of life. They learn from their mistakes and then build on this knowledge to create their own success. Owning up to your mistakes is great career advice. First, you have to own up to them privately. This is the only way to get past them and move forward to career success. Second, you have to own up to your mistakes publicly. Admit them to your colleagues and coworkers. Take responsibility when you let down others. You'll build strong relationships by being forthright.

Success Tweet 139

Become widely trusted. Deliver on what you say you'll do. If you can't meet a commitment, let the other person know right away.

The career advice in this tweet is a no brainer. Yet I'm constantly surprised by how many people miss deadlines and don't keep commitments – and never bother to mention it. Almost all of the work that you do has an impact on other people. Your output is often the input they need to get their work done.

You can build your career success simply by doing what you say you'll do. I have found that this bit of career advice is overlooked way too often. Too many people feel comfortable missing deadlines. Worse yet, they don't even mention that they'll be late to people who are waiting for their work.

I'm a big believer in taking personal responsibility for your life and career success. I always tell my career success coach clients that saying, "I'm late on my project because Joe – or Sue – didn't get me the information I needed" doesn't cut it. I tell them to seek out the information they need and get it so they can finish their project on time.

On the other hand, I tell them that they have a responsibility to Joe or Sue or anybody who is waiting for their work to get it to them on time. And if they are going to miss a deadline, let Joe or Sue know as soon as possible so they can adjust their work planning. This is not only common courtesy, it's good business and career success advice.

When you meet your commitments consistently – or let others know when you are going to be unable to do so – you gain a reputation as someone who can be trusted. And as I've mentioned in a previous post, trust is the glue that binds relationships.

I have built my consulting and career success coach business by doing what I say I'll do. I try to go beyond what I promise, to over-deliver. In this way, I have built some client relationships that have exceeded 20 years. These people hire me again and again. And they refer me to their friends and colleagues – all because I do what I say I'll do.

I once flew all night from Seattle to Detroit to do a workshop. I made a wrong notation in my calendar and ended up having to be in Seattle until 6:00 one day, and in Detroit to do a workshop at 10:00 the next day. When I told one of my friends about the problem I had created for myself, he suggested I cancel one of the engagements. I couldn't do that; both were part of larger programs that had been scheduled months in advance by my clients. I couldn't let them down. A little lost sleep was a small price to pay for keeping my reputation as a guy who keeps his commitments intact.

This blog demonstrates my commitment to keeping my commitments. Twenty-seven weeks and four days ago I wrote the first post in this series. In that post, I said that I would write a series of posts that further explain the ideas in each tweet in *Success Tweets*. I committed to writing five posts a week. I've done that. Next Monday, I will post about Success Tweet 141. I've posted every day, Monday through Friday, for 28 weeks. I've posted when I've been working from my home office, when I've been traveling for business, and when I've been on vacation. I did this because I committed to doing it – to myself, and to readers of this blog. I take the career advice in Success Tweet 139 seriously. I suggest that you do too.

Finally, the subtitle of *Success Tweets* is *140 bits of Common Sense Career Success Advice, All in 140 Characters or Less.* If you've downloaded the book, you've probably noticed that it has 141 tweets. I did this on purpose -- to over-deliver on the promise I make on the front cover. This is a small, silly even, example of how I go out of my way to make sure that people see me as someone who keeps his commitments. What are some of the small things you do to demonstrate that you are someone who keeps commitments and can be trusted?

The common sense career success coach point here is simple. If you want to become a life and career success you have to build a reputation as someone who can be trusted. Follow the career advice in Tweet 139 in Success Tweets. "Become widely trusted. Deliver on what you say you'll do. If you can't meet a commitment, let the other person know right away." I've built a thriving business by following this career advice. And you can create the life and career success you want by following it. I think it goes without saying that while it is important to let other people know when you will be missing a deadline or can't keep a commitment, it is more important to do whatever you must do to make deadlines and keep your commitments. This can inconvenience you at times, but it is great career advice that will pay off in the long run.

Success Tweet 140

Social networks allow you to help others. Give value, and you'll be able to build some great online relationships.

In this post, I'd like to focus on building relationships on the Internet. The Internet gives you the opportunity to maintain relationships with people you know well, strengthen relationships with people you know only a little and build new relationships with people who can help you create the successful life and career you want and deserve.

I believe that LinkedIn is the best social network for professionals. Facebook, Plaxo and Twitter are OK too. Regardless of the social network you choose, there are some common sense points you should follow if you want to build solid relationships. While these points focus primarily on LinkedIn, there are similar functions on just about every social network.

Your profile is the place to begin. It can help you build your brand. A good profile will attract others, educate them about you and influence their feelings towards you – even if you've never met in person. Experts say that you have three seconds to communicate your brand on your LinkedIn profile. Make those seconds count.

My professional description on LinkedIn used to read "Bud Bilanich, The Common Sense Guy." Now it reads, "Bud Bilanich: I help individuals, teams and entire organizations succeed by helping them apply their common sense." I don't know about you, but I think that the second professional description is much stronger, communicates better and makes the most out of my three seconds.

You can leverage your social network profiles in several ways. Invite everyone you know to connect with you. Most social networking sites have a reconnect function. Use it. LinkedIn calls this the "colleagues and classmates reconnect function." It can be a lot of fun to reconnect with people you used to know. If you use Microsoft Outlook, download the Outlook toolbar. It will let you know the LinkedIn status of everyone from whom you receive an email. Ask your existing LinkedIn connections to introduce you to their connections. In this way, you can build a large network of people who will be exposed to your brand.

The LinkedIn "What you are working on now" function can help build your brand. Update it regularly. Post all of the interesting things you are doing – at work and in your life. This will help others get to know you better and it will showcase the depth and breadth of your experience. Think of it as a longer tweet. Twitter limits you to 140 characters per post. Here you can post three or four sentences and go into a little more detail. And, just like Twitter, people can respond to your LinkedIn "What you are working on now" posts. This creates the opportunity for you to engage in dialogue with the people you meet on LinkedIn, strengthening your relationships.

LinkedIn Groups are another powerful way to leverage the power of LinkedIn. You can find groups to join by seeing which groups people with interests similar to your own join. You can use the LinkedIn search tool for this. Start slowly, join no more than three groups at first. Spend some time in these groups. See if they appeal to you. If they do, become active by participating in conversations; sharing your thoughts and ideas and links that you find helpful. If you don't like a group, drop out and find another. Participating in groups can be time consuming. Set your default to receive emails from groups once a week. Then set aside a specific period each week to read the recent post and reply to the relevant ones.

Remember, the career advice here is to build on line relationships the same way you build in person relationships. Give with no expectation of return. Establish yourself as a person of value first – someone who not only has something to give, but someone who is willing to help others. In this way, when the time comes, you'll be in a great position to ask for the help you need in creating your life and career success.

The common sense career success coach point here is simple. Successful people follow the career advice in Tweet 140 in Success Tweets. "Social networks allow you to help others. Give value, and you'll be able to build some great online relationships." Build strong, lasting mutually beneficial relationships – in person and on line. While there is no substitute for face-to-face interaction when it comes to building relationships, the Internet has opened up a lot of opportunities to reconnect with old friends and to make new ones. For my money, LinkedIn is the best social network for professionals. However, Facebook, Plaxo and Twitter are good too. Offering something of value is the best way to get people to befriend you on social networking sites. This can be as simple as retweeting a Twitter post you found interesting. Or, you can offer advice by answering questions people posts in forums. The idea is to offer value – not hype yourself. Keep in mind the Zig Ziglar quote, "You will get what you want in life if you help enough other people get what they want." Social networks allow you to help others get what they want. So give value – and you'll find that you'll be able to build some great on line relationships that will help you create the life and career success you want and deserve.

Success Tweet 141

Knowing is not enough. Successful people will read the advice in these tweets. And they will act on it. Be a successful person.

Much of the career advice in this book focuses on taking personal responsibility for your life and career success. I want to revisit that idea here. Personal responsibility means using this material once you learn it. I wrote Success Tweets and these career advice blog posts to provide you with useful information and knowledge on becoming a success in your career and life. But, as the U.S. Steel pencils my Dad brought home from work used to say, "Knowing is not enough."

When I was a kid, I was really fascinated and puzzled by these pencils. "Knowing is not enough – what the hell does that mean?" I used to think. I spent hours struggling with that idea. I was too stubborn to ask a grown-up.

When I got to Penn State, I took Philosophy 101 my freshman year. We had to read Johann von Goethe. One day, as I was plowing through an assignment, I came across this quote: "Knowing is not enough, we must do. Willing is not enough, we must apply."

Boy, was I glad I took that course! It solved one of the profound mysteries of my childhood: "Knowing is not enough." You have to take what you learn and use it, or what you've learned isn't very valuable. That's part of personal responsibility, and a huge part of creating the life and career success you want and deserve.

I've tried to present this material in such a manner that it provides you with some ideas of what to do to become a success in your life and career. It's up to you to think about what's here and decide if and how you are going to use it.

A Message to Garcia is one of the best-known writings on the idea of personal responsibility. It is an inspirational essay written in 1899 by Elbert Hubbard that has been made into two movies, reprinted as a pamphlet and a book, translated into 37 languages, and was well-known in American popular and business culture until the middle of the twentieth century. It was originally published as a filler without a title in the March 1899 issue of *Philistine* magazine.

A Message to Garcia celebrates the initiative of a soldier who was assigned and accomplished a daunting mission. "He asked no questions, made no objections, requested no help, and accomplished the mission." The soldier was Andrew Summers Rowan, a class of 1881 West Point graduate.

The essay suggests that the reader should apply this attitude to his or her own life as an avenue to success. Its wide popularity at the time was reflective of the general appeal of self-reliance and energetic problem solving in American culture. Its "don't ask questions, get the job done" message was often used by business leaders as a motivational message to their employees. It was given to every United States Sailor and Marine in both World Wars and was often memorized by schoolchildren.

The essay is about an event in the Spanish-American War in 1898. As the American army prepared to invade the Spanish colony of Cuba, they needed to contact the leader of the Cuban insurgents (the insurgents were on our side in that war), Calixto Iniguez Garcia. Garcia had been fighting the Spanish for Cuban independence since 1868 and sought the help of the United States.

Here are some selected excerpts from *A Message to Garcia*:

> "In all this Cuban business there is one man who stands out on the horizon of my memory like Mars at perihelion. When war broke out between Spain and the United States, it was very necessary to communicate quickly with the leader of the Insurgents. Garcia was somewhere in the mountain fastnesses of Cuba – no one knew where. No mail or telegraph could reach him. The President must secure his co-operation, and quickly.

> "What to do!

> "Someone said to the President, 'There is a fellow by the name of Rowan who will find Garcia for you, if anybody can.'

> "Rowan was sent for and given a letter to be delivered to Garcia...

> "McKinley gave Rowan a letter to be delivered to Garcia; Rowan took the letter and did not ask, 'Where is he?'

"By the Eternal! There is a man whose form should be cast in deathless bronze and the statue placed in every college of the land. It is not book-learning young men need, nor instruction about this or that, but a stiffening of the vertebrae which will cause them to be loyal to a trust, to act promptly, concentrate their energies: do the thing – 'Carry a message to Garcia...'

Knowing is not enough. You have to do. We all have to do. Be like Rowan. Treat all of your tasks as "a message to Garcia." If you would like to have the full text of *A Message to Garcia*, go to http://BudBilanich.com/garcia.

I've enjoyed writing these posts. It was fun to look back on my career and to distill the nuggets that have become my personal rules for success into a series of tweets. It was even more fun to write this series of blog posts delving deeper into each tweet.

But you should remember that these tweets are ideas that I have found helpful in my personal journey to professional success. One size does not fit all. Change, adapt, discard ideas that don't work for you. Add new ideas that you find helpful, or that you've learned in other places.

I am using Success Tweet and the Success Tweets blog to start a community of success seekers – one in which we freely exchange ideas, helping one another to learn, grow and succeed. I will be launching a combination membership site and group coaching site very soon. I hope to make it into a lively community. It takes more than one person to create a community though, that's why I hope you will join and actively participate on the blog.

While I will encourage open discussion of ideas on the coaching calls, you can email me at Bud@BudBilanich.com if you have any career advice questions you would like me to answer in private.

I am offering a free 30-minute coaching session. If you are interested in taking me up on this offer, send an email to Bud@Bilanich.com with the words "free coaching session" in the subject line. Send your phone number and a few good times to call you.

The common sense career success coach point here is simple. Follow the career advice in Tweet 141 in Success Tweets. "Knowing is not enough. Successful people will read the advice in these tweets. And they will act on it.   Be a successful person." I really want you to succeed, and I want to help you succeed in any way I can. Please keep reading my daily blog posts at www.BudBilanich.com. Comment when you have something to add. Ask questions for clarification. I wish you the very best in creating the life and career success you want and deserve.